A SENTIMENTAL CHRISTMAS

ISBN 978-1-5400-5471-5

Visit Hal Leonard Online at
www.halleonard.com

Contact us:
Hal Leonard
7777 West Bluemound Road
Milwaukee, WI 53213
Email: info@halleonard.com

In Europe, contact:
Hal Leonard Europe Limited
42 Wigmore Street
Marylebone, London, W1U 2RN
Email: info@halleonardeurope.com

In Australia, contact:
Hal Leonard Australia Pty. Ltd.
4 Lentara Court
Cheltenham, Victoria, 3192 Australia
Email: info@halleonard.com.au

Registration Guide

- Match the Registration number on the song to the corresponding numbered category below. Select and activate an instrumental sound available on your instrument.
- Choose an automatic rhythm appropriate to the mood and style of the song. (Consult your Owner's Guide for proper operation of automatic rhythm features.)
- Adjust the tempo and volume controls to comfortable settings.

Registration

1	Mellow	Flutes, Clarinet, Oboe, Flugel Horn, Trombone, French Horn, Organ Flutes
2	Ensemble	Brass Section, Sax Section, Wind Ensemble, Full Organ, Theater Organ
3	Strings	Violin, Viola, Cello, Fiddle, String Ensemble, Pizzicato, Organ Strings
4	Guitars	Acoustic/Electric Guitars, Banjo, Mandolin, Dulcimer, Ukulele, Hawaiian Guitar
5	Mallets	Vibraphone, Marimba, Xylophone, Steel Drums, Bells, Celesta, Chimes
6	Liturgical	Pipe Organ, Hand Bells, Vocal Ensemble, Choir, Organ Flutes
7	Bright	Saxophones, Trumpet, Mute Trumpet, Synth Leads, Jazz/Gospel Organs
8	Piano	Piano, Electric Piano, Honky Tonk Piano, Harpsichord, Clavi
9	Novelty	Melodic Percussion, Wah Trumpet, Synth, Whistle, Kazoo, Perc. Organ
10	Bellows	Accordion, French Accordion, Mussette, Harmonica, Pump Organ, Bagpipes

CONTENTS

All I Want for Christmas Is You

Registration 5
Rhythm: Swing

Words and Music by Mariah Carey
and Walter Afanasieff

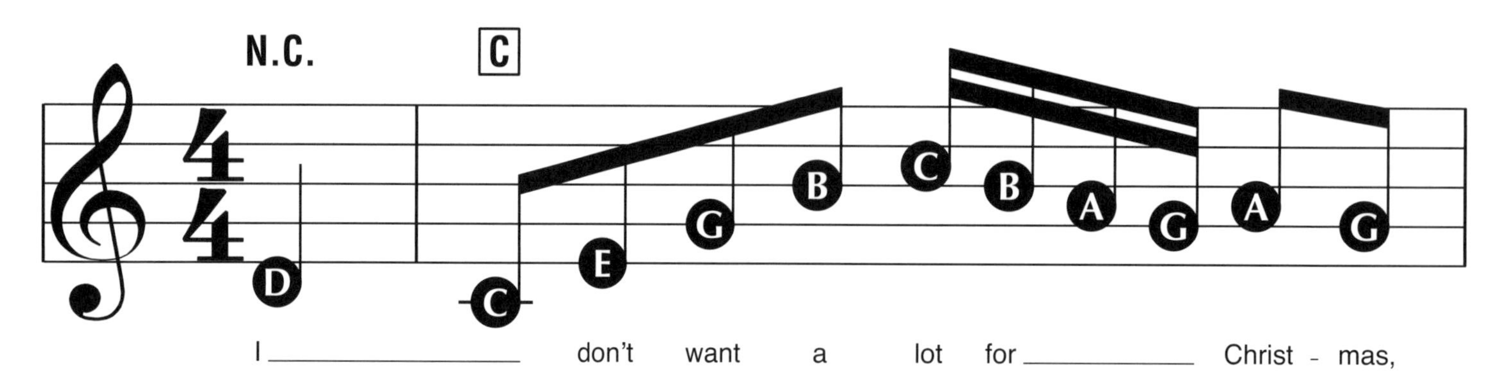

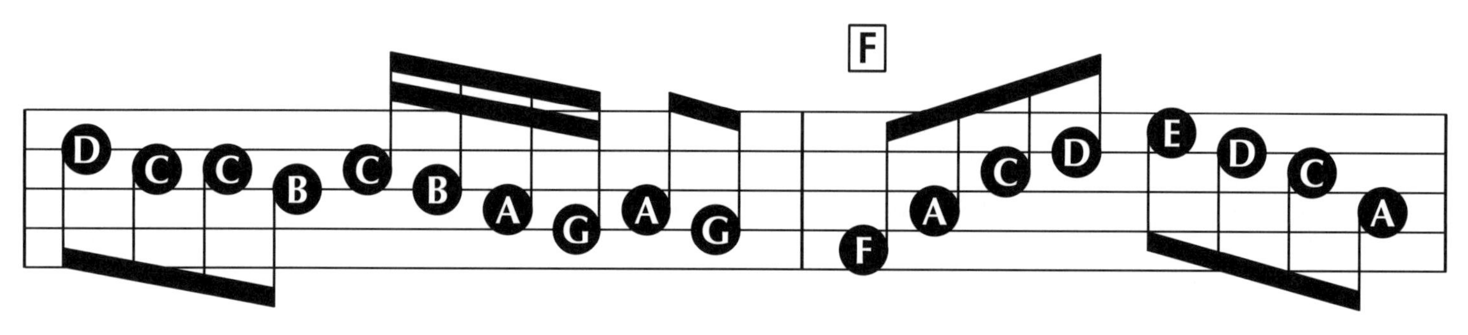

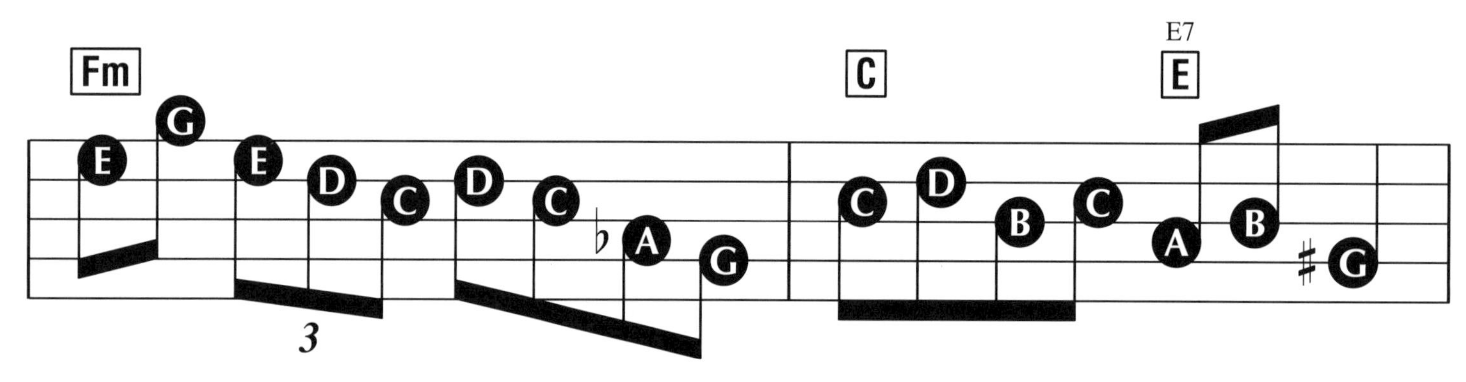

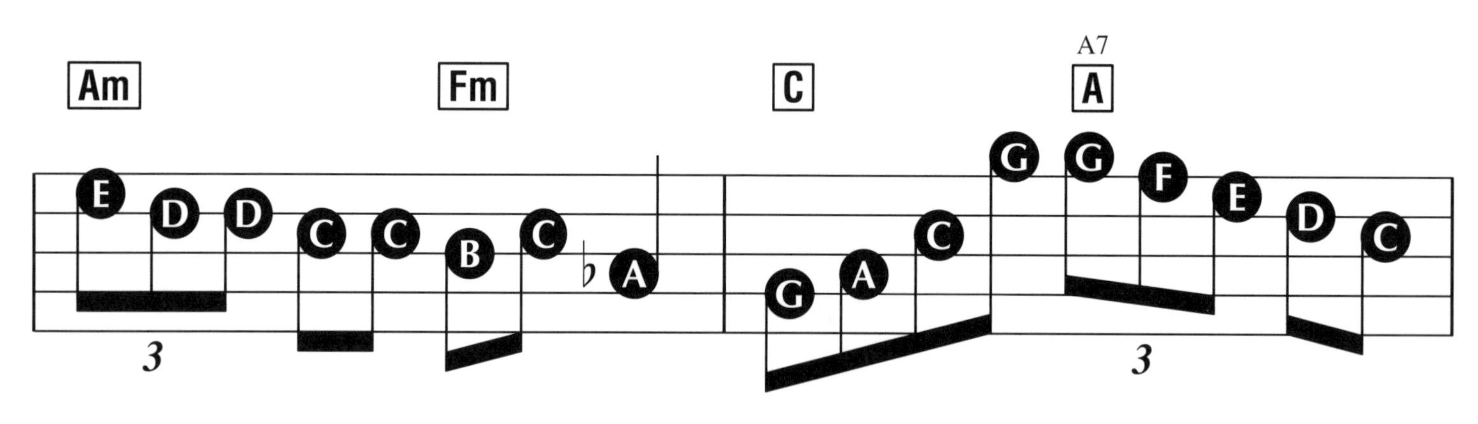

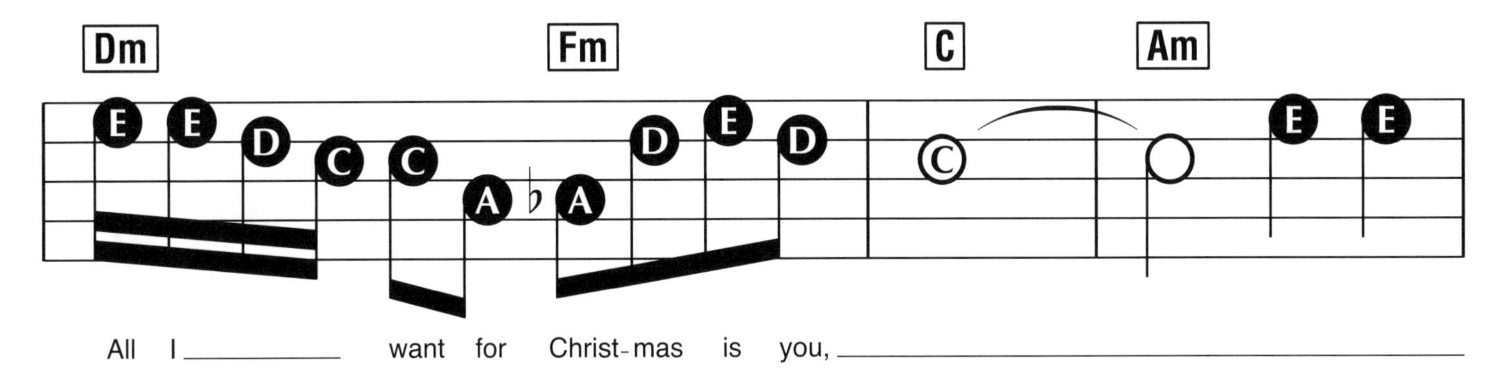
Dm
Fm
C
Am
E E D C C A A D E D C E E
All I want for Christ-mas is you,

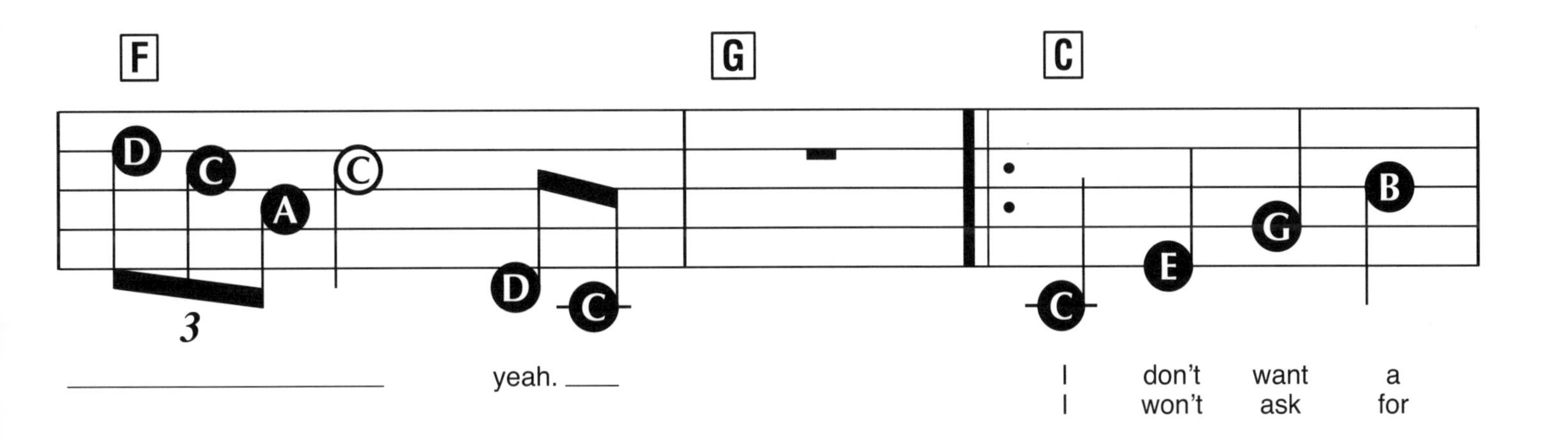
F
G
C
D C A C D C C E G B
3
yeah.
I don't want a
I won't ask for

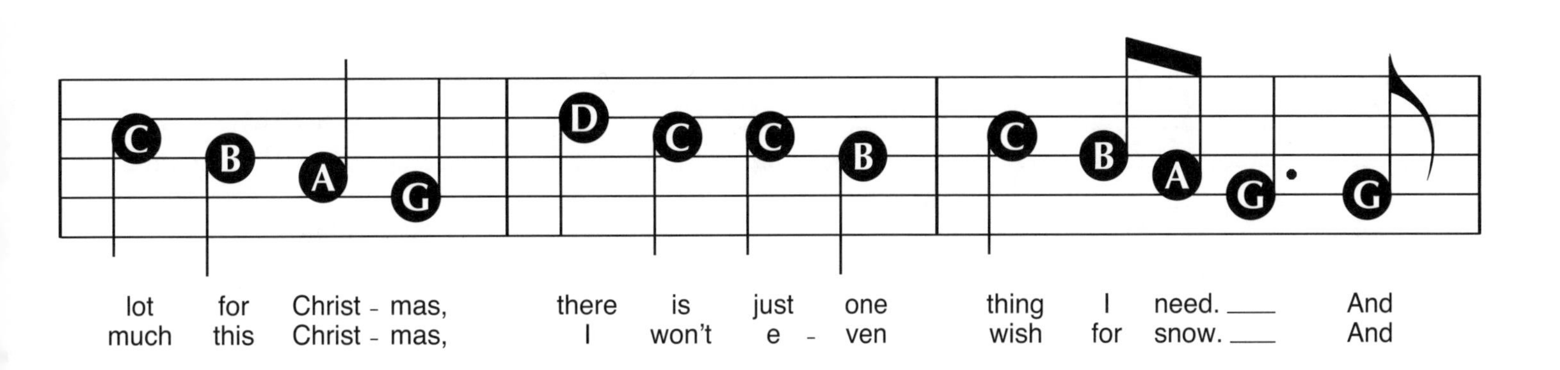
C B A G D C C B C B A G G
lot for Christ - mas, there is just one thing I need. And
much this Christ - mas, I won't e - ven wish for snow. And

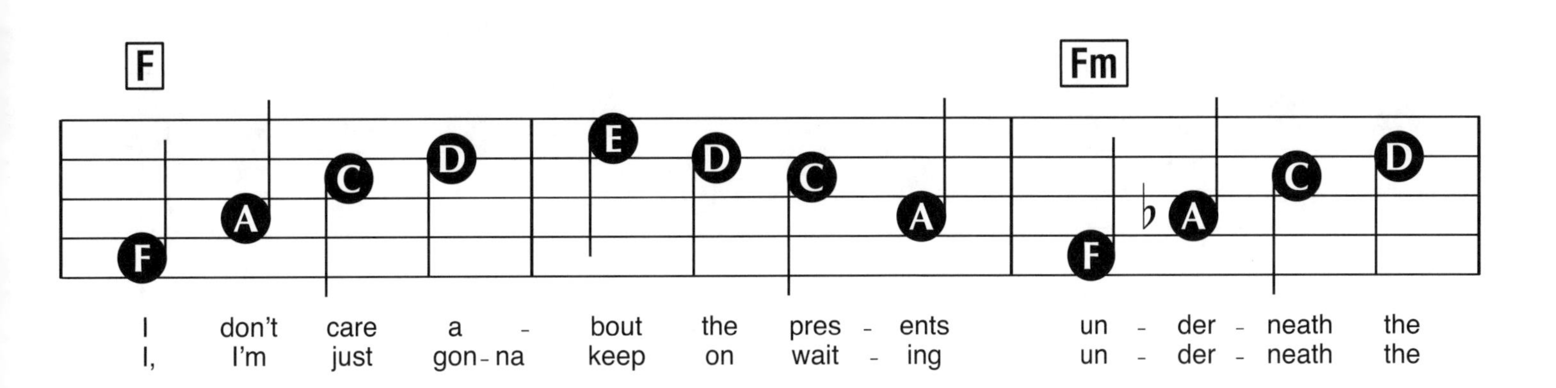
F
Fm
F A C D E D C A F A C D
I don't care a - bout the pres - ents un - der - neath the
I, I'm just gon-na keep on wait - ing un - der - neath the

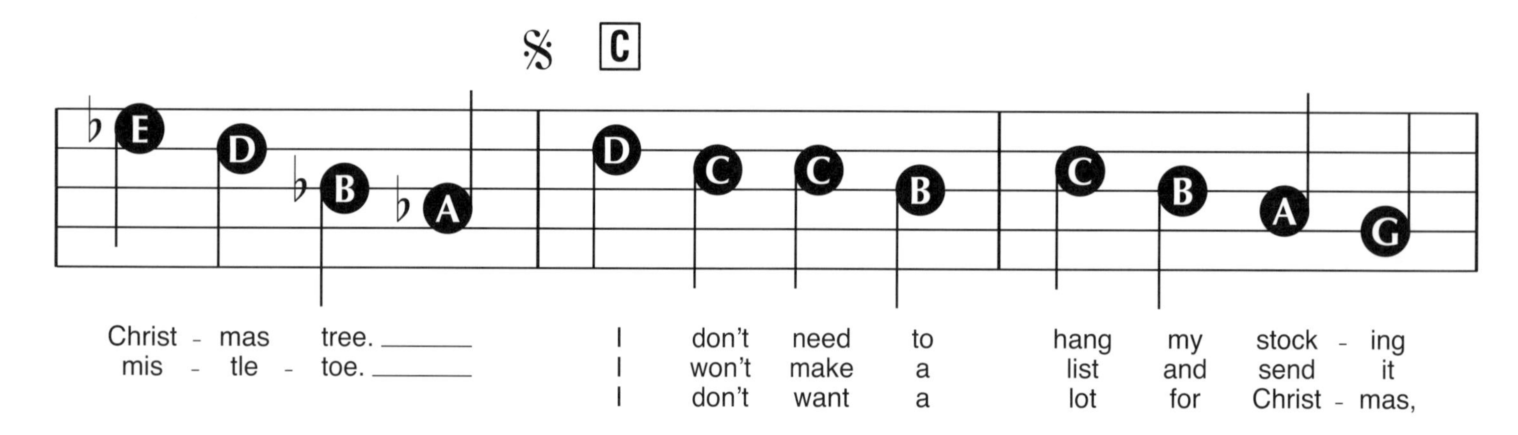
C
Christ - mas tree.
mis - tle - toe.
I don't need to hang my stock - ing
I won't make a list and send it
I don't want a lot for Christ - mas,

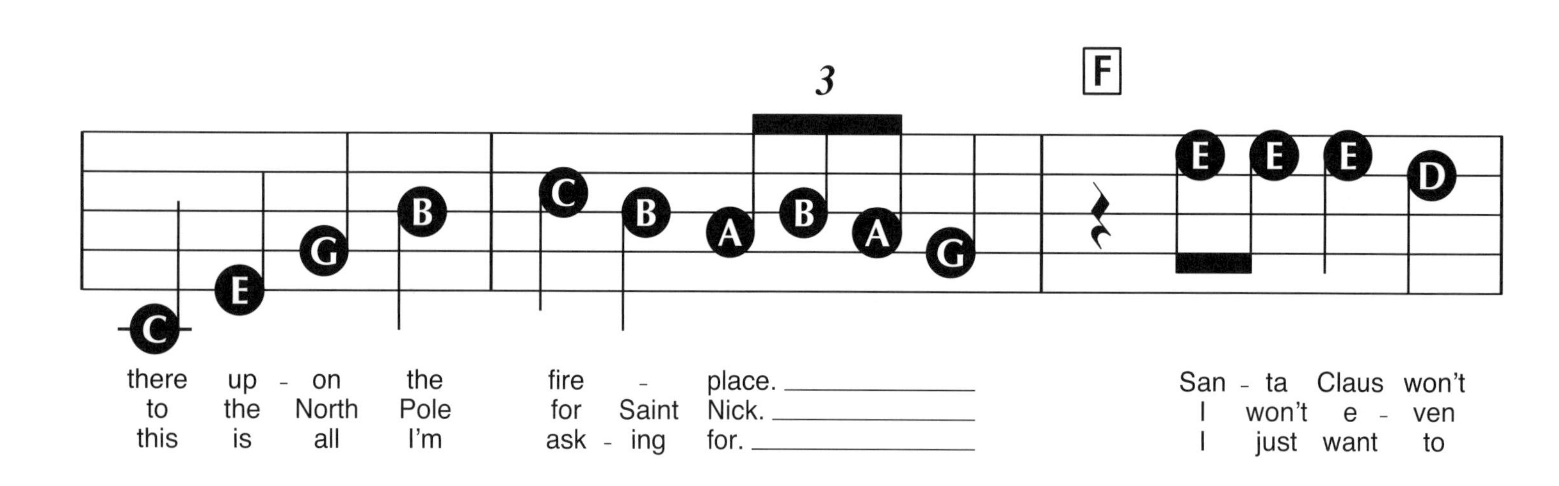
3
F
there up - on the fire - place.
to the North Pole for Saint Nick.
this is all I'm ask - ing for.
San - ta Claus won't
I won't e - ven
I just want to

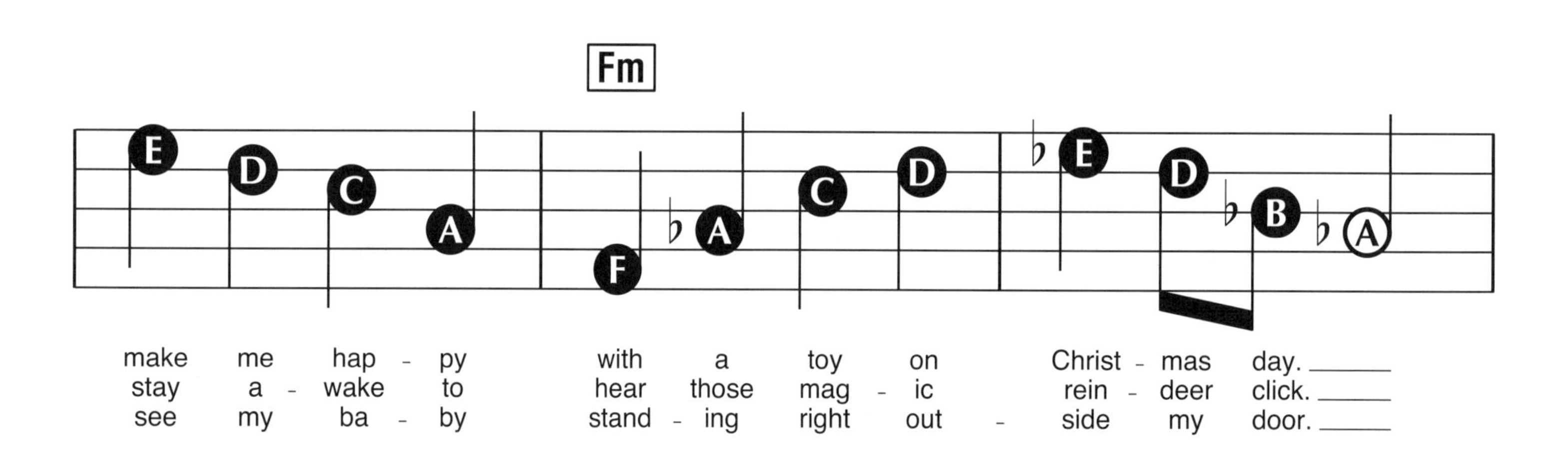
Fm
make me hap - py with a toy on Christ - mas day.
stay a - wake to hear those mag - ic rein - deer click.
see my ba - by stand - ing right out - side my door.

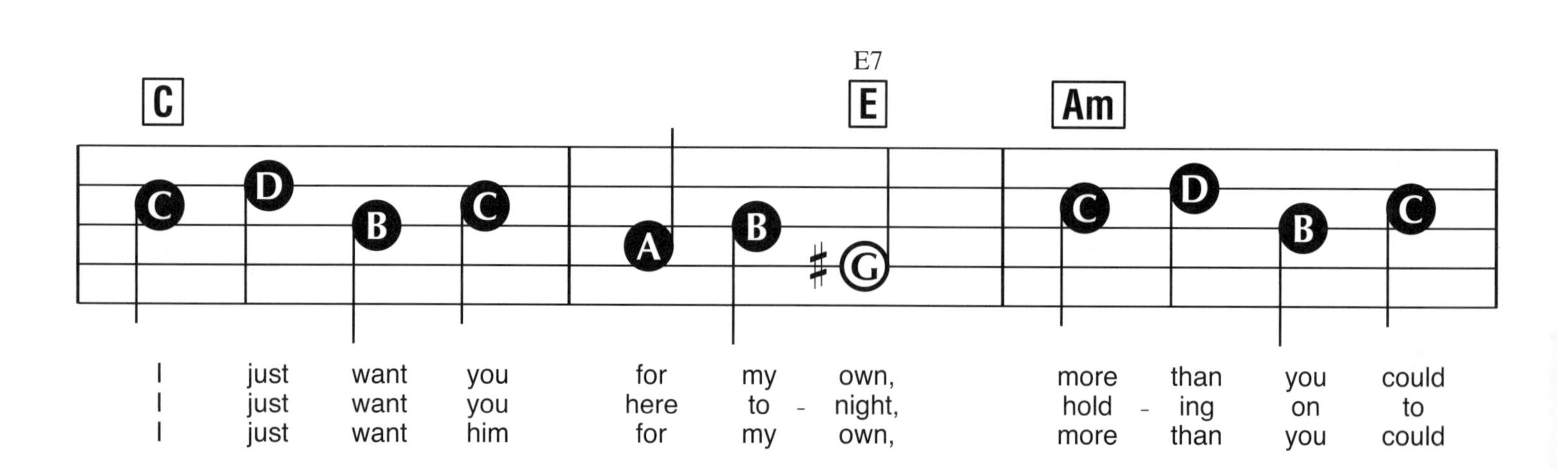
C
E7
E
Am
I just want you for my own, more than you could
I just want you here to - night, hold - ing on to
I just want him for my own, more than you could

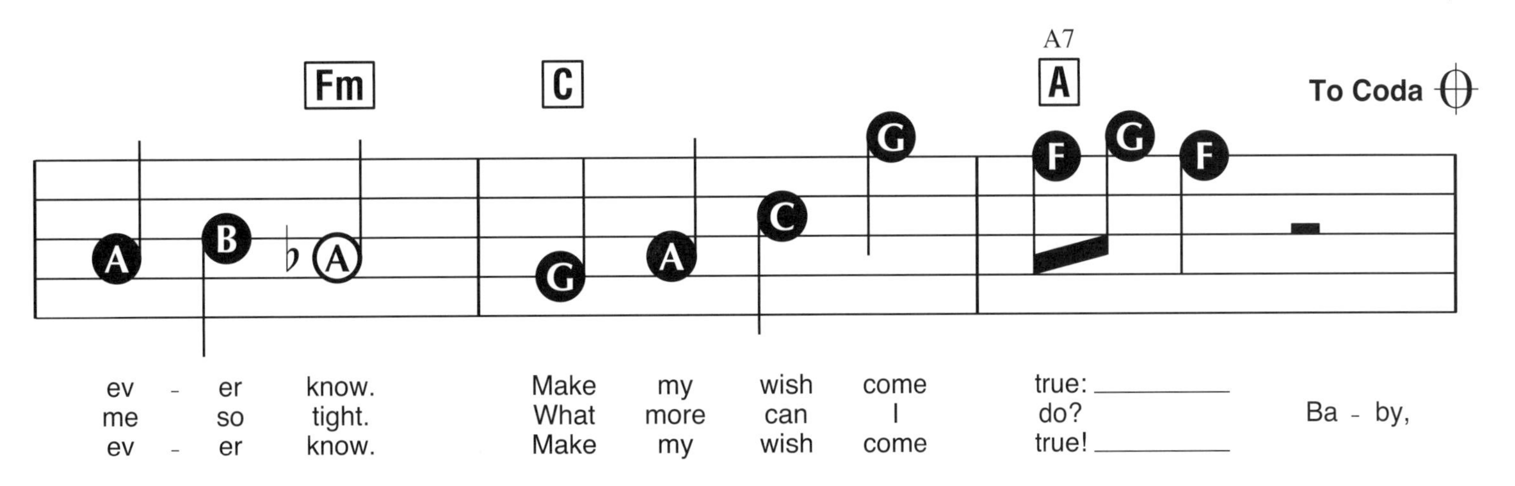
Fm
C
A7
A
To Coda
A B A
G A C G
F G F
ev - er know.
me so tight.
ev - er know.
Make my wish come
What more can I
Make my wish come
true:
do?
true!
Ba - by,

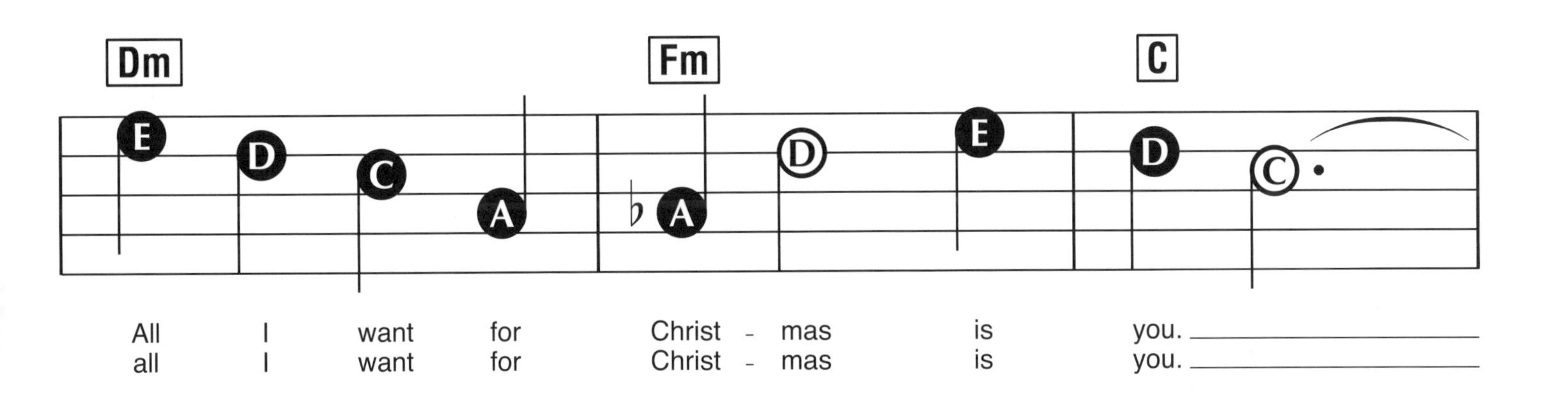
Dm
Fm
C
E D C A
A D E
D C
All I want for Christ - mas is you.
all I want for Christ - mas is you.

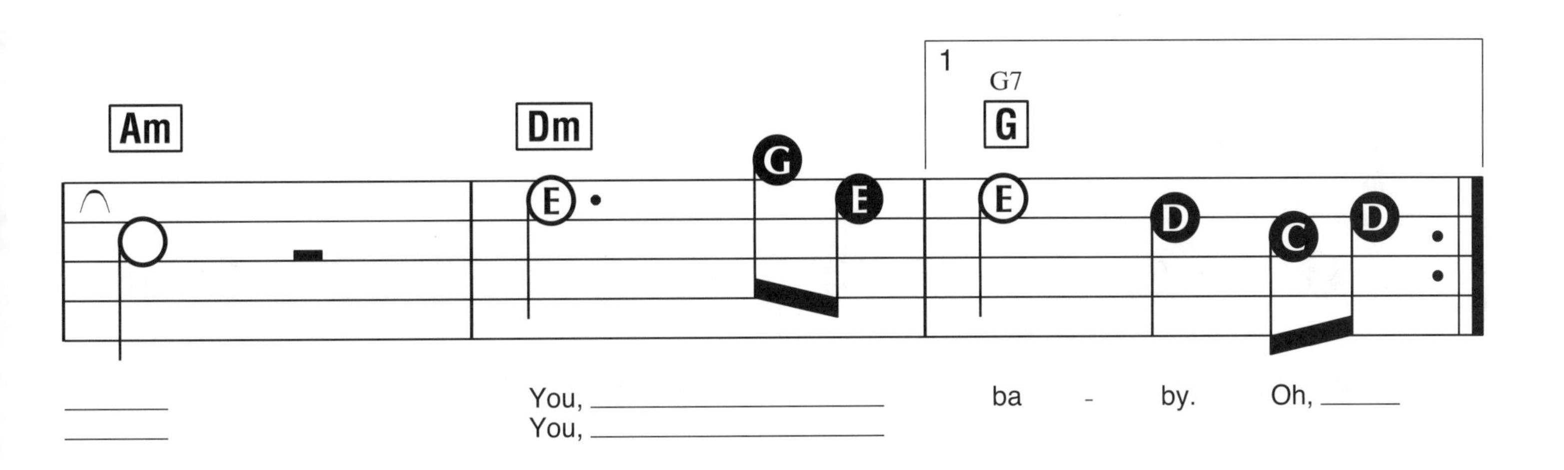
Am
Dm
1
G7
G
E G E
E D C D
You,
You,
ba - by. Oh,

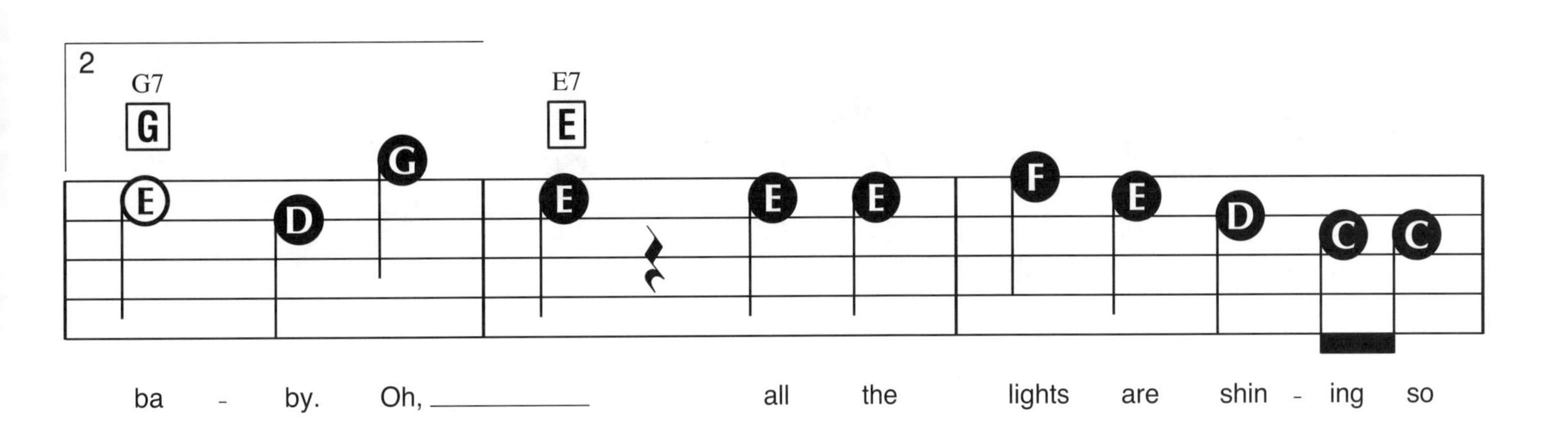
2
G7
G
E7
E
E D G
E E E
F E D C C
ba - by. Oh,
all the lights are shin - ing so

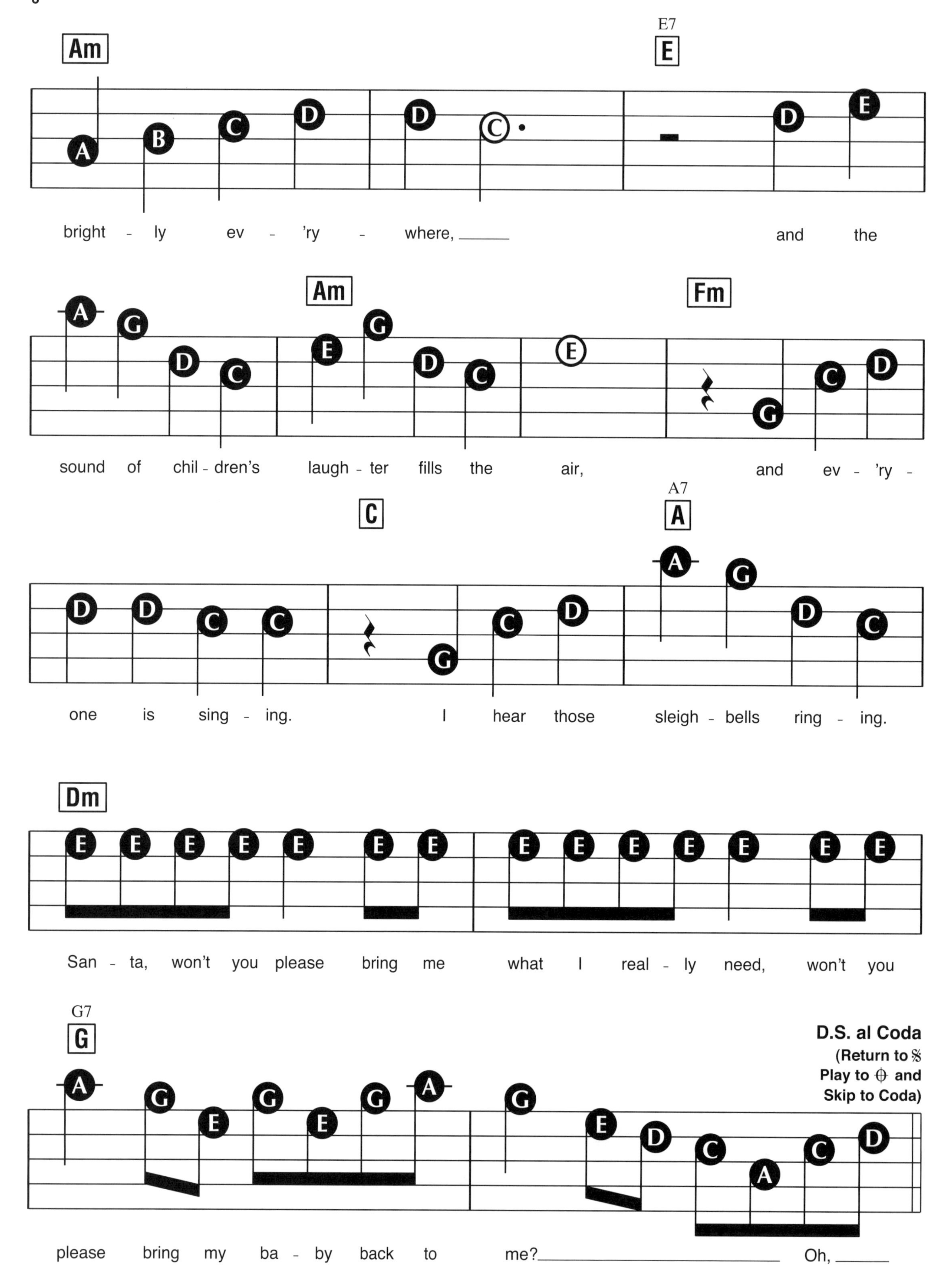
Am
E7
E
bright - ly ev - 'ry - where, and the
Am
Fm
sound of chil - dren's laugh - ter fills the air, and ev - 'ry -
C
A7
A
one is sing - ing. I hear those sleigh - bells ring - ing.
Dm
San - ta, won't you please bring me what I real - ly need, won't you
G7
G
D.S. al Coda
(Return to 𝄋
Play to 𝄌 and
Skip to Coda)
please bring my ba - by back to me? Oh,

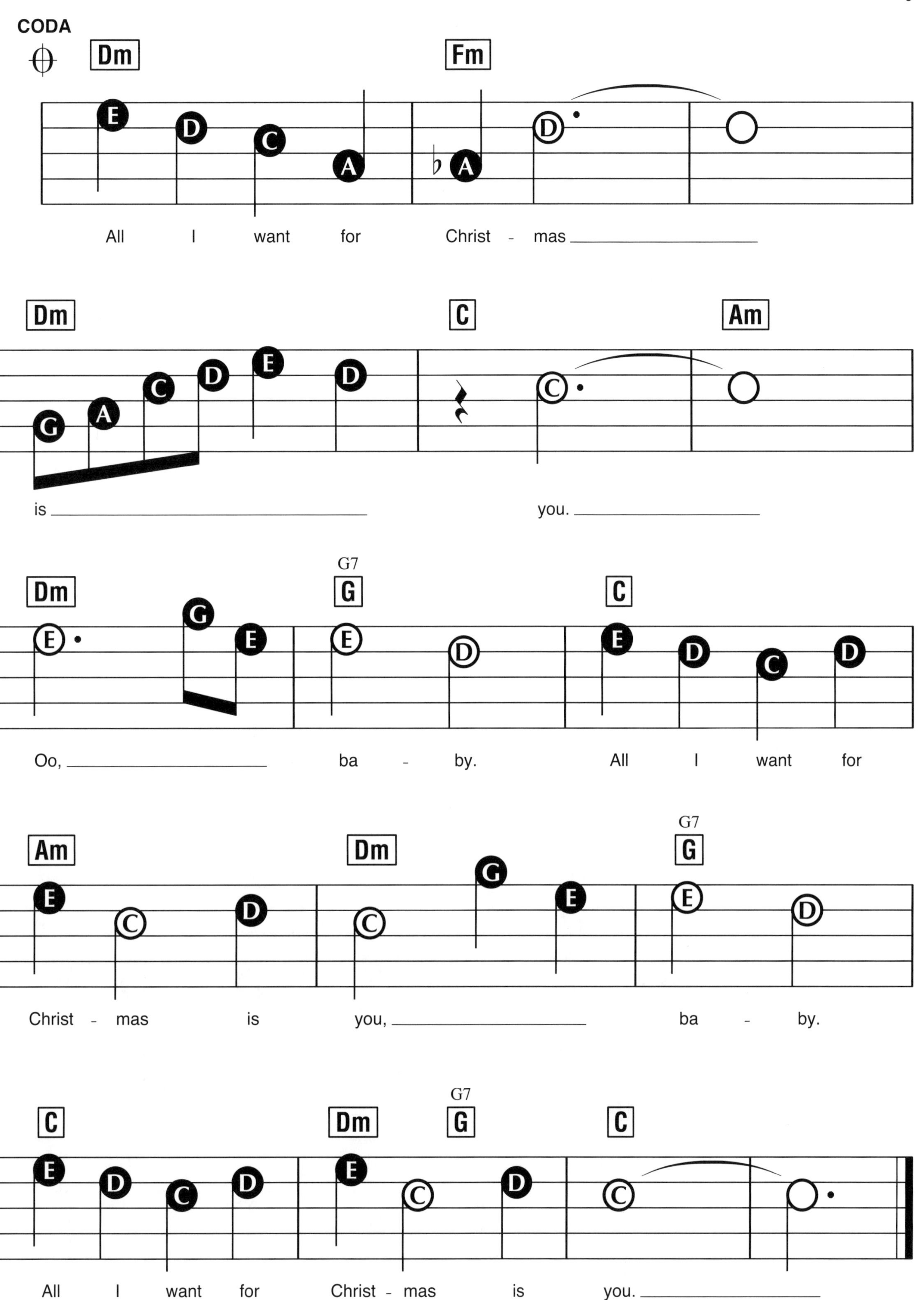
CODA
Dm
Fm
E D C A A D
All I want for Christ - mas
Dm
C
Am
G A C D E D C
is you.
Dm
G7
G
C
E G E E D E D C D
Oo, ba - by. All I want for
Am
Dm
G7
G
E C D C G E E D
Christ - mas is you, ba - by.
C
Dm
G7
G
C
E D C D E C D C
All I want for Christ - mas is you.

Blue Christmas

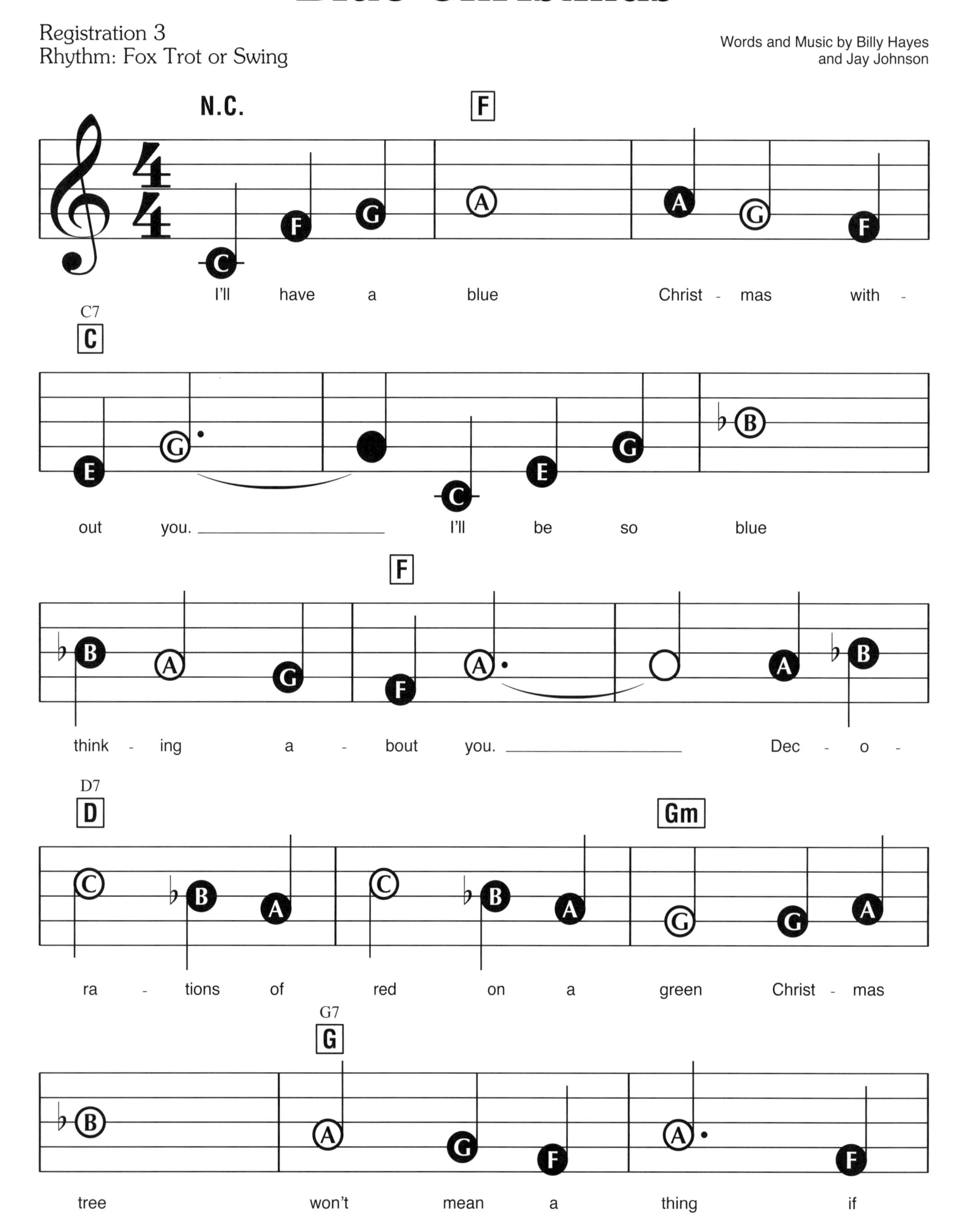

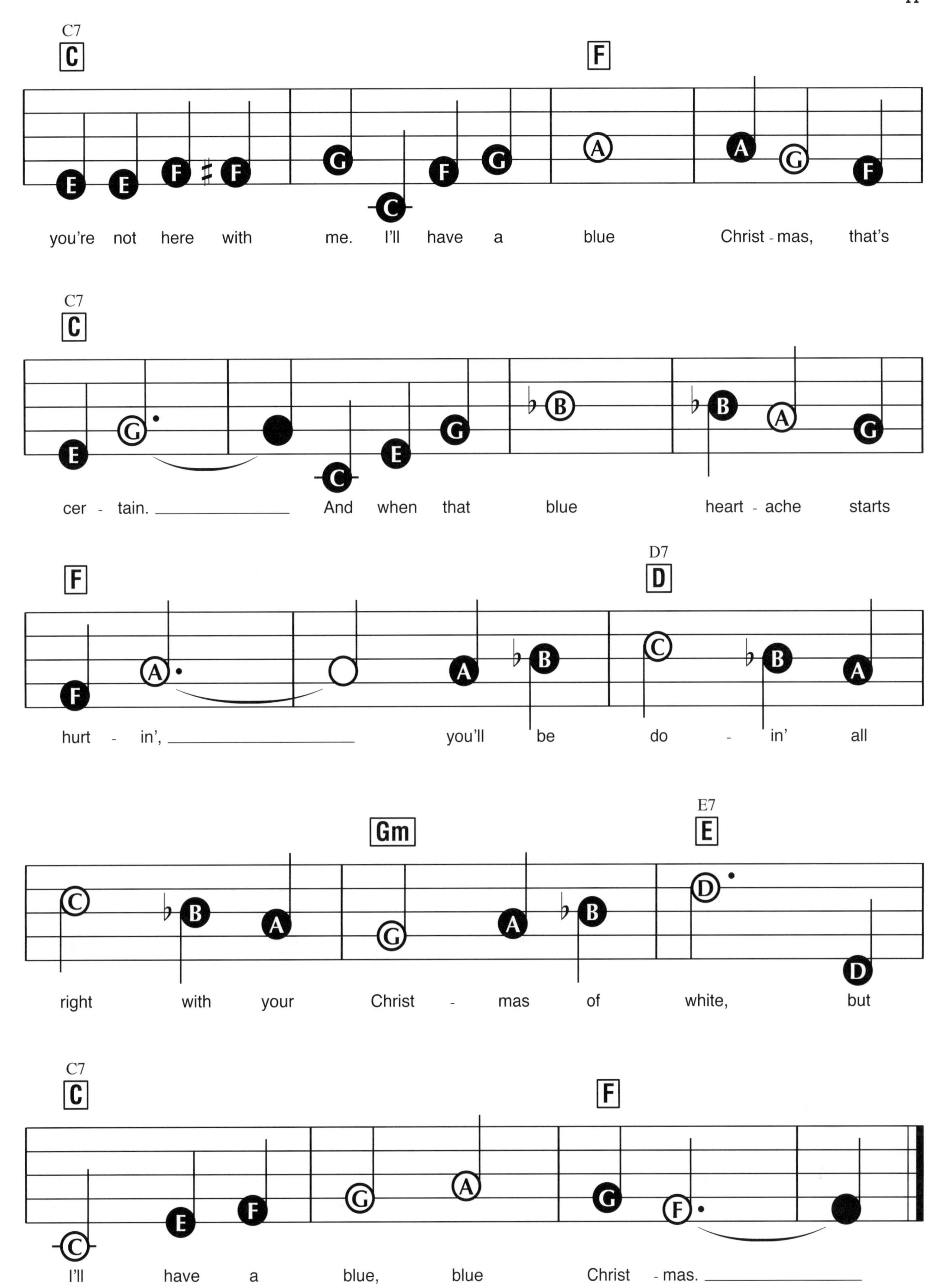
C7 C F
E E F ♯F G C F G A A G F
you're not here with me. I'll have a blue Christ - mas, that's
C7 C
E G G C E G ♭B ♭B A G
cer - tain. And when that blue heart - ache starts
F D7 D
F A A ♭B C ♭B A
hurt - in', you'll be do - in' all
Gm E7 E
C ♭B A G A ♭B D D
right with your Christ - mas of white, but
C7 C F
C E F G A G F
I'll have a blue, blue Christ - mas.

Christmas Lights

Registration 8
Rhythm: 4/4 Ballad

Words and Music by Guy Berryman,
Will Champion, Chris Martin and Jonny Buckland

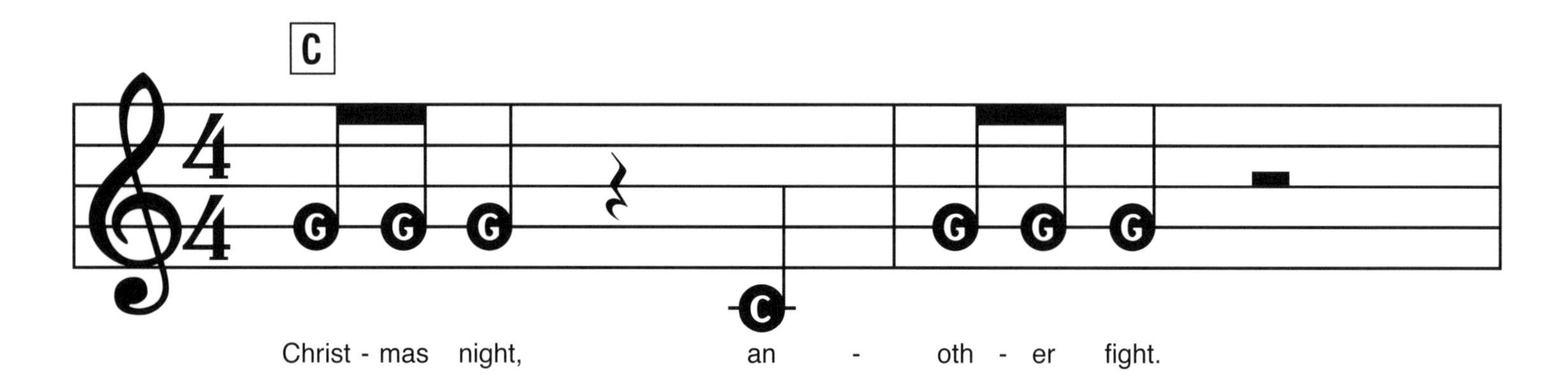

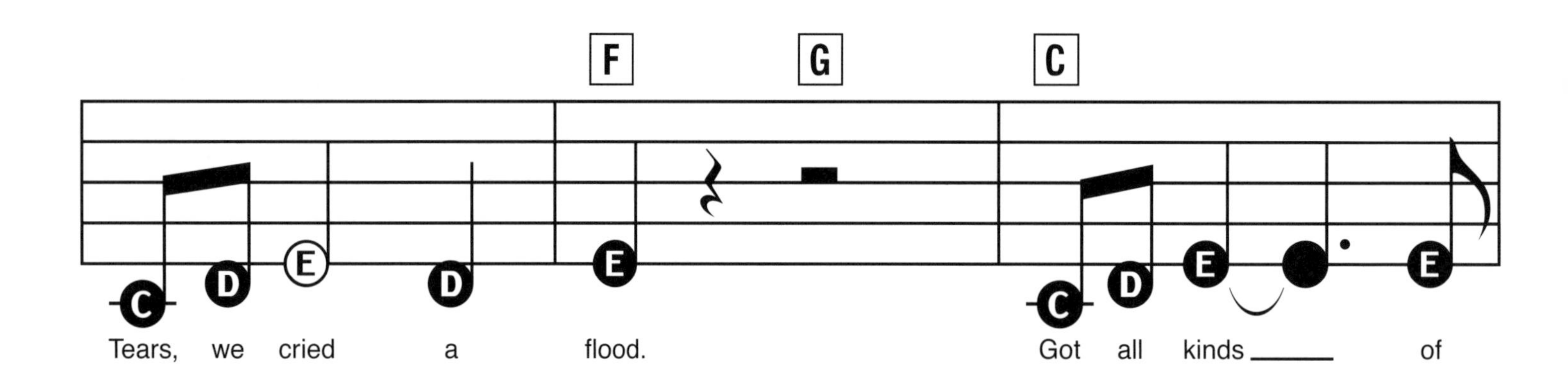

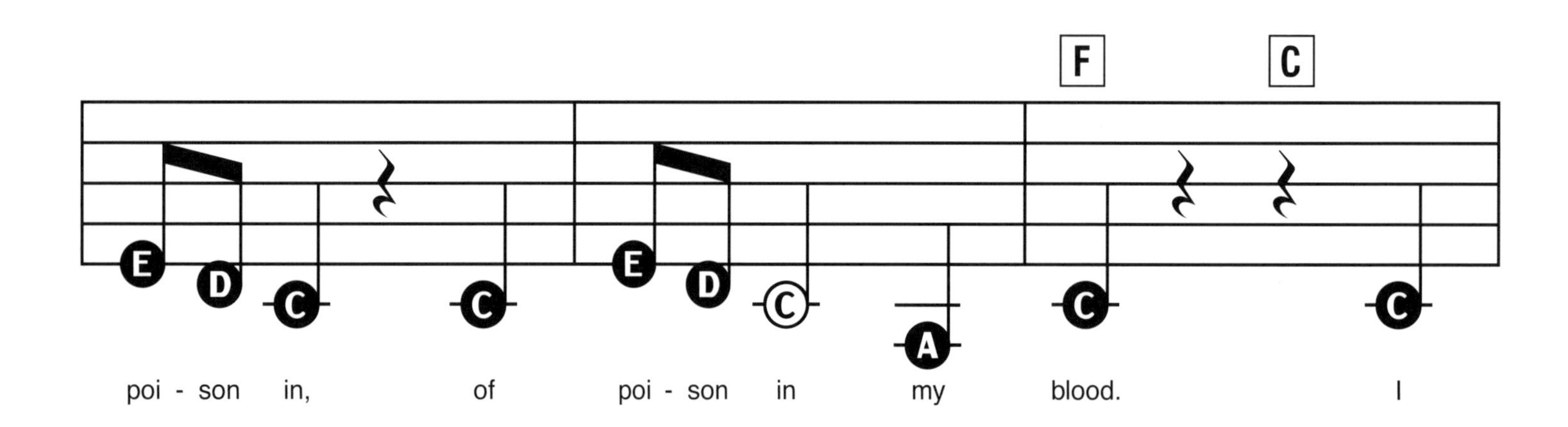

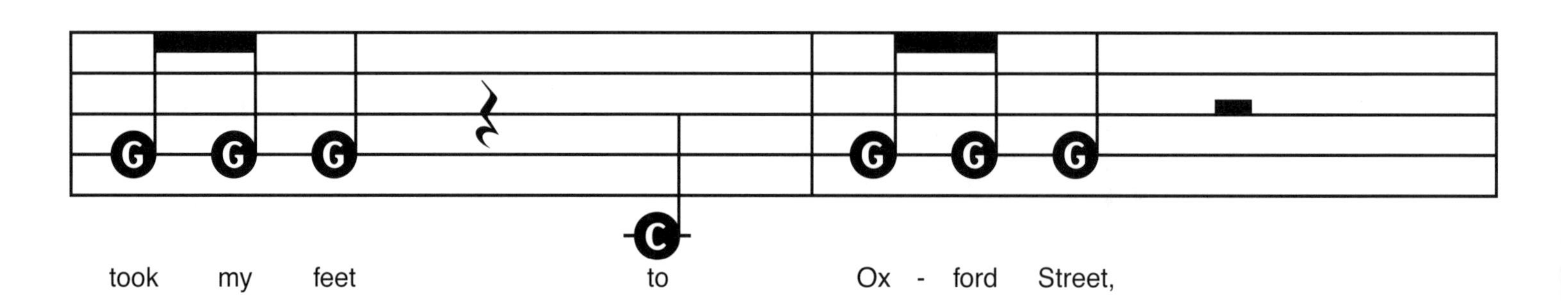

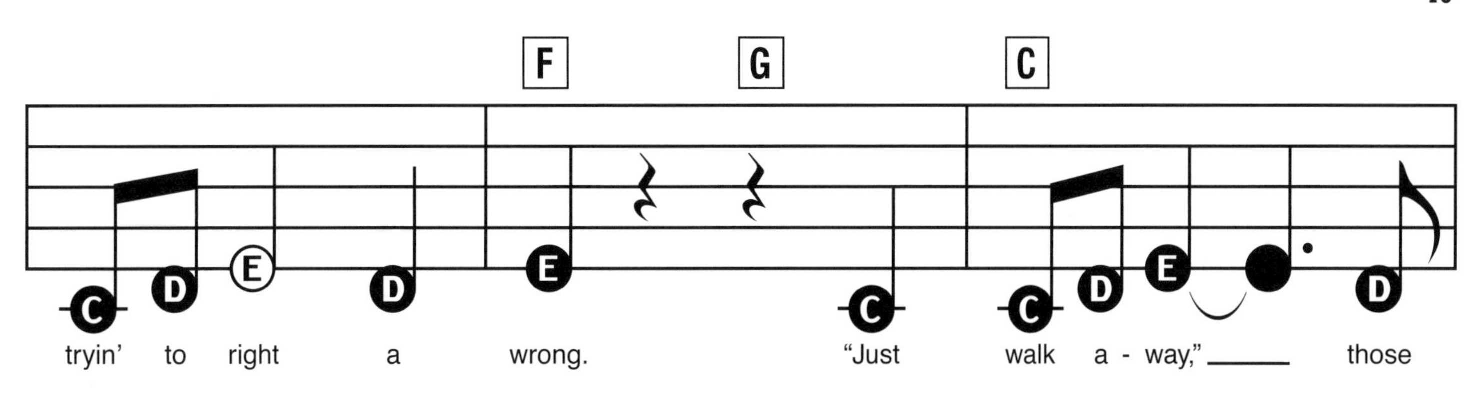
F G C
tryin' to right a wrong. "Just walk a - way," those

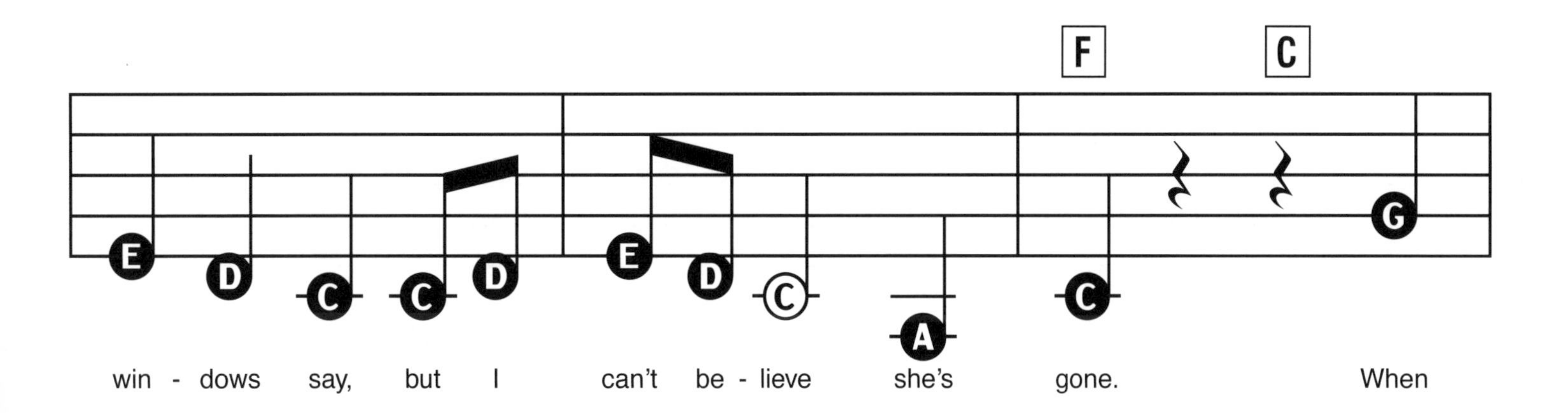
F C
win - dows say, but I can't be - lieve she's gone. When

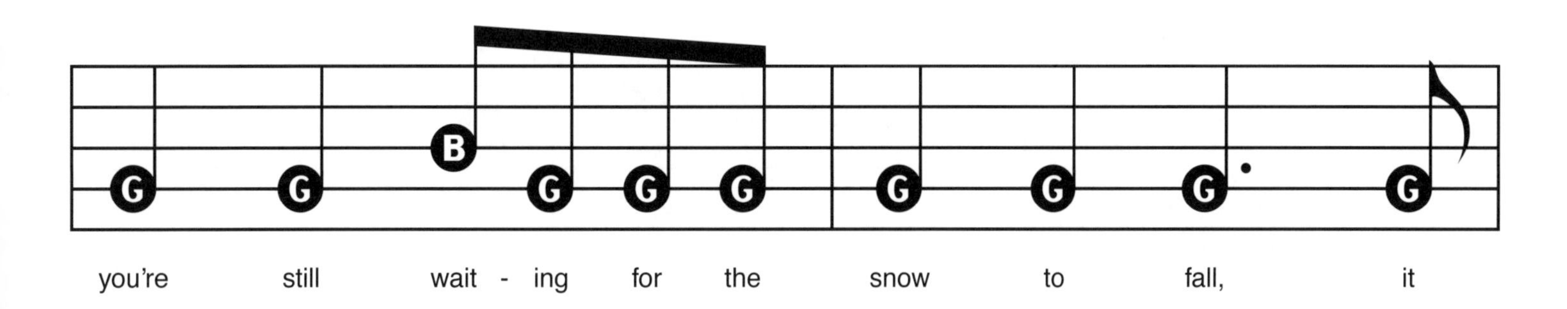
you're still wait - ing for the snow to fall, it

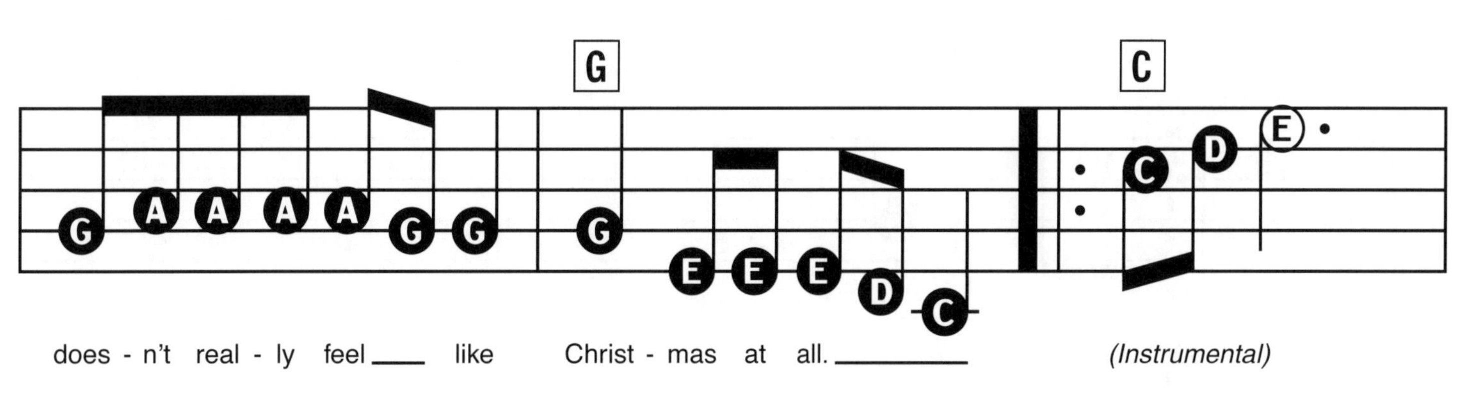
G C
does - n't real - ly feel like Christ - mas at all.
(Instrumental)

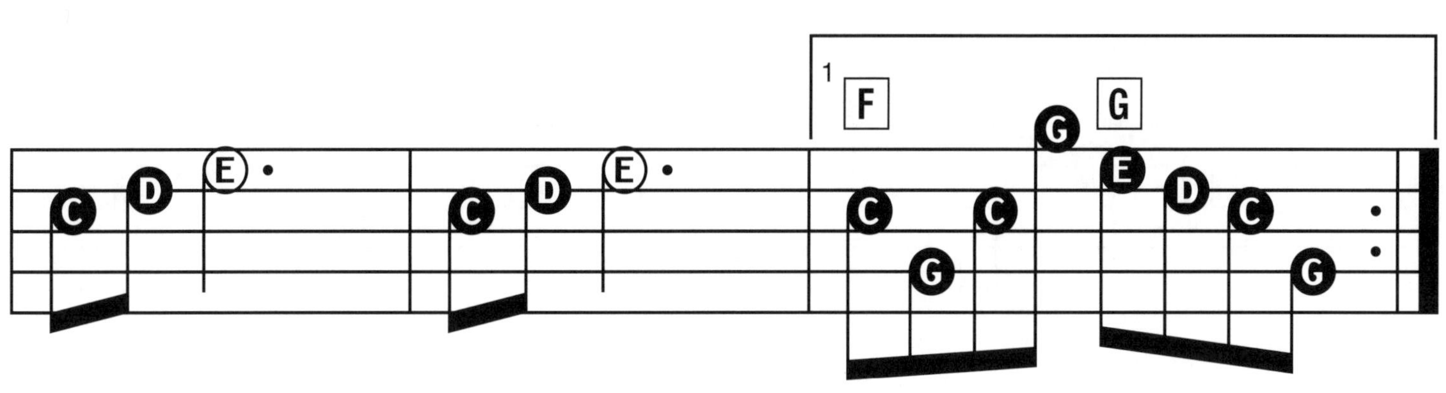
1
F G

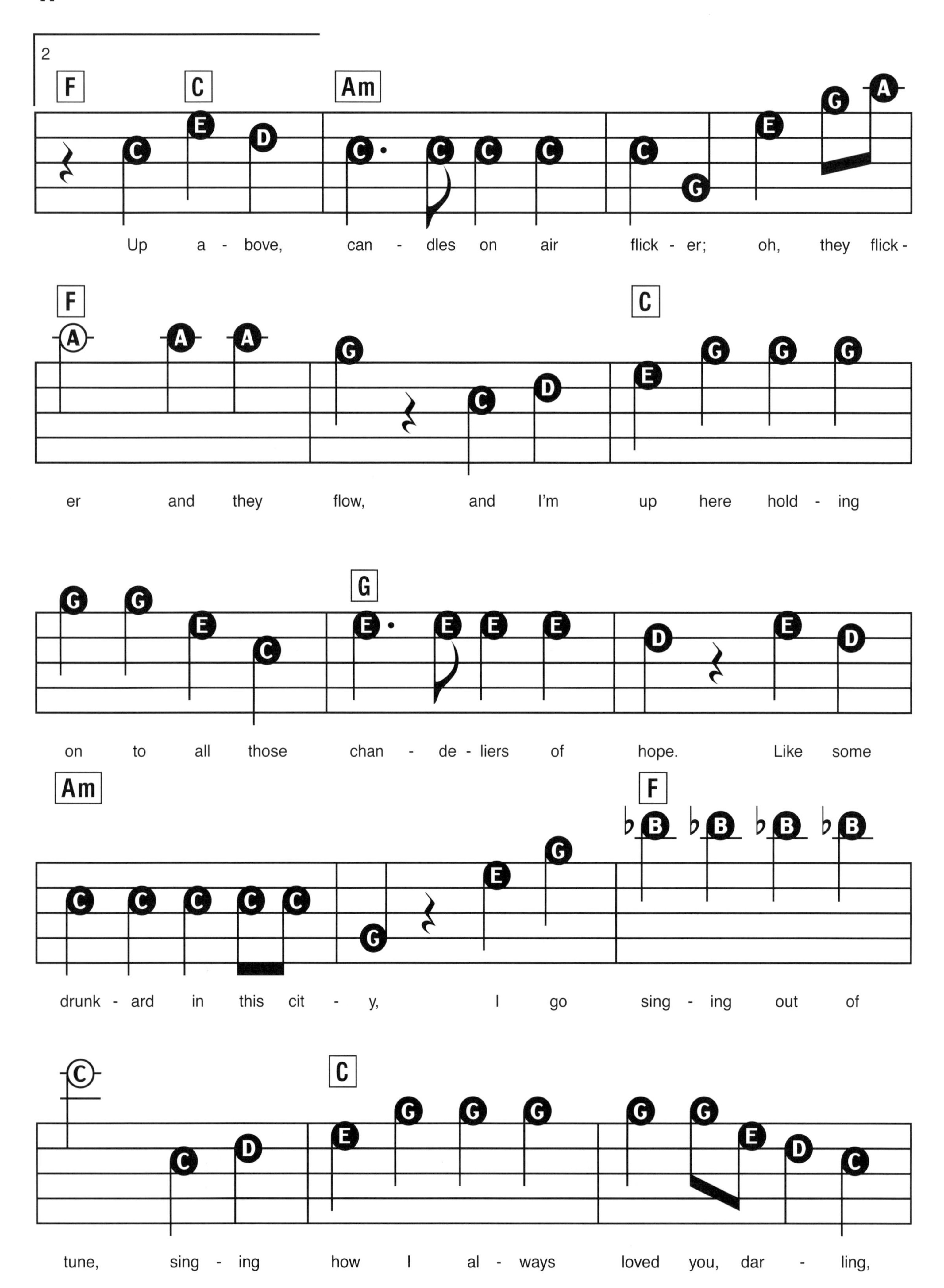
2
F C Am
Up a - bove, can - dles on air flick - er; oh, they flick -
F C
er and they flow, and I'm up here hold - ing
G
on to all those chan - de - liers of hope. Like some
Am F
drunk - ard in this cit - y, I go sing - ing out of
C
tune, sing - ing how I al - ways loved you, dar - ling,

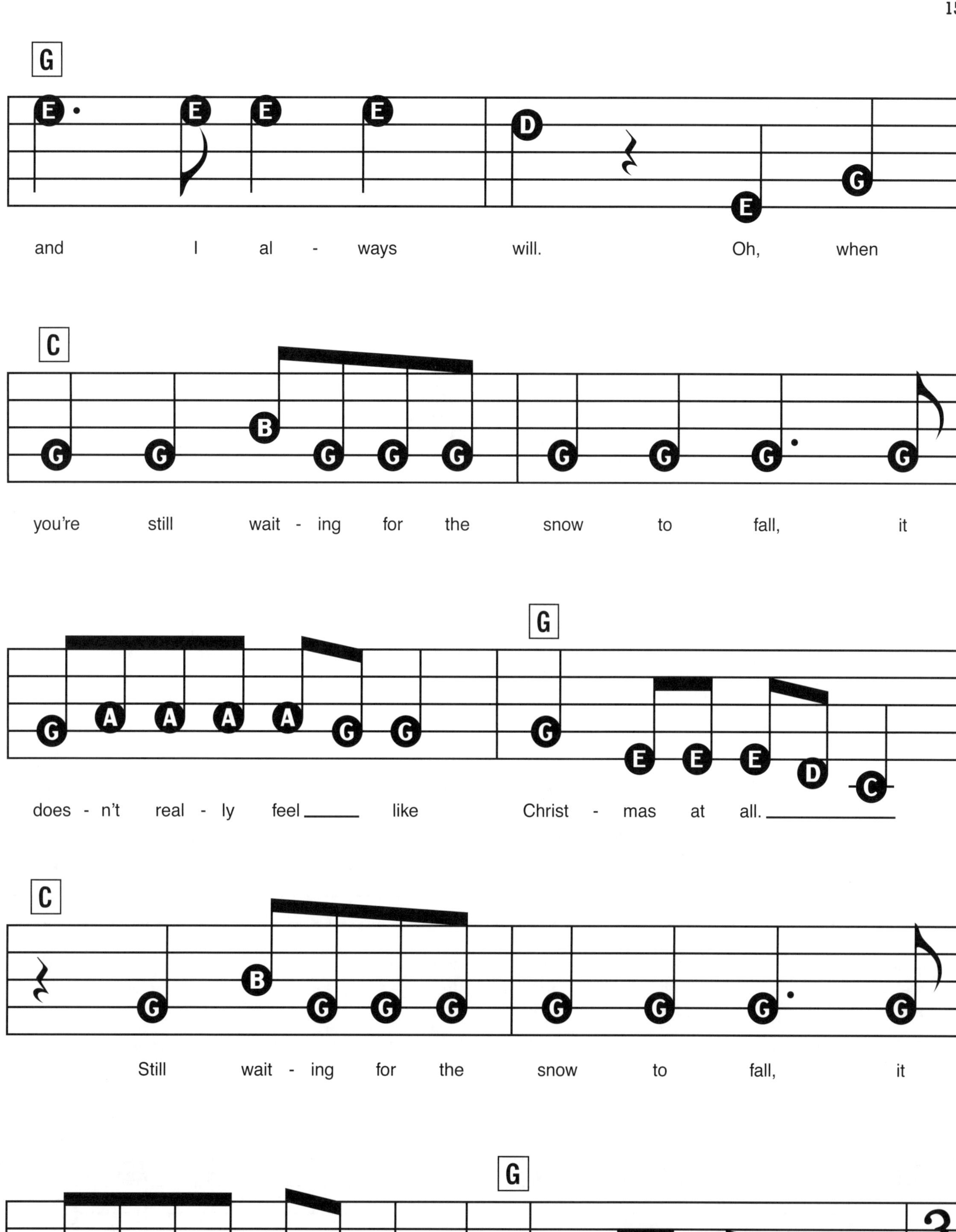
G
E E E E D E G
and I al - ways will. Oh, when
C
G G B G G G G G G G
you're still wait - ing for the snow to fall, it
G
G A A A A G G G E E E D C
does - n't real - ly feel like Christ - mas at all.
C
G B G G G G G G G
Still wait - ing for the snow to fall, it

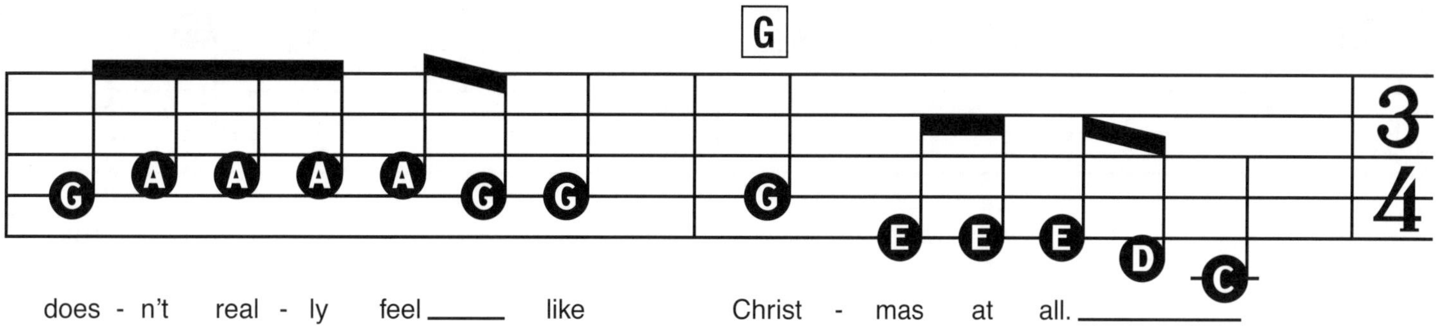
G
G A A A A G G G E E E D C
does - n't real - ly feel like Christ - mas at all.
3
4

Change to Waltz
C
E E D C E C A
These Christ - mas lights light up the
lights light up the
lights, light up the
F
G C E G A G G C
street, down where the sea and cit - y
street, may - be they'll bring her back to
street, light up the fi - re - works in
C
F
To Coda
E C E G A C A G
meet. May all your trou - bles soon be
me. Then all my trou - bles will be
me. May all your trou -
Am
C
E E E D C E E B
gone. Oh, Christ - mas lights, keep shin - ing
gone. Oh, Christ - mas lights, keep shin - ing

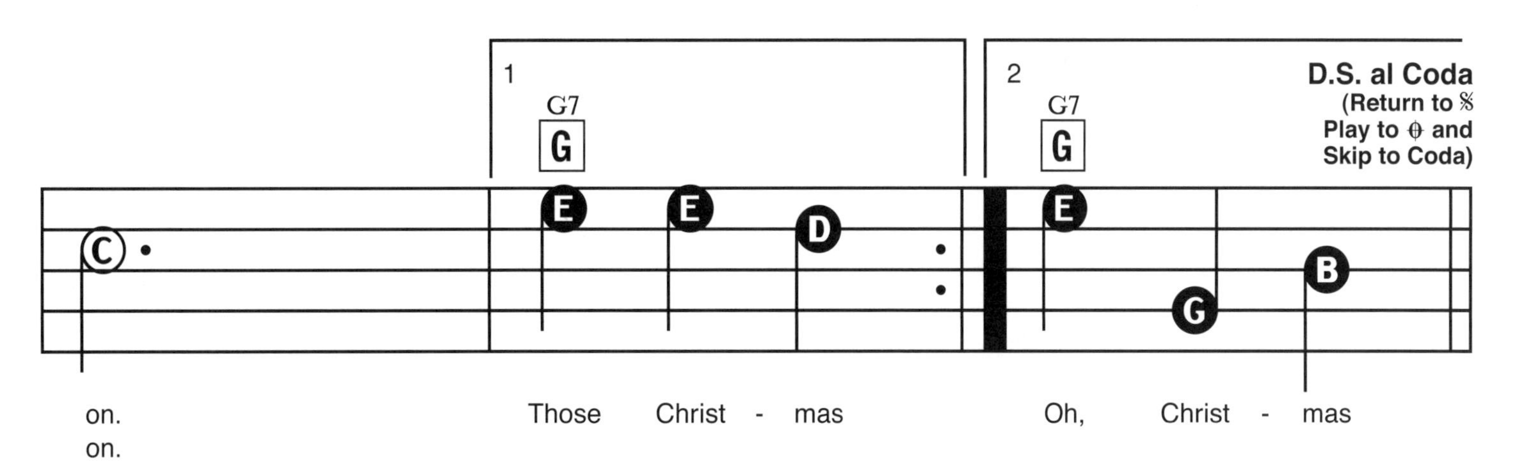
1
G7
G
2
G7
G
D.S. al Coda
(Return to 𝄋
Play to ⊕ and
Skip to Coda)
on.
on.
Those Christ - mas
Oh, Christ - mas

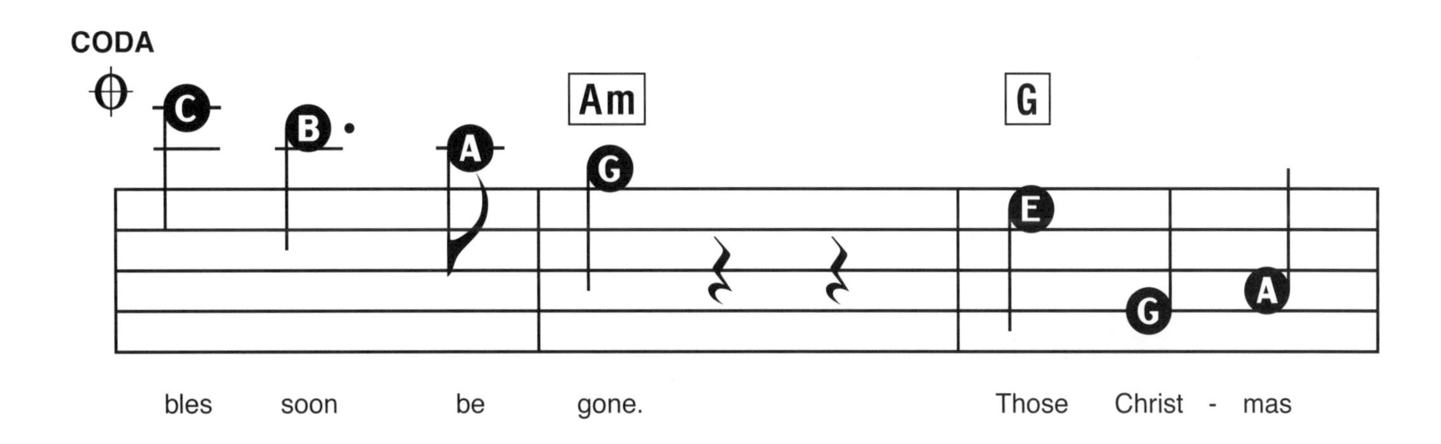
CODA
Am
G
bles soon be gone.
Those Christ - mas

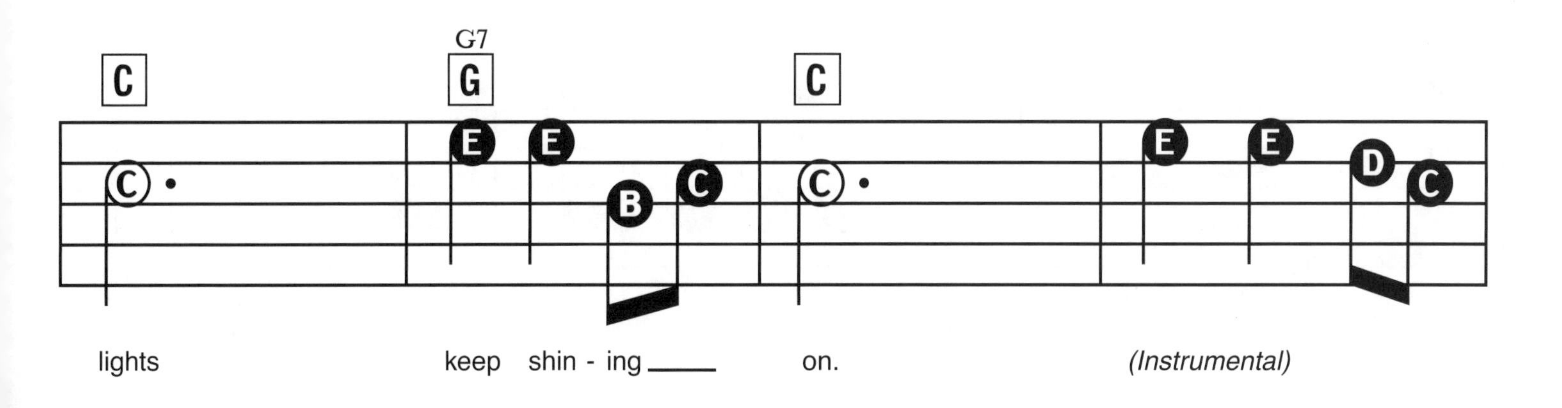
C
G7
G
C
lights
keep shin - ing
on.
(Instrumental)

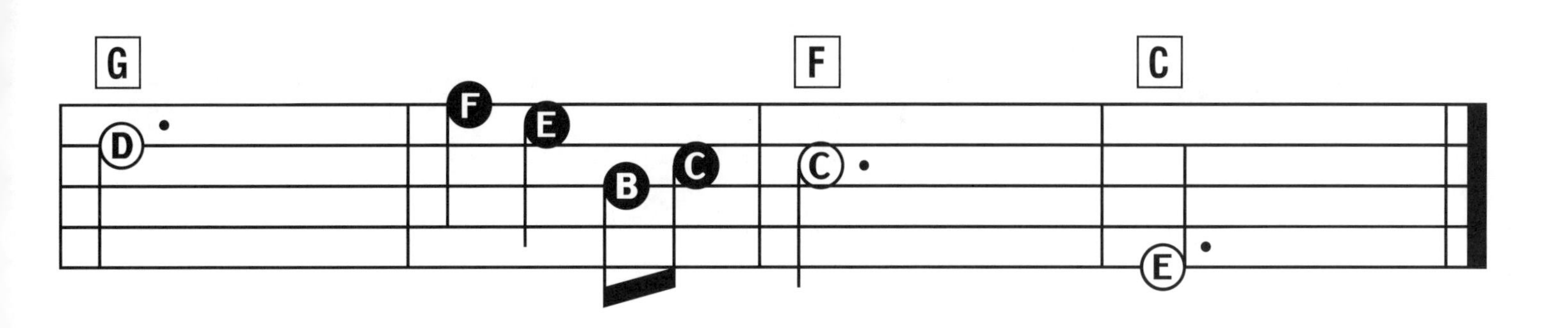
G
F
C

The Christmas Shoes

Registration 2
Rhythm: 4/4 Ballad or Fox Trot

Words and Music by Leonard Ahlstrom
and Eddie Carswell

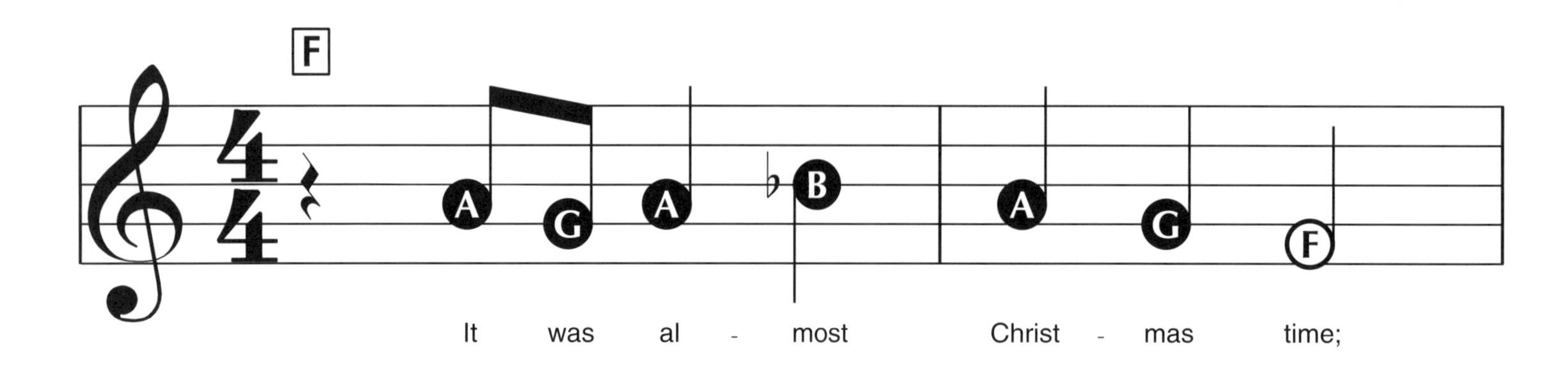

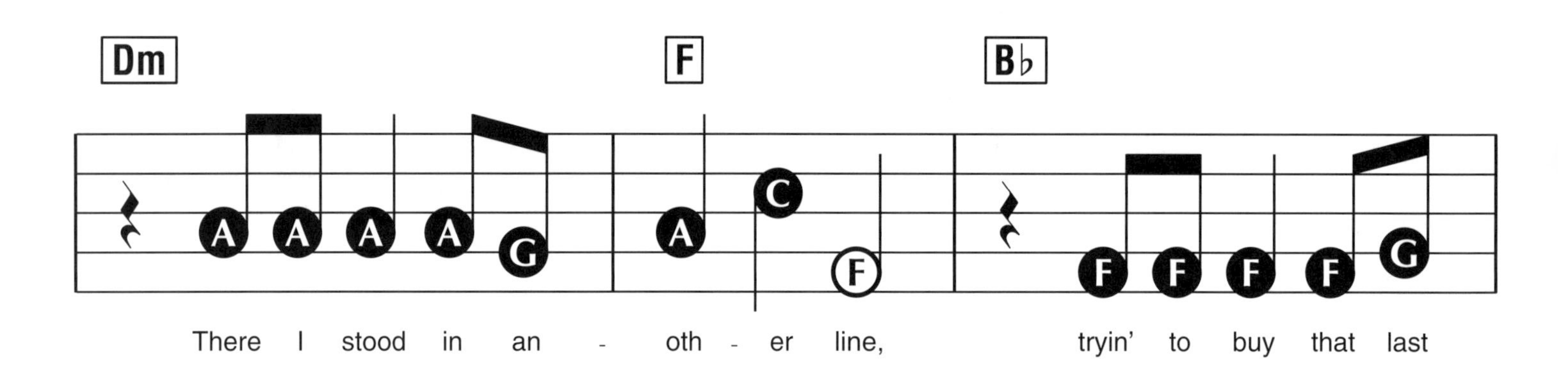

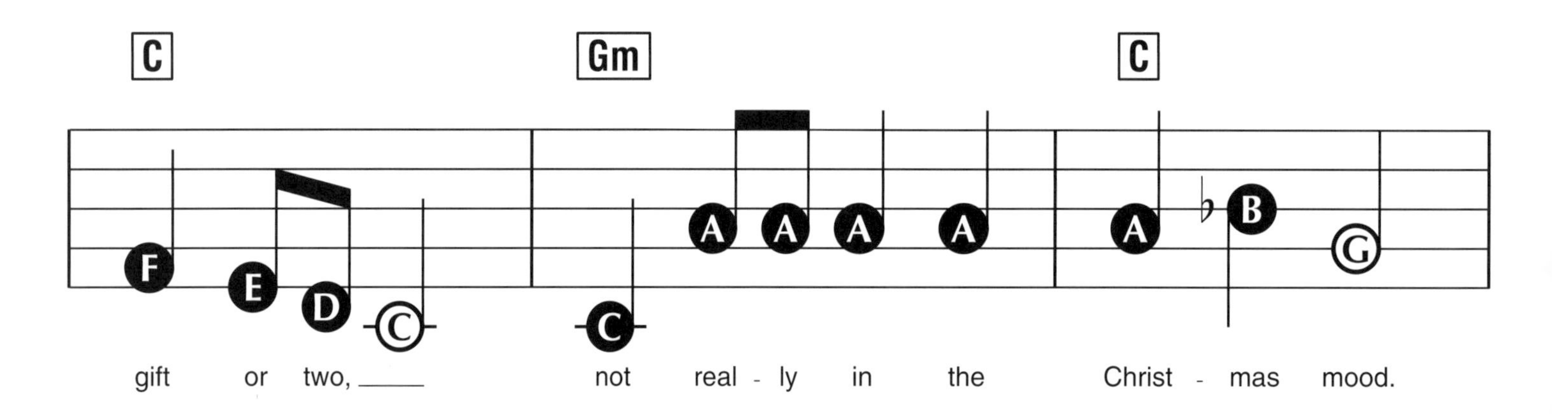

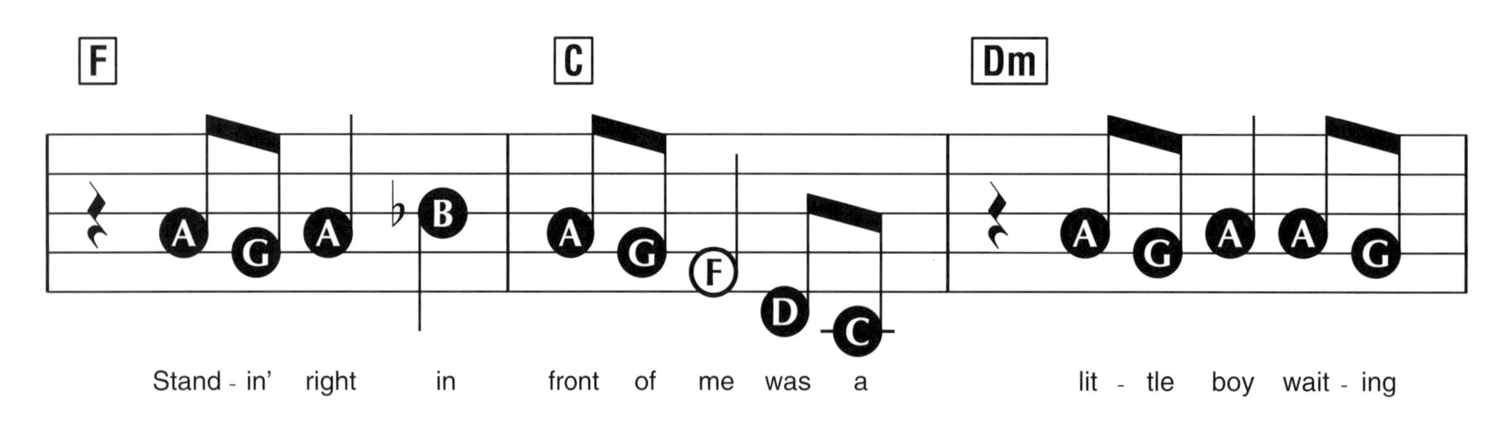

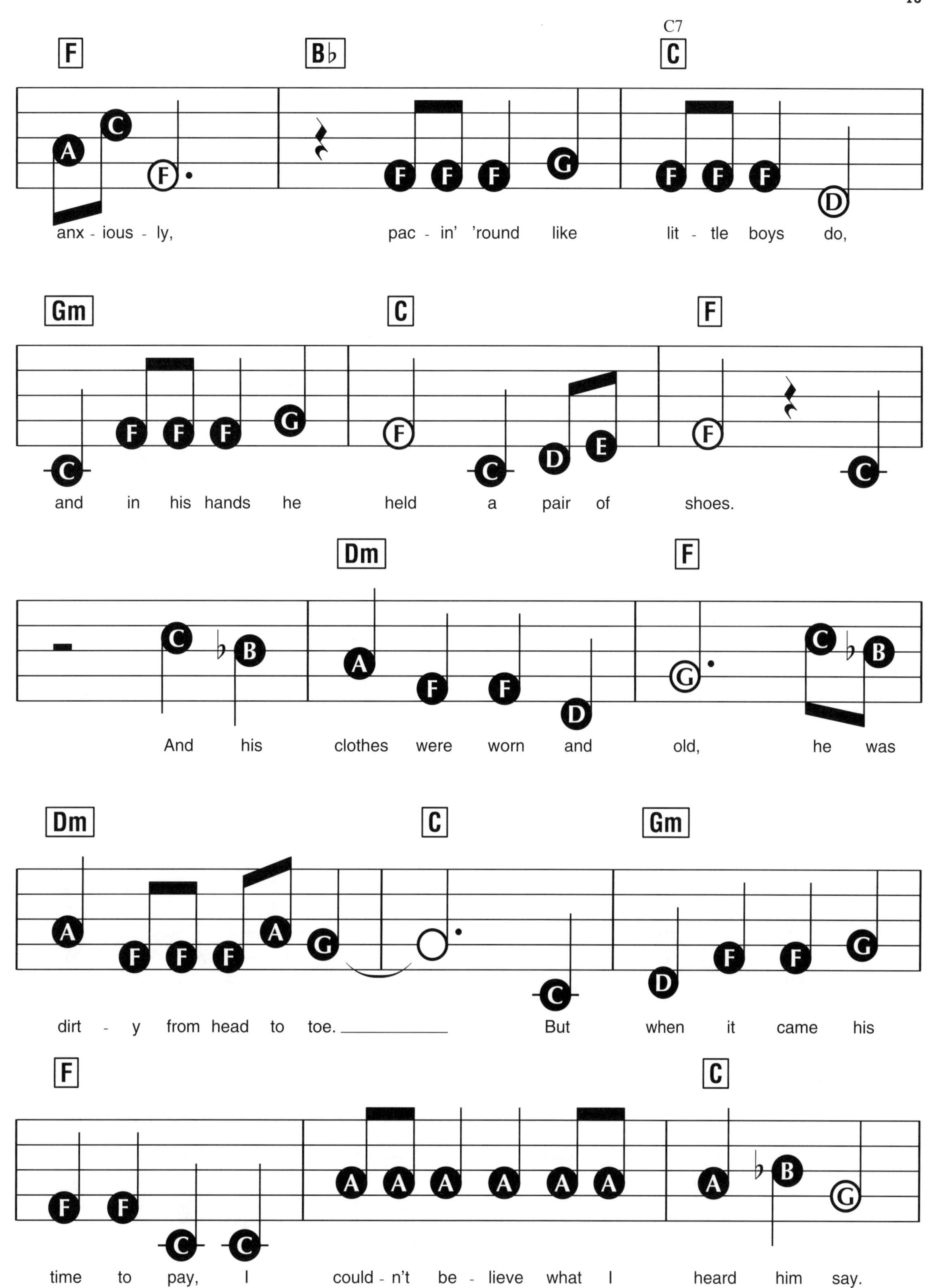

F
B♭
C7
C
A
C
F
F
F
F
G
F
F
F
D
anx - ious - ly,
pac - in' 'round like
lit - tle boys do,
Gm
C
F
C
F
F
F
G
F
C
D
E
F
C
and in his hands he
held a pair of
shoes.
Dm
F
C
B
A
F
F
D
G
C
B
And his
clothes were worn and
old, he was
Dm
C
Gm
A
F
F
F
A
G
C
D
F
F
G
dirt - y from head to toe.
But
when it came his
F
C
F
F
C
C
A
A
A
A
A
A
A
B
G
time to pay, I
could - n't be - lieve what I
heard him say.

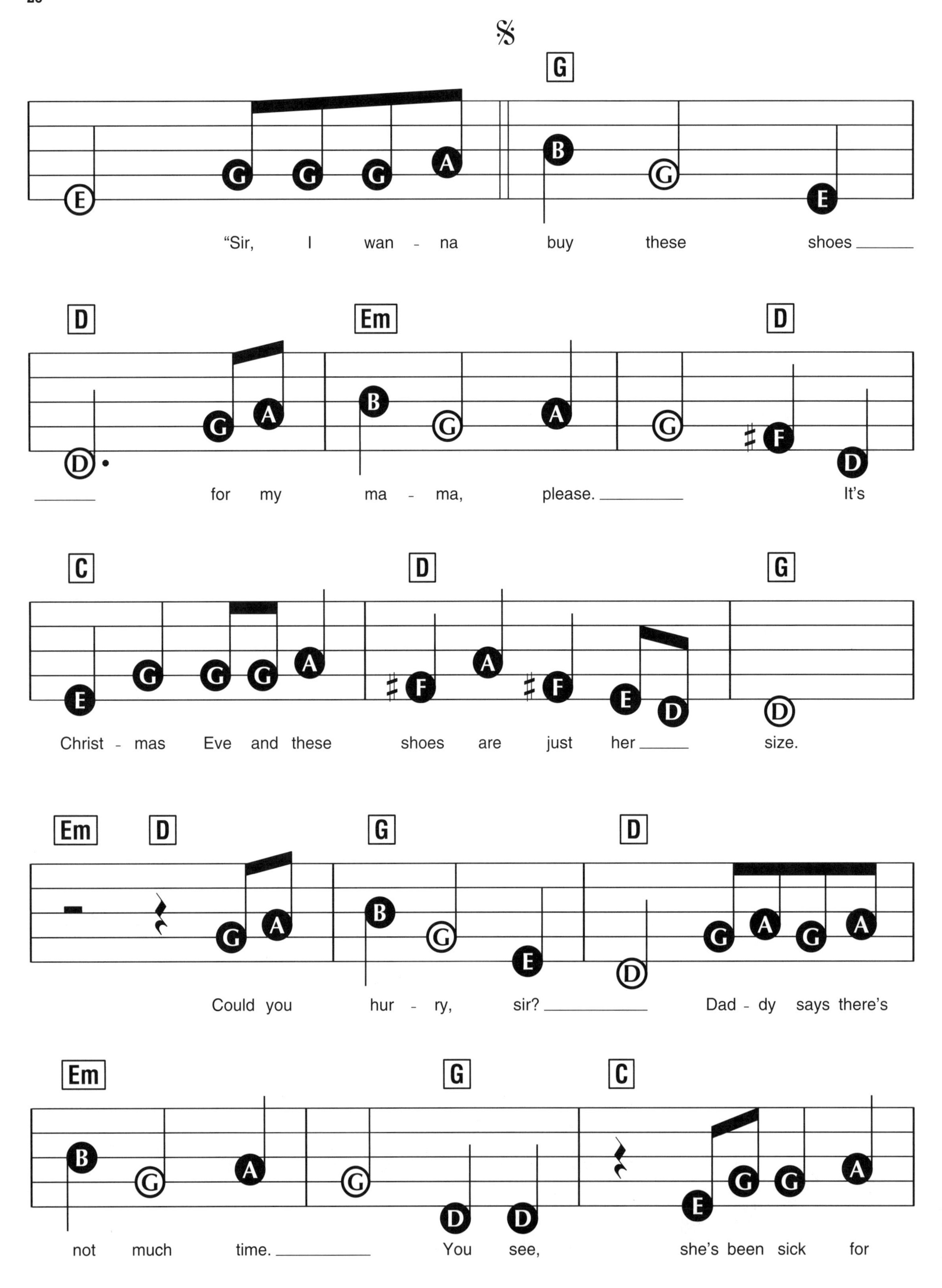
G
"Sir, I wan - na buy these shoes
D
Em
D
for my ma - ma, please.
It's
C
D
G
Christ - mas Eve and these shoes are just her size.
Em
D
G
D
Could you hur - ry, sir?
Dad - dy says there's
Em
G
C
not much time.
You see,
she's been sick for

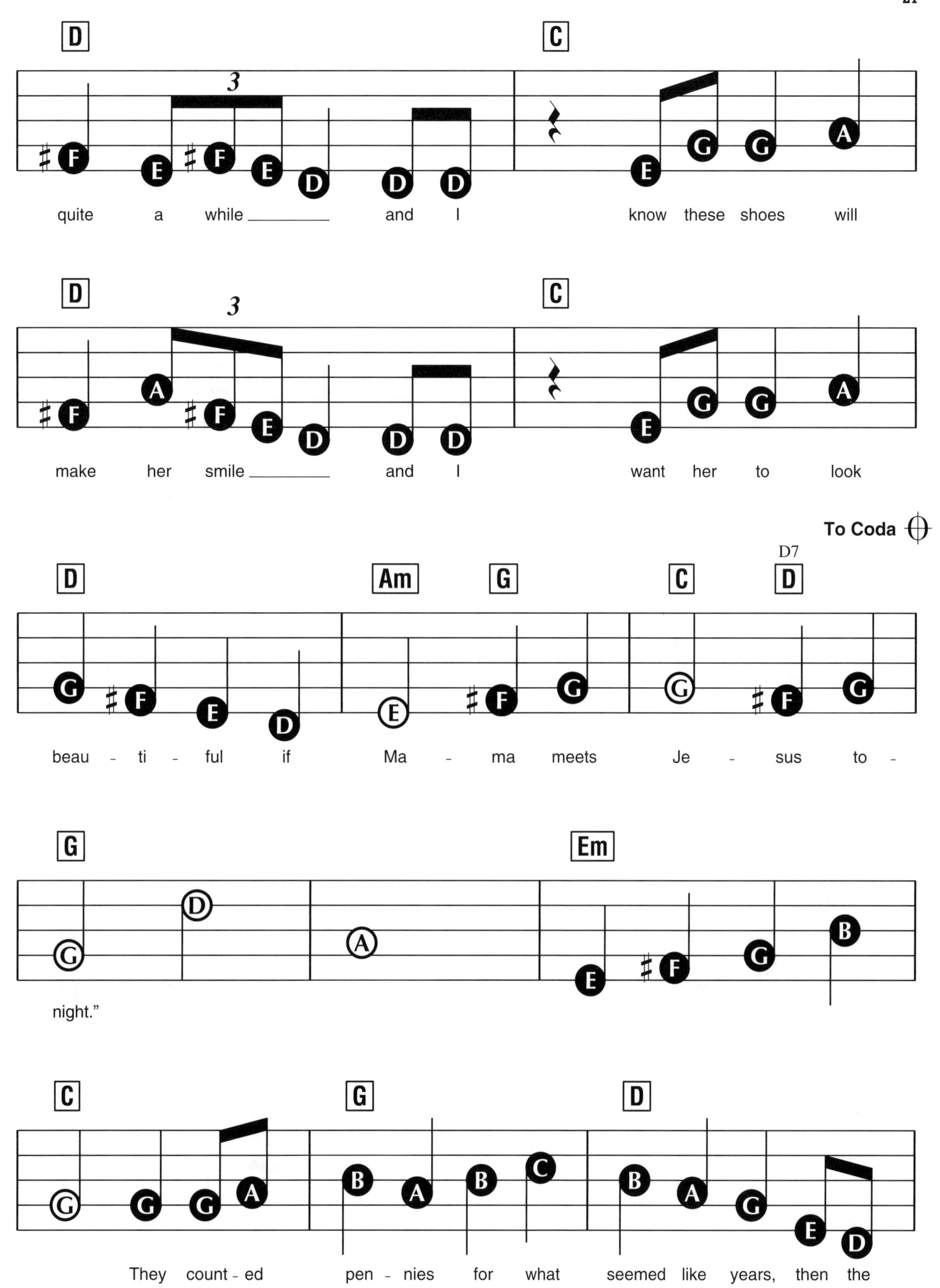
D
C
3
quite a while and I
know these shoes will
D
C
3
make her smile and I
want her to look
To Coda
D7
D
Am
G
C
D
beau - ti - ful if
Ma - ma meets
Je - sus to -
G
Em
night."
C
G
D
They count - ed
pen - nies for what
seemed like years, then the

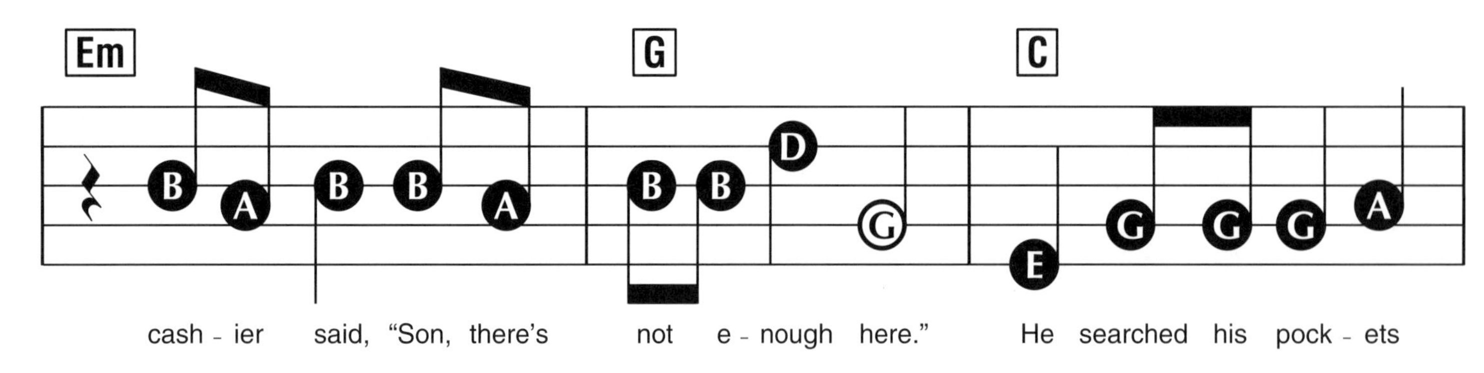
Em
G
C
cash - ier said, "Son, there's not e - nough here." He searched his pock - ets

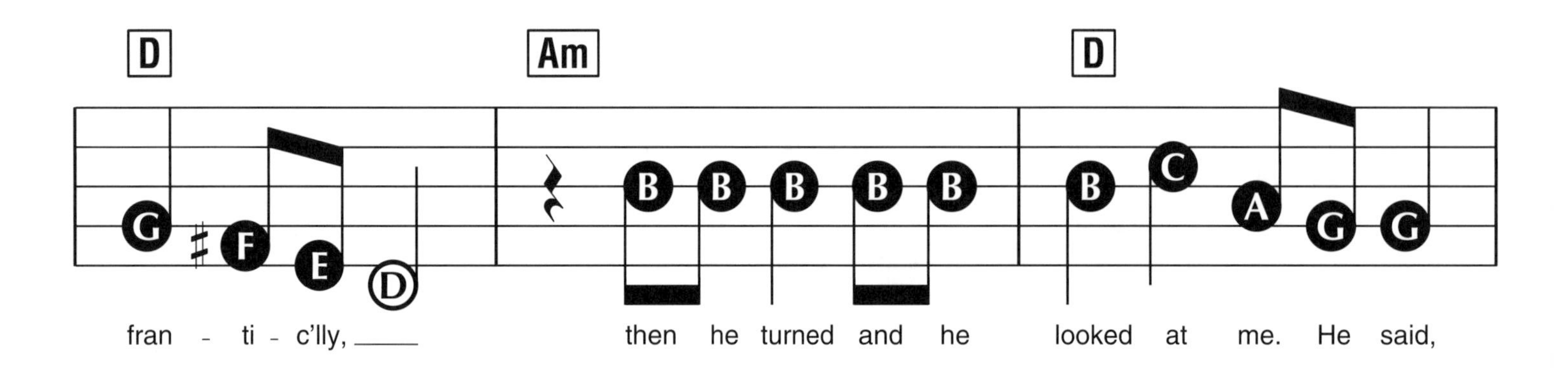
D
Am
D
fran - ti - c'lly, then he turned and he looked at me. He said,

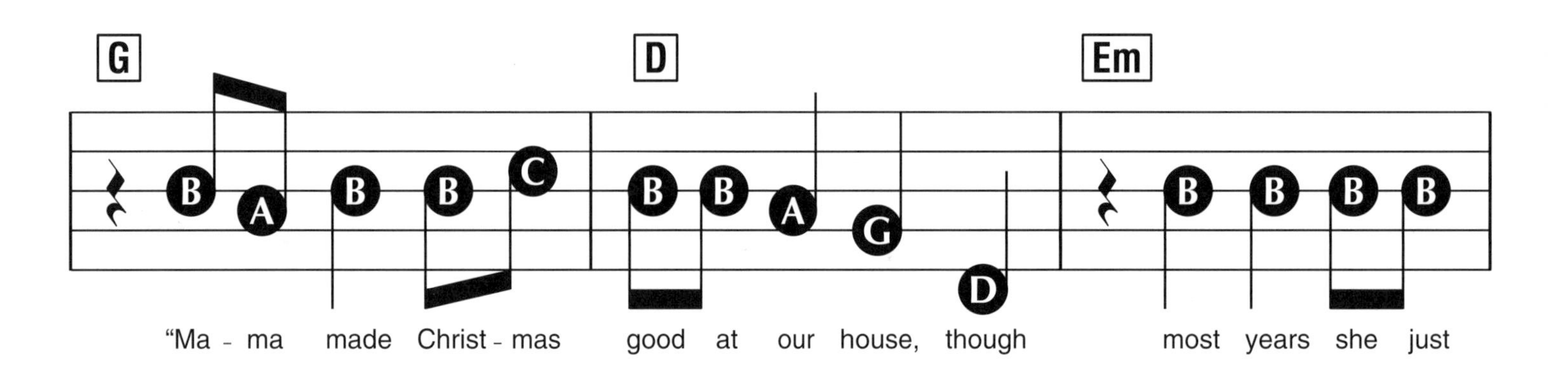
G
D
Em
"Ma - ma made Christ - mas good at our house, though most years she just

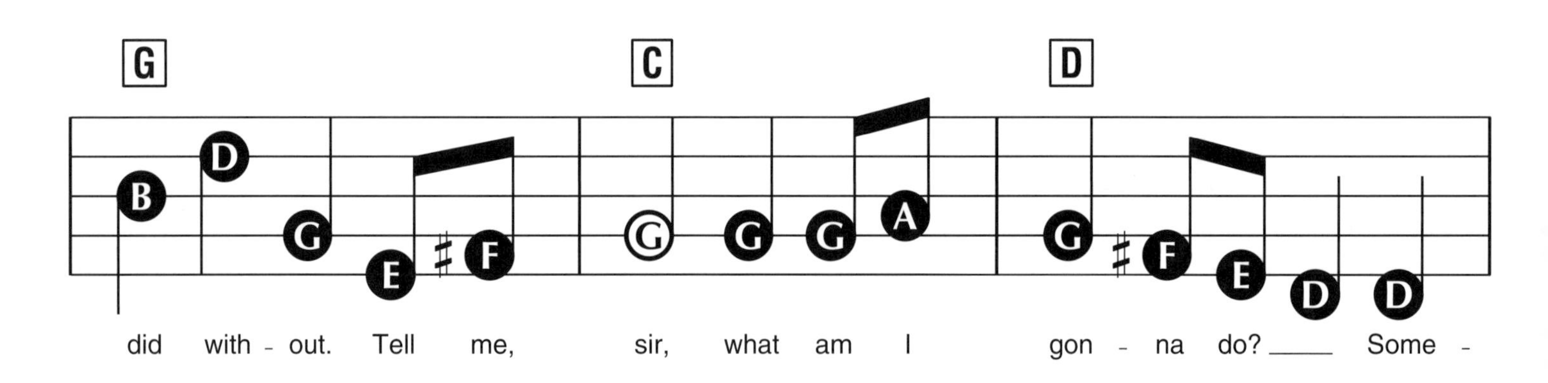
G
C
D
did with - out. Tell me, sir, what am I gon - na do? Some -

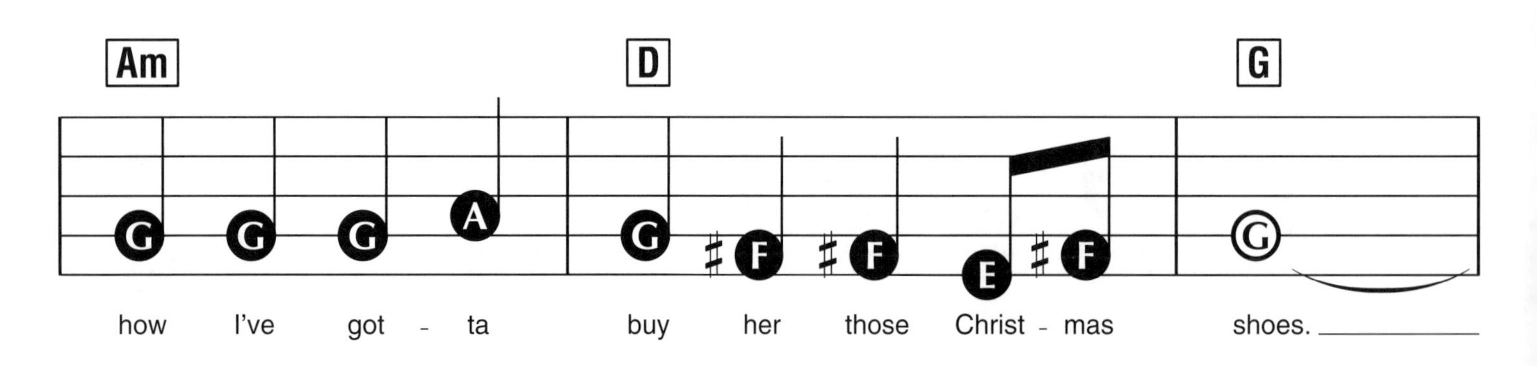
Am
D
G
how I've got - ta buy her those Christ - mas shoes.

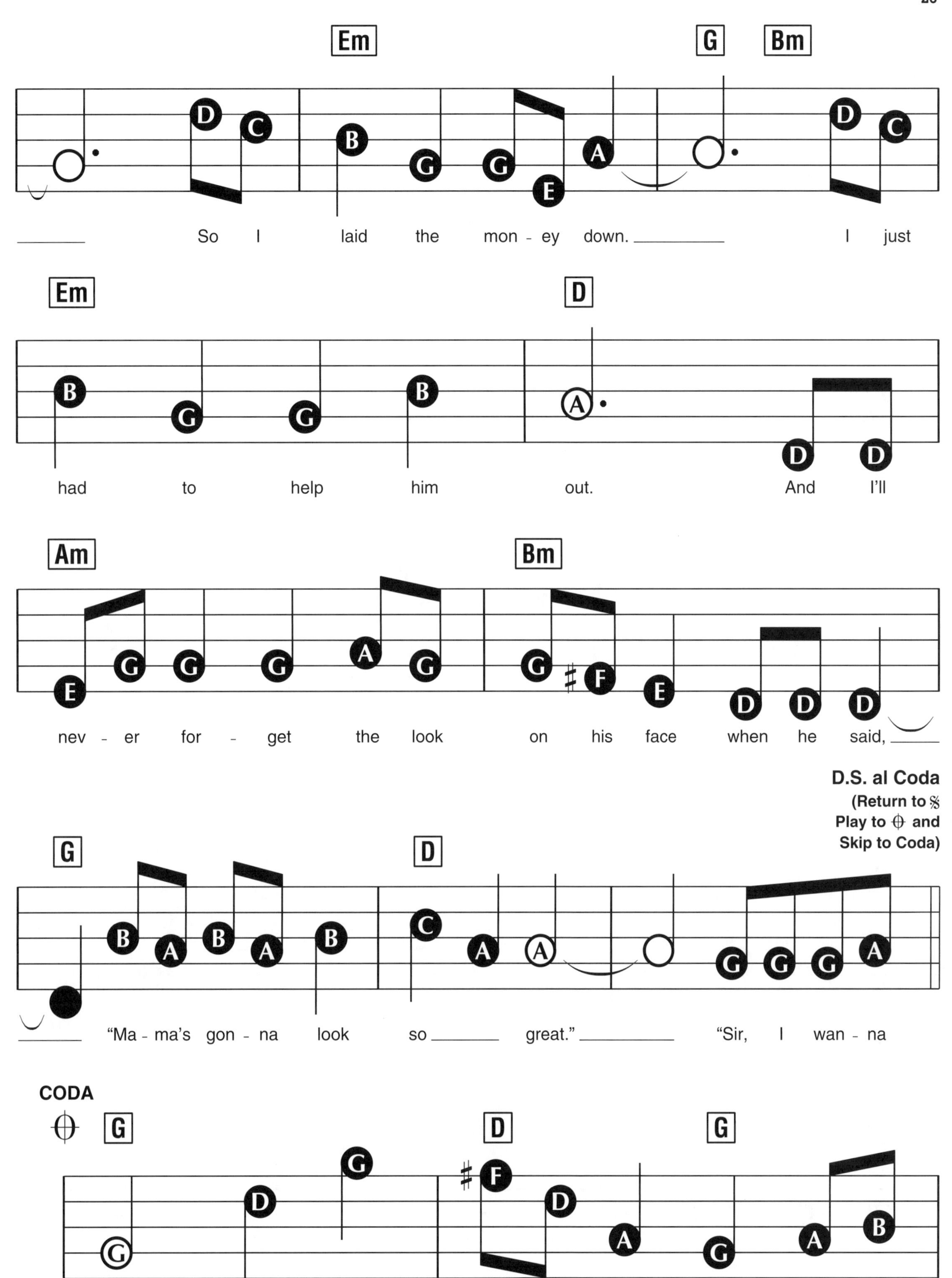
Em
G
Bm
So I laid the mon - ey down.
I just
Em
D
had to help him out.
And I'll
Am
Bm
nev - er for - get the look on his face when he said,
D.S. al Coda
(Return to 𝄋
Play to ⊕ and
Skip to Coda)
G
D
"Ma - ma's gon - na look so great."
"Sir, I wan - na
CODA
G
D
G
night."
I knew I

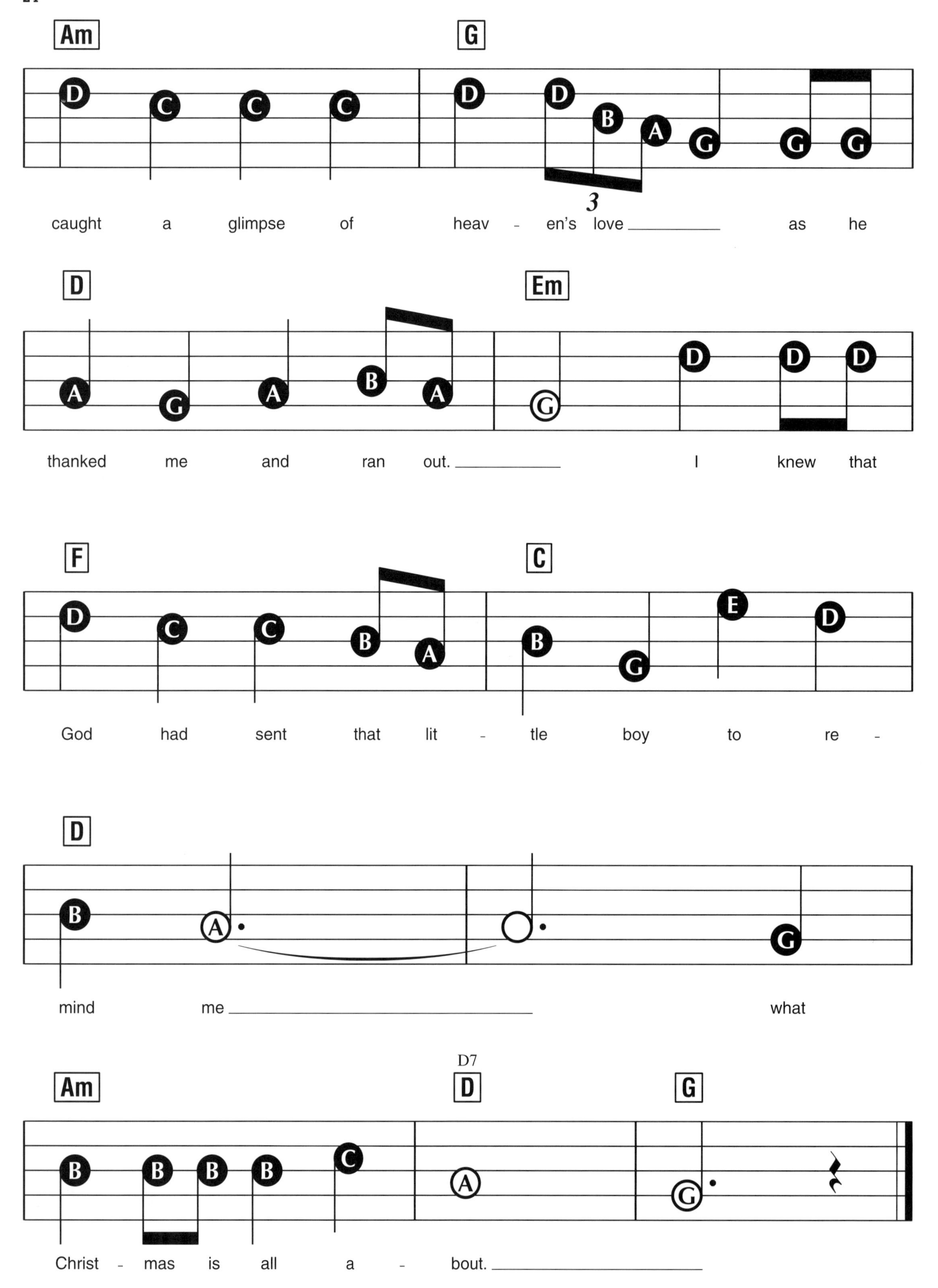
Am
G
caught a glimpse of heav - en's love as he
3
D
Em
thanked me and ran out. I knew that
F
C
God had sent that lit - tle boy to re -
D
mind me what
Am
D7
D
G
Christ - mas is all a - bout.

Fairytale of New York

Registration 8
Rhythm: 4/4 Ballad

Words and Music by Jeremy Finer
and Shane MacGowan

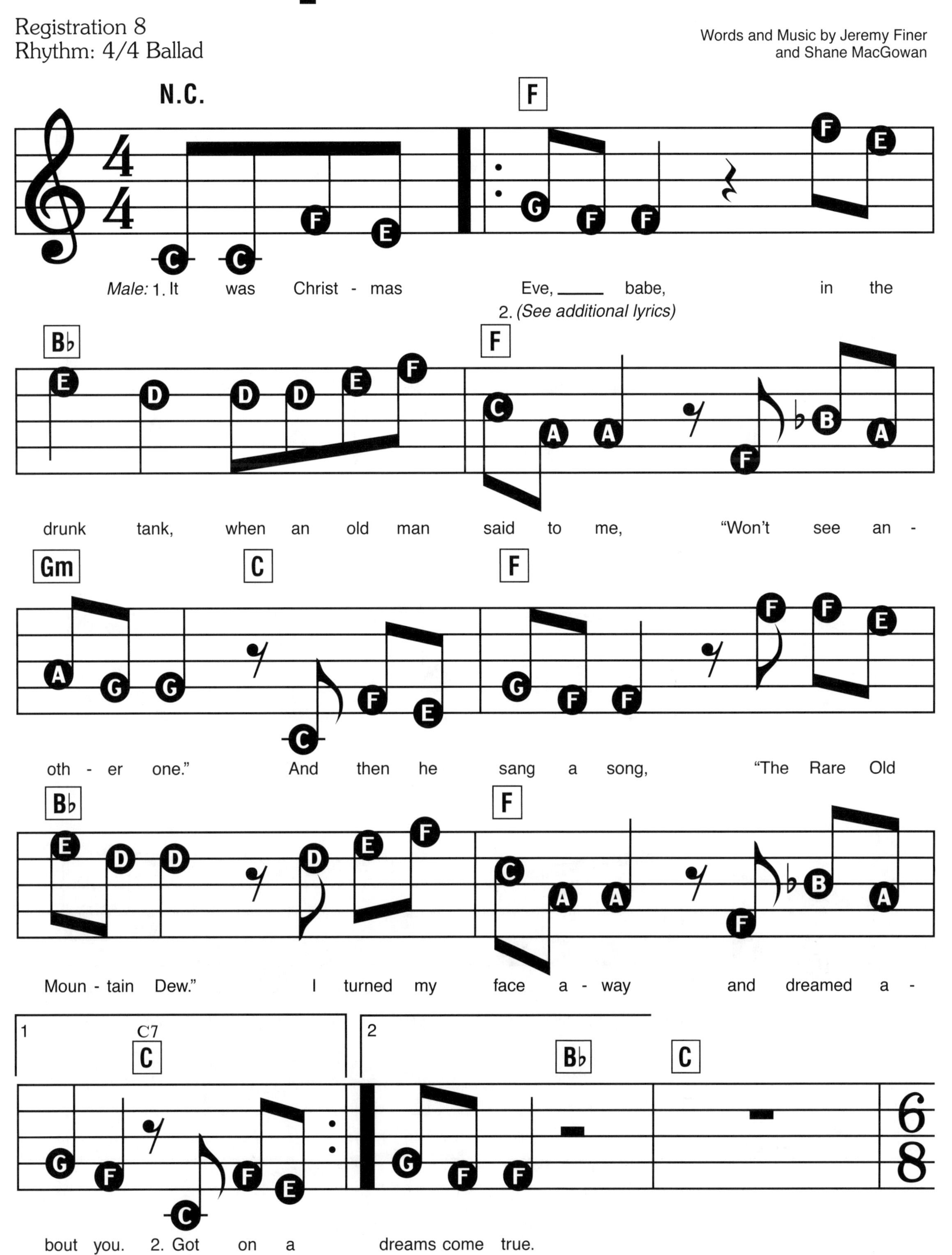

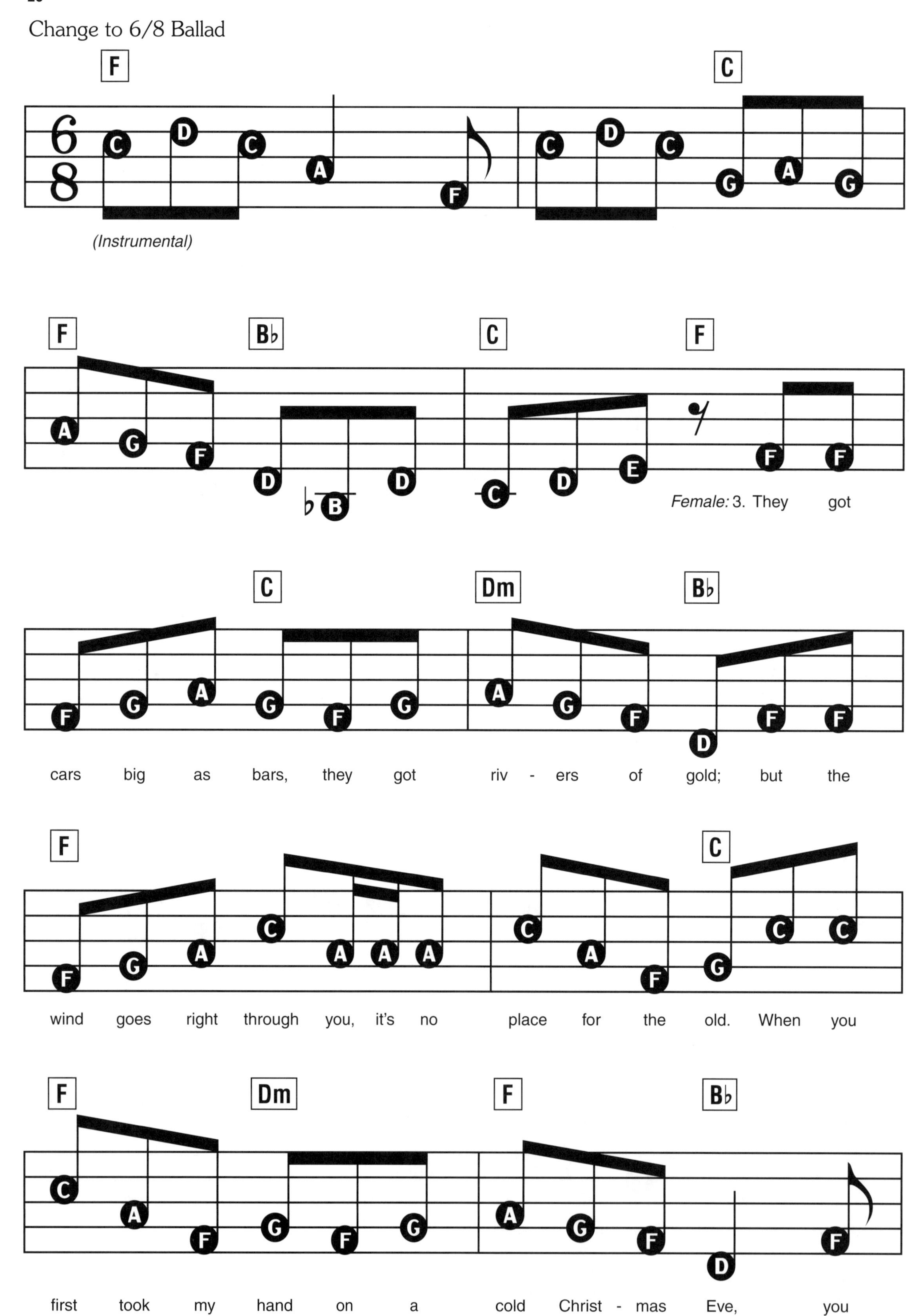
Change to 6/8 Ballad
F
C
(Instrumental)
F
B♭
C
F
Female: 3. They got
C
Dm
B♭
cars big as bars, they got riv - ers of gold; but the
F
C
wind goes right through you, it's no place for the old. When you
F
Dm
F
B♭
first took my hand on a cold Christ - mas Eve, you

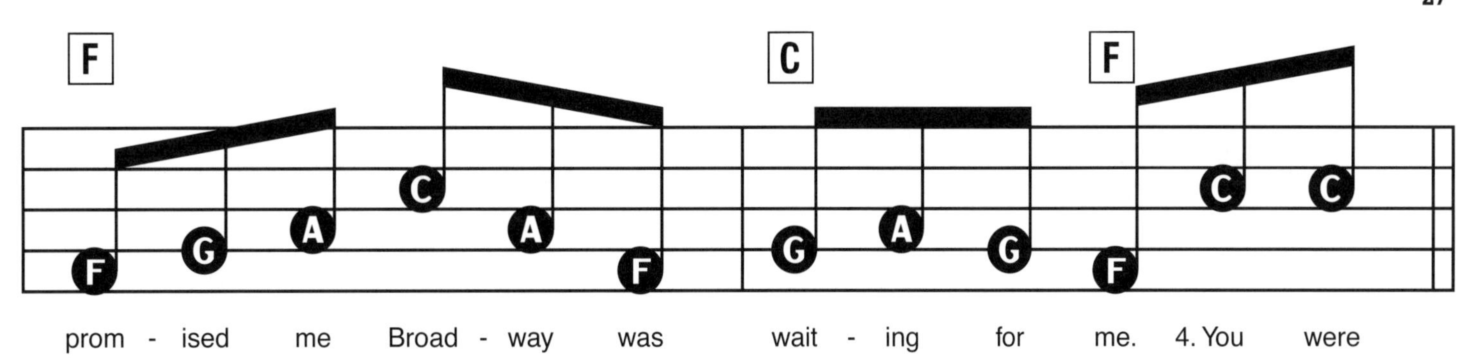
F
C
F
prom - ised me Broad - way was wait - ing for me. 4. You were

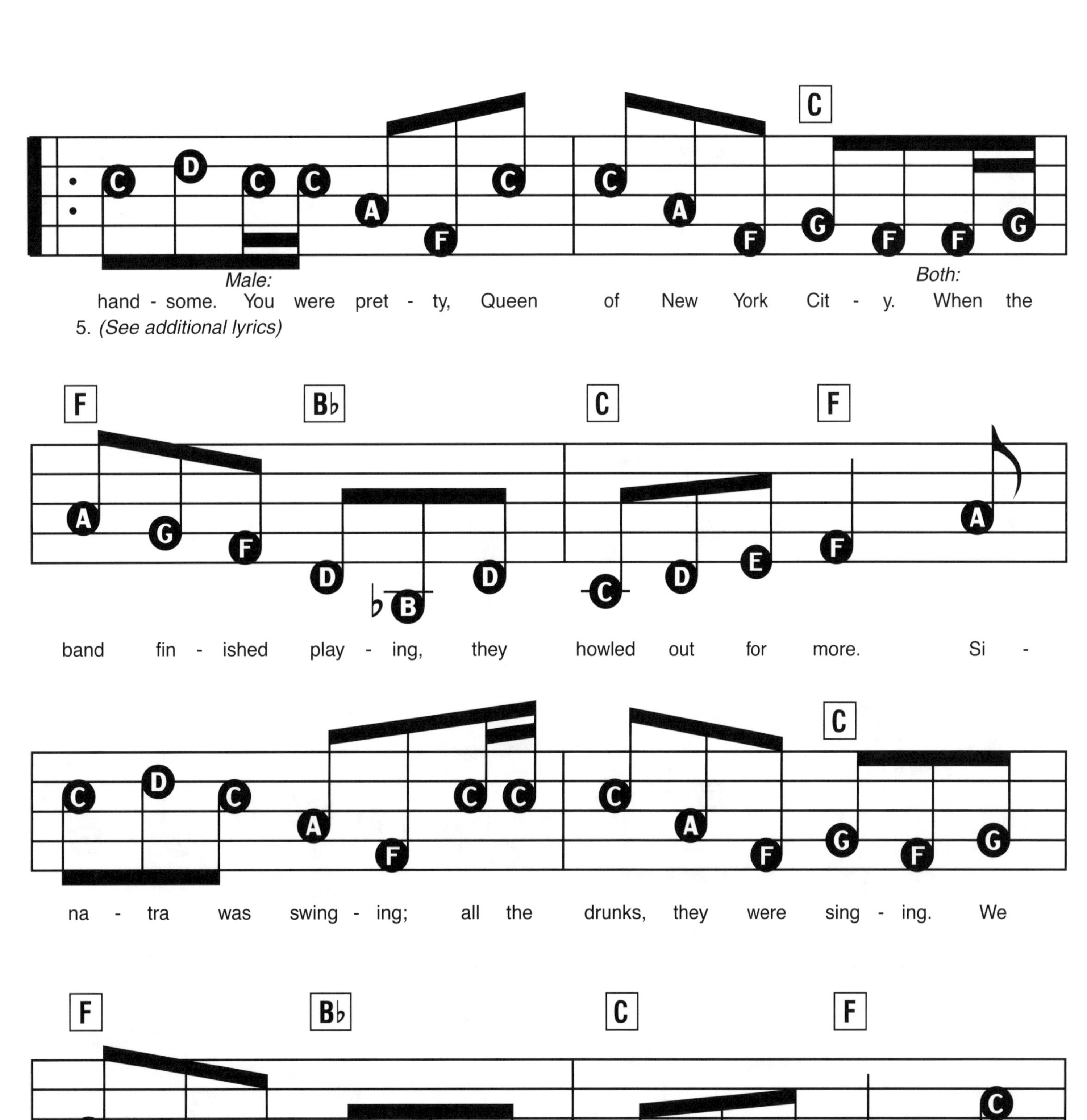
C
Male:
Both:
hand - some. You were pret - ty, Queen of New York Cit - y. When the
5. (See additional lyrics)
F
B♭
C
F
band fin - ished play - ing, they howled out for more. Si -
C
na - tra was swing - ing; all the drunks, they were sing - ing. We
F
B♭
C
F
kissed on the cor - ner, then danced through the night. The

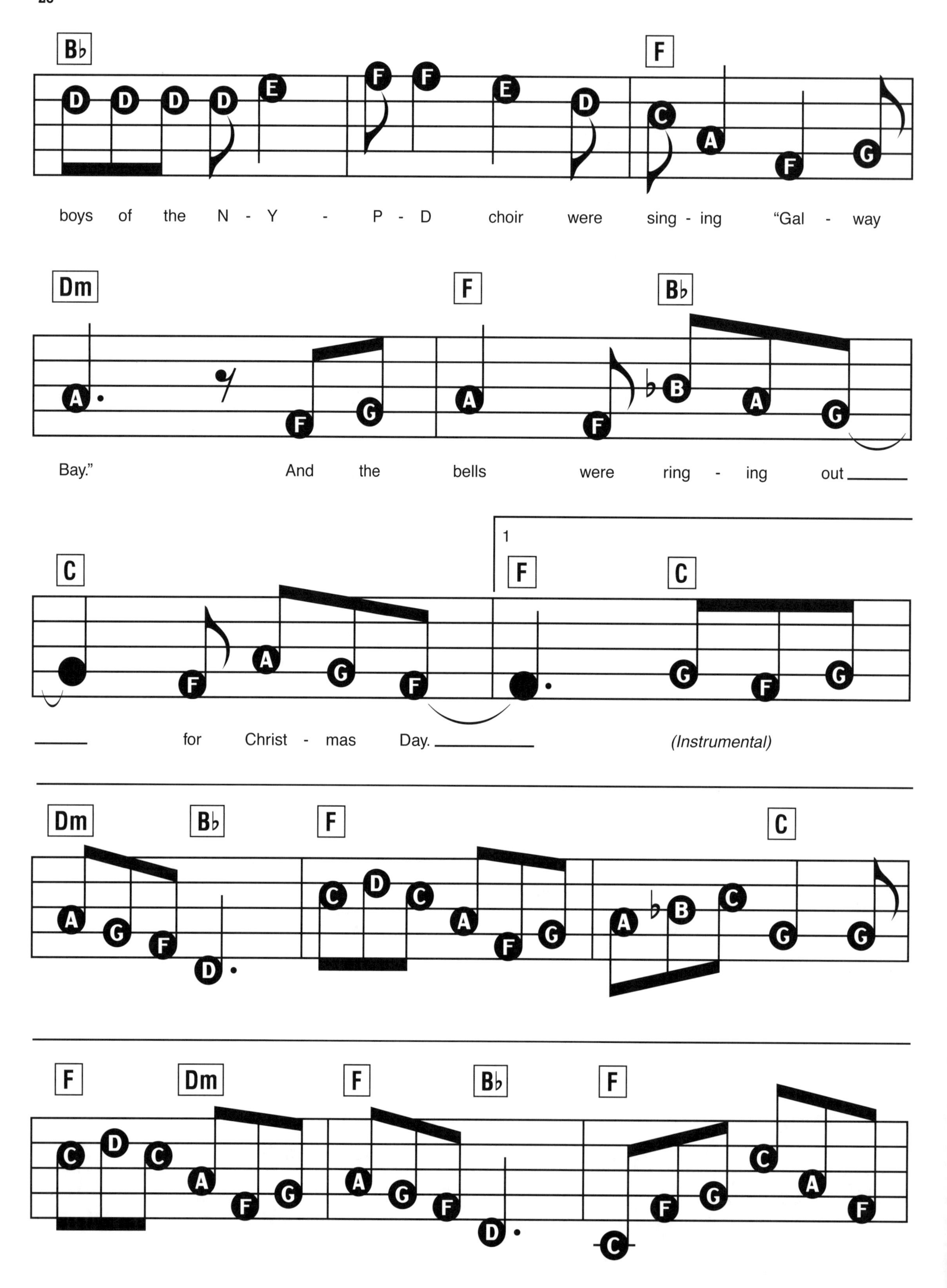
B♭
F
boys of the N - Y - P - D choir were sing - ing "Gal - way
Dm
F
B♭
Bay." And the bells were ring - ing out
C
1
F
C
for Christ - mas Day.
(Instrumental)
Dm
B♭
F
C
F
Dm
F
B♭
F

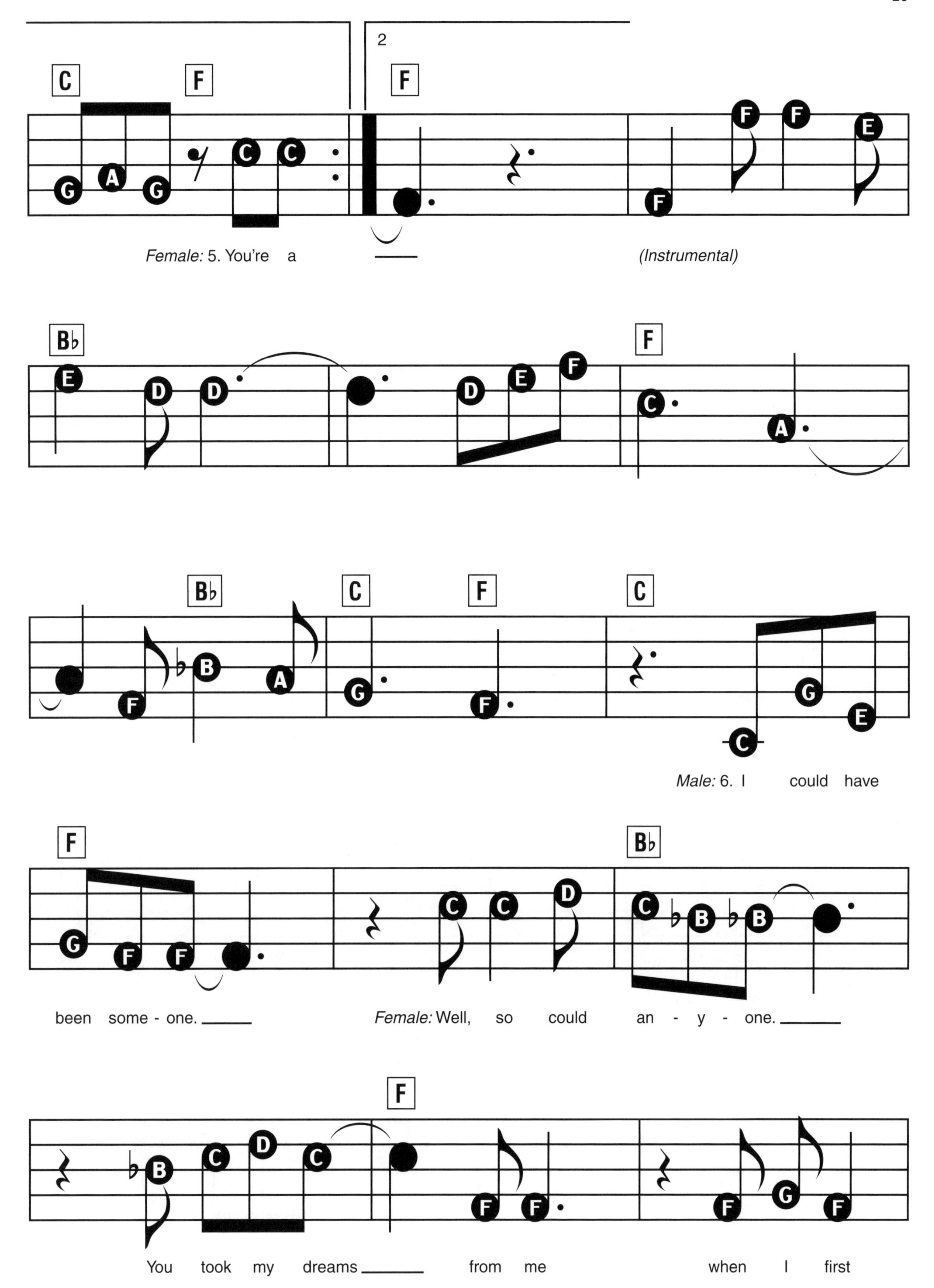
2
C
F
F
G
A
G
C
C
F
F
F
F
E
Female: 5. You're a
(Instrumental)
B♭
F
E
D
D
D
E
F
C
A
B♭
C
F
C
F
B
A
G
F
C
G
E
Male: 6. I could have
F
B♭
G
F
F
C
C
D
C
B
B
been some - one.
Female: Well, so could an - y - one.
F
B
C
D
C
F
F
F
G
F
You took my dreams from me when I first

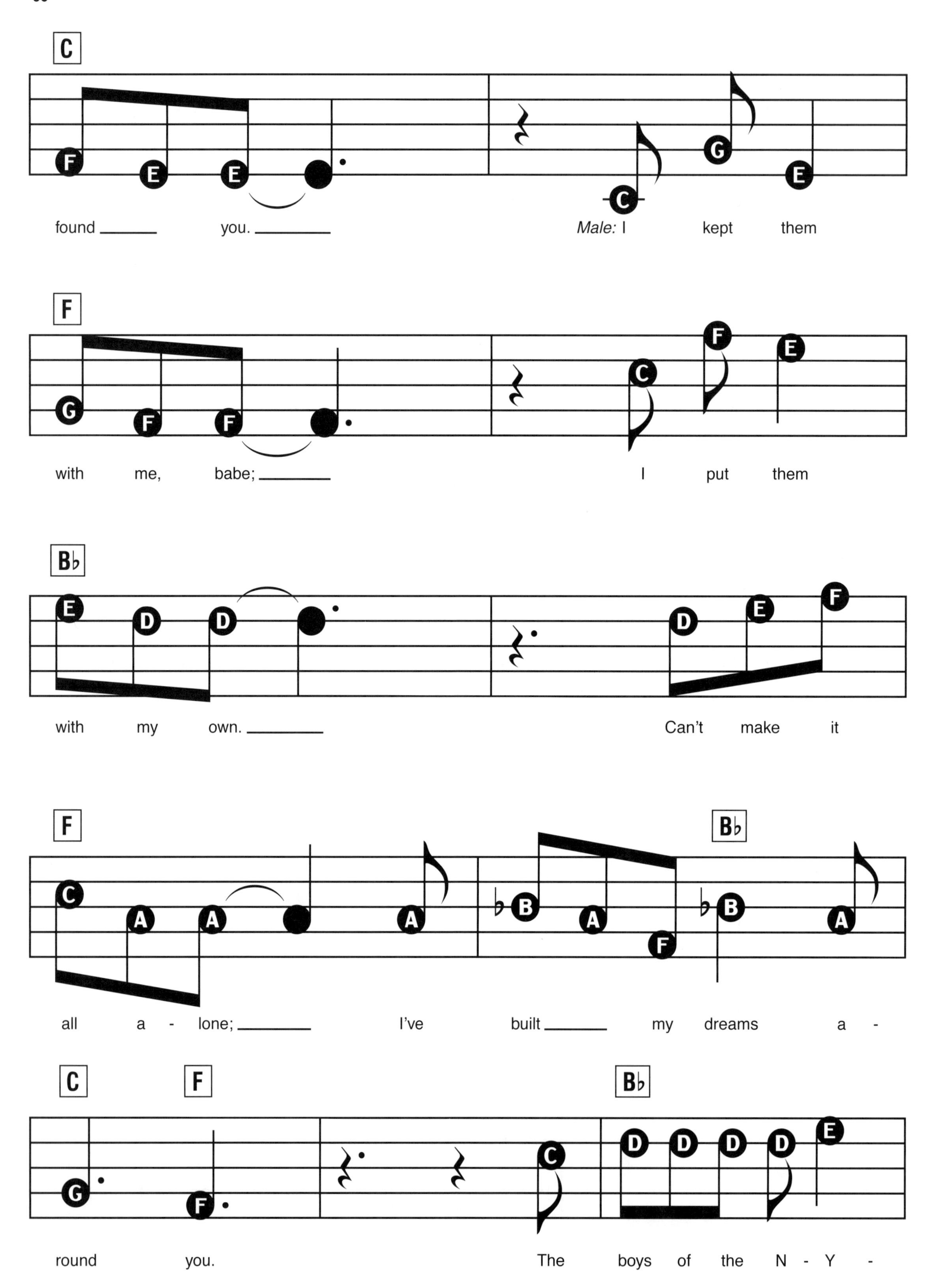
C
found ___ you. ___
Male: I kept them
F
with me, babe; ___
I put them
B♭
with my own. ___
Can't make it
F
B♭
all a - lone; ___ I've built ___ my dreams a -
C
F
B♭
round you.
The boys of the N - Y -

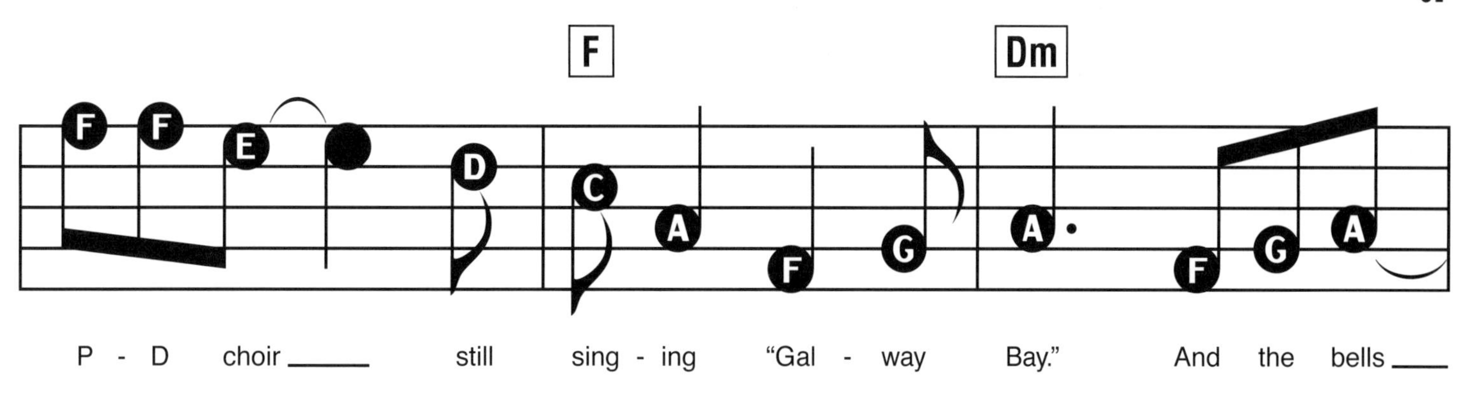

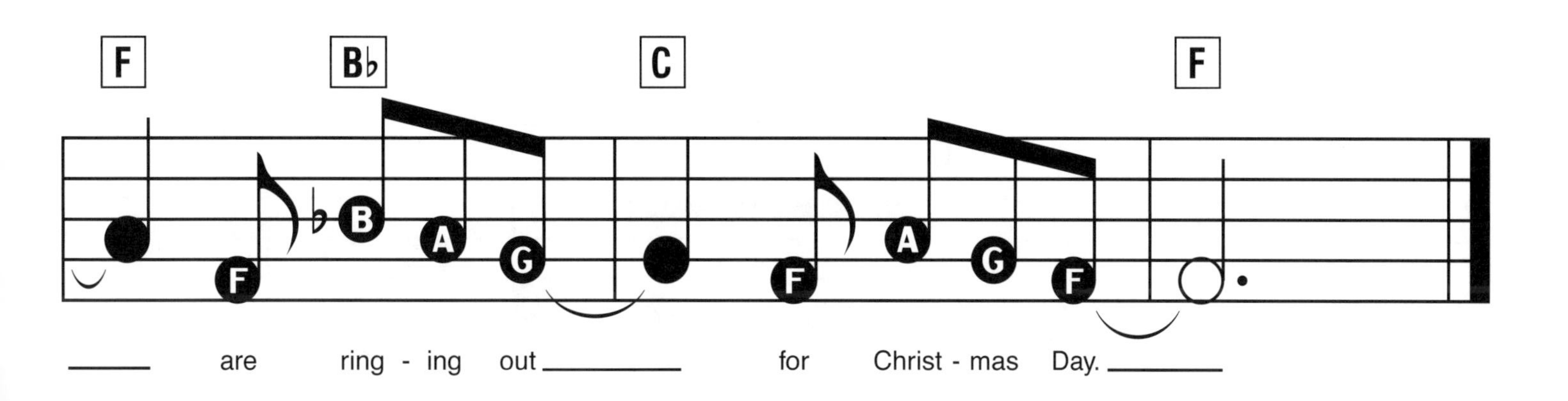

Additional Lyrics

2. Got on a lucky one, came in eighteen to one;
   I've got a feeling this year's for me and you.
   So happy Christmas; I love you, baby.
   I can see a better time when all our dreams come true.

5. *(Female)* You're a bum, you're a punk!
   (Male) You're an old slut on junk,
   Lying there almost dead on a drip in that bed!
   (Female) You scumbag! You maggot!
   You cheap lousy faggot!
   Happy Christmas, your arse!
   I pray God it's our last.

The Christmas Song
(Chestnuts Roasting on an Open Fire)

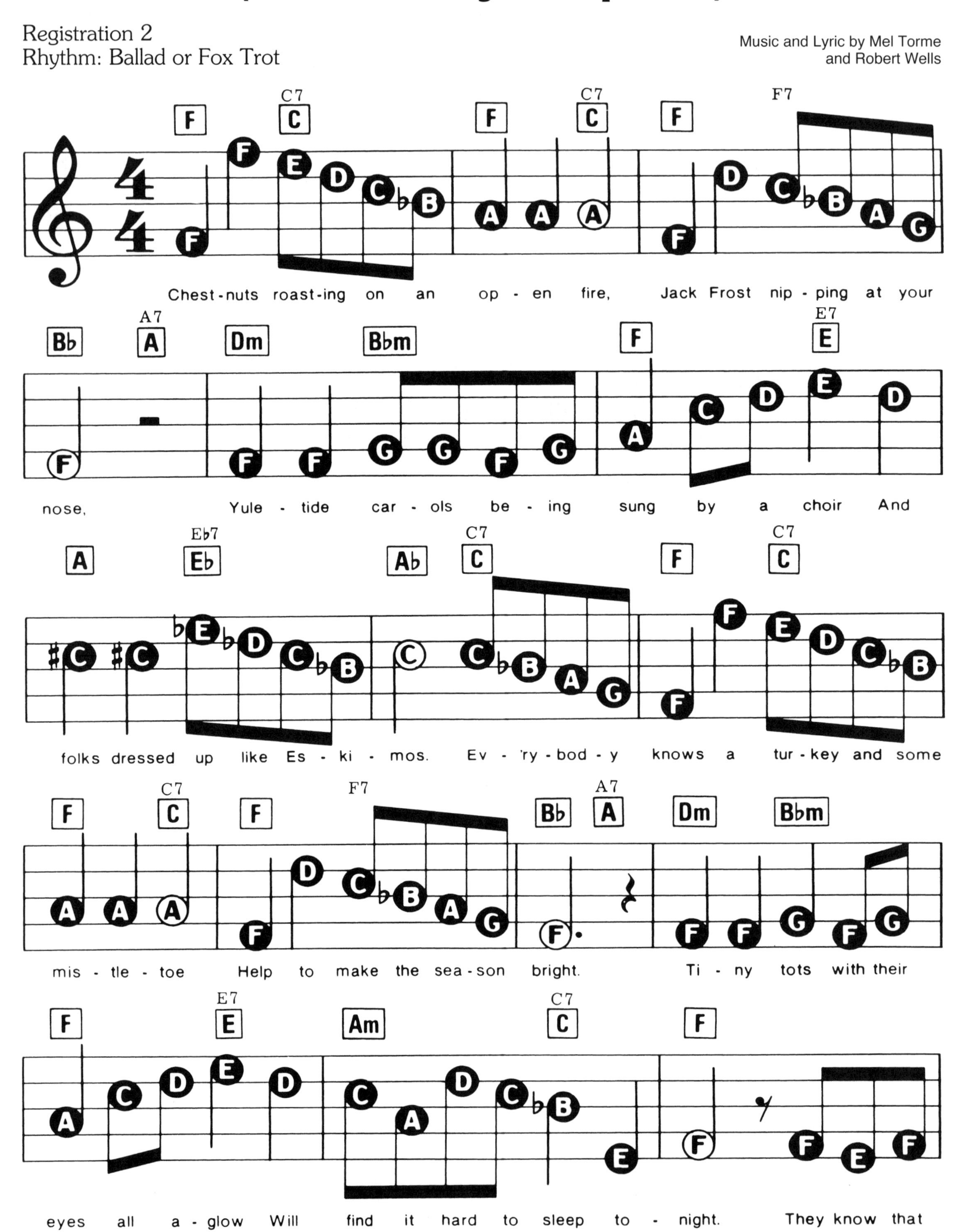

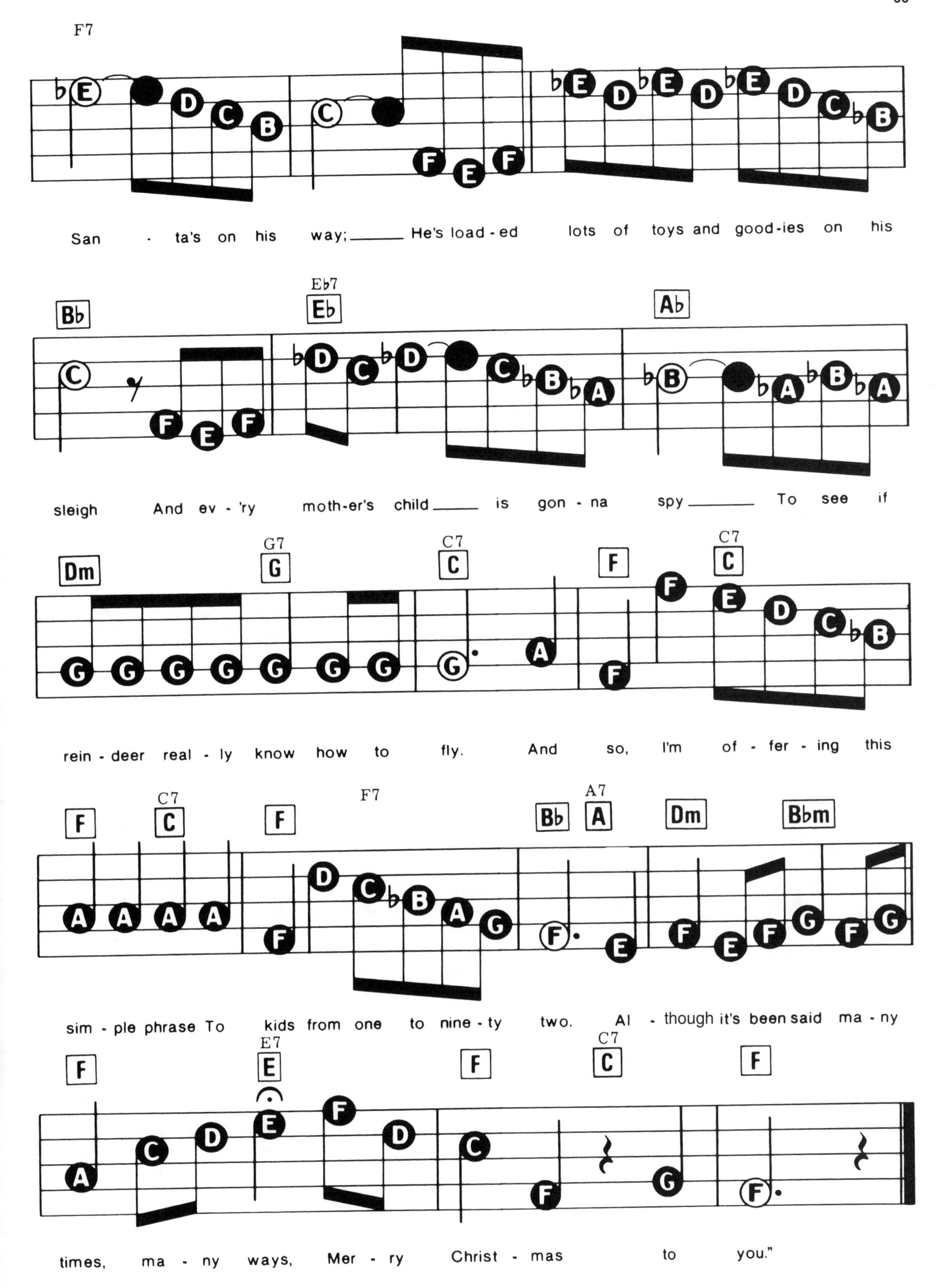
F7
San - ta's on his way; He's load - ed lots of toys and good - ies on his
Bb Eb7 Eb Ab
sleigh And ev - 'ry moth - er's child is gon - na spy To see if
Dm G7 G C7 C F C7 C
rein - deer real - ly know how to fly. And so, I'm of - fer - ing this
F C7 C F F7 Bb A7 A Dm Bbm
sim - ple phrase To kids from one to nine - ty two. Al - though it's been said ma - ny
F E7 E F C7 C F
times, ma - ny ways, Mer - ry Christ - mas to you."

Christmas Time Is Here

from a CHARLIE BROWN CHRISTMAS

Registration 8
Rhythm: Waltz

Words by Lee Mendelson
Music by Vince Guaraldi

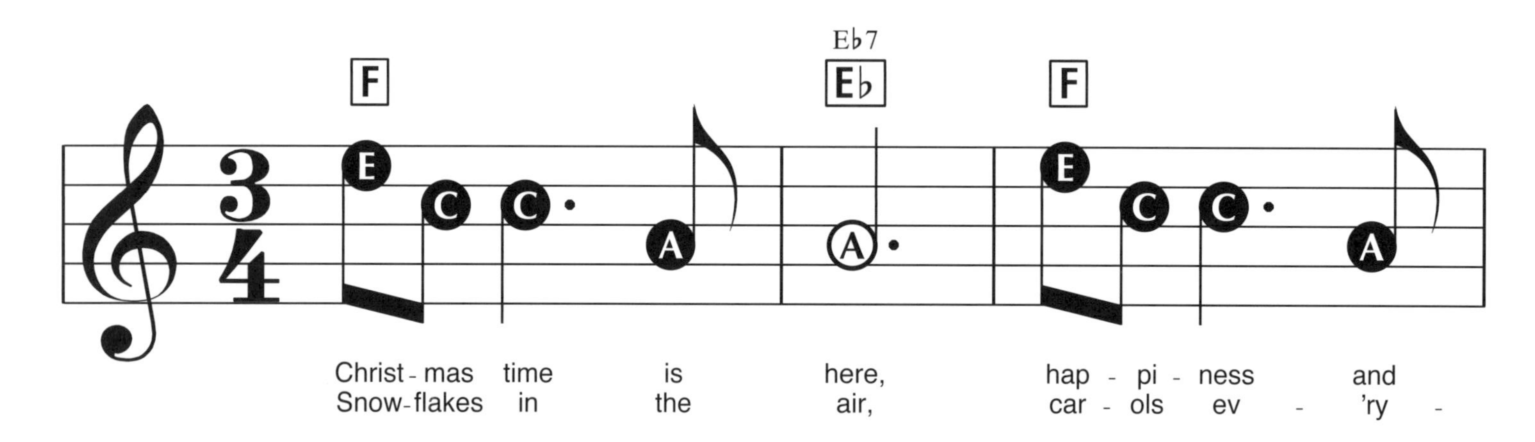

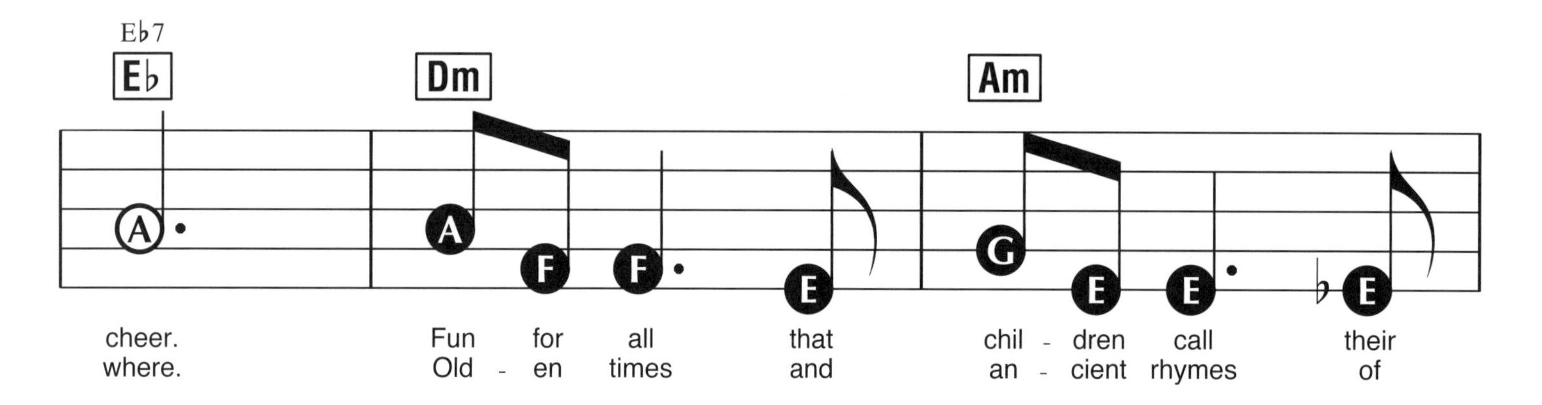

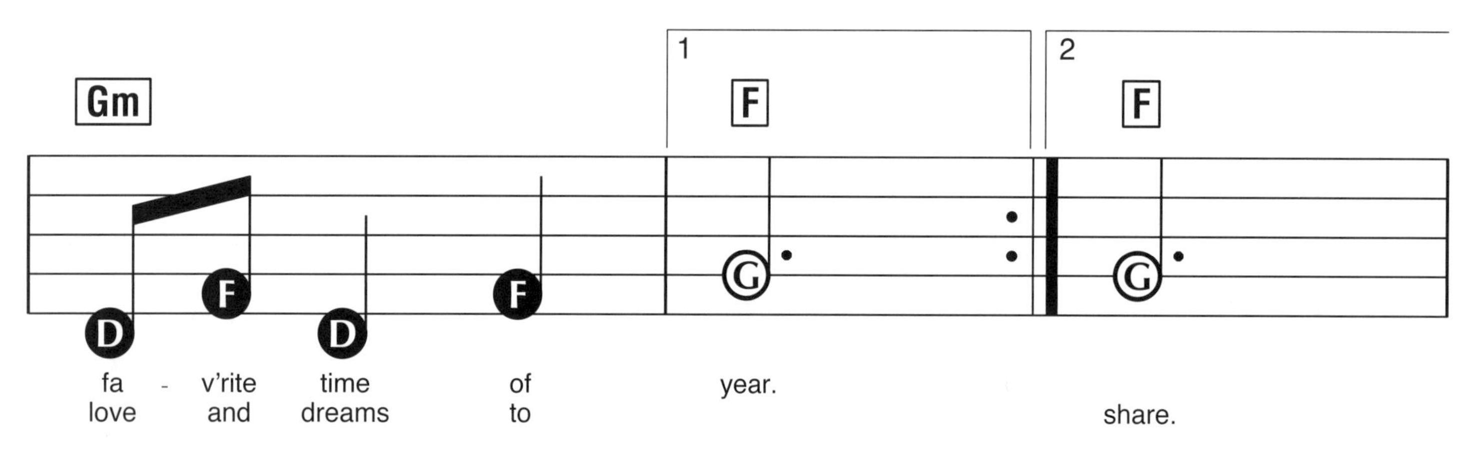

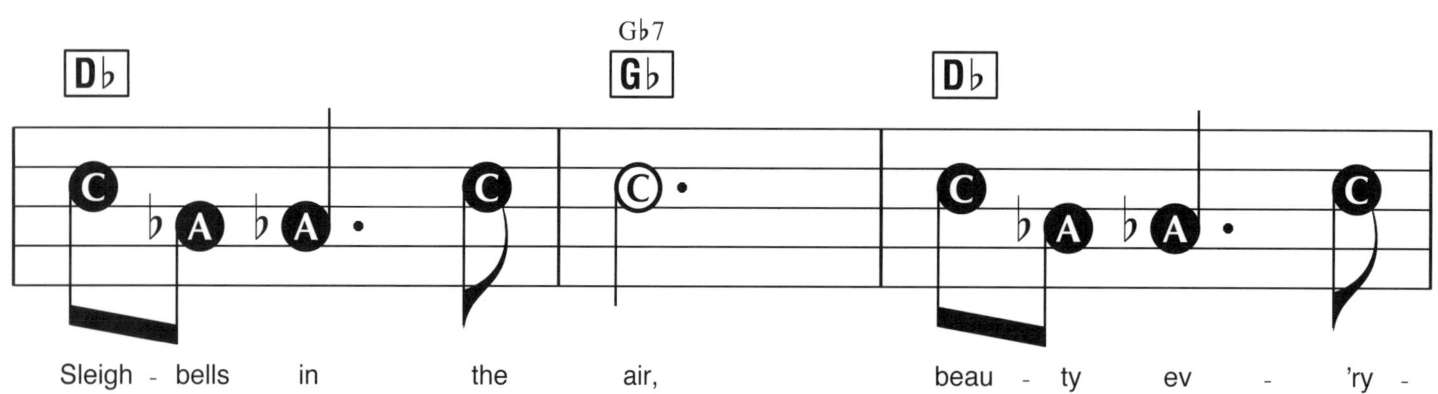

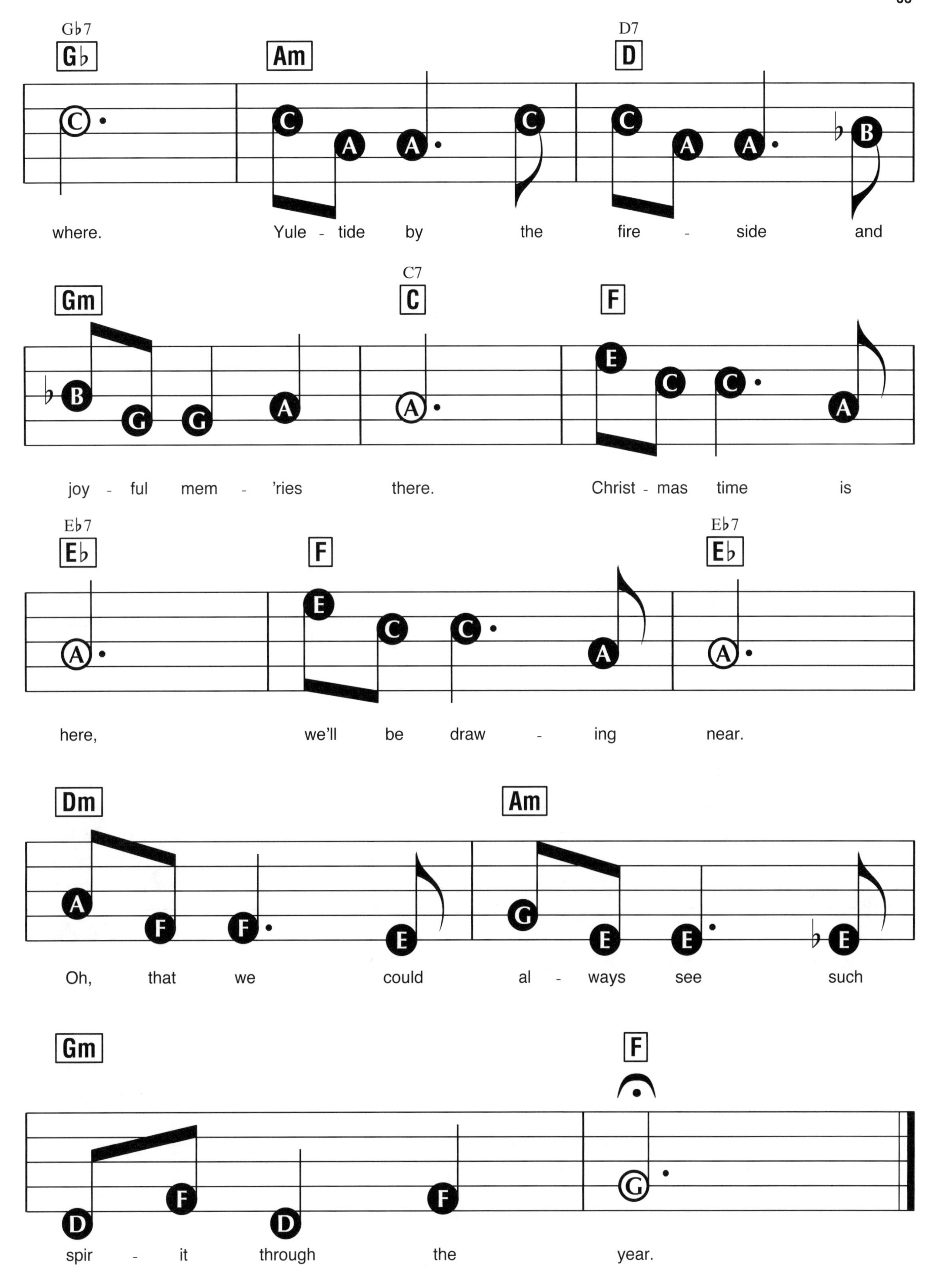
G♭7 G♭ Am D7 D
where. Yule - tide by the fire - side and
Gm C7 C F
joy - ful mem - 'ries there. Christ - mas time is
E♭7 E♭ F E♭7 E♭
here, we'll be draw - ing near.
Dm Am
Oh, that we could al - ways see such
Gm F
spir - it through the year.

Christmases When You Were Mine

Registration 4
Rhythm: 4/4 Ballad

Words and Music by Nathan Chapman,
Liz Rose and Taylor Swift

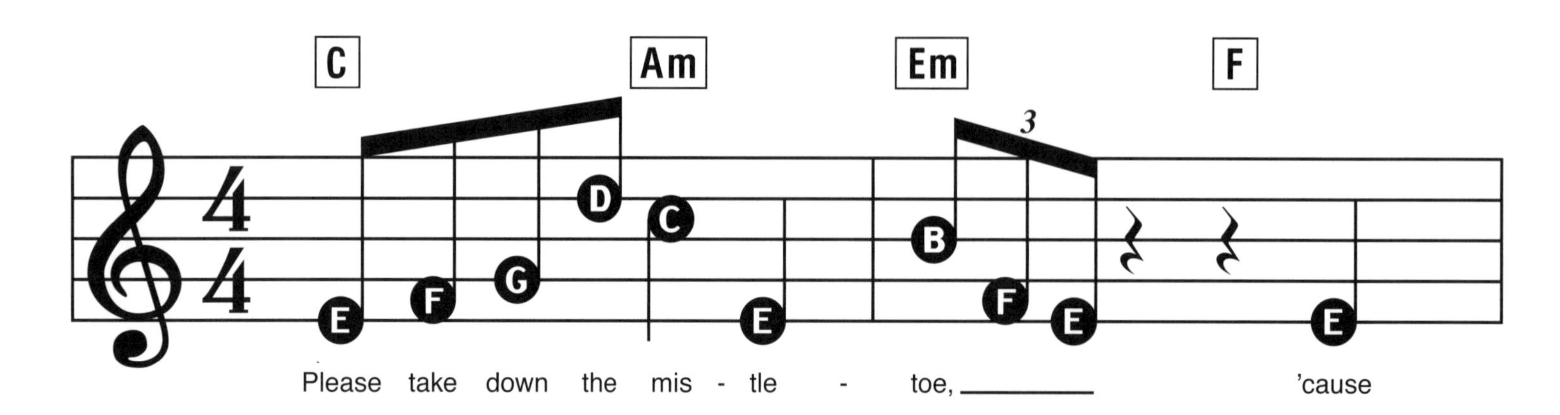

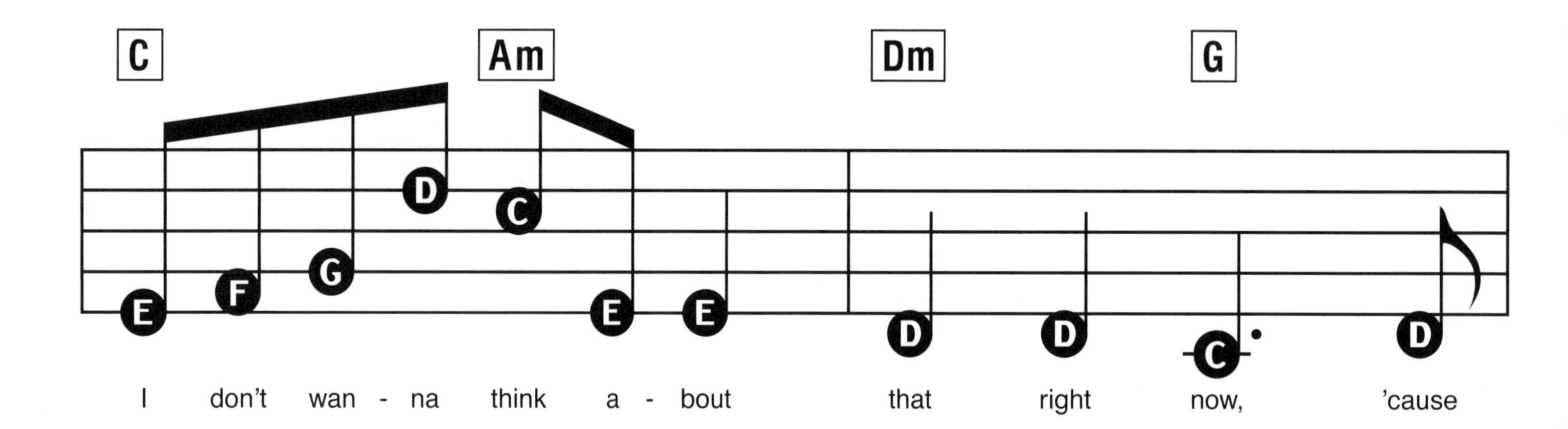

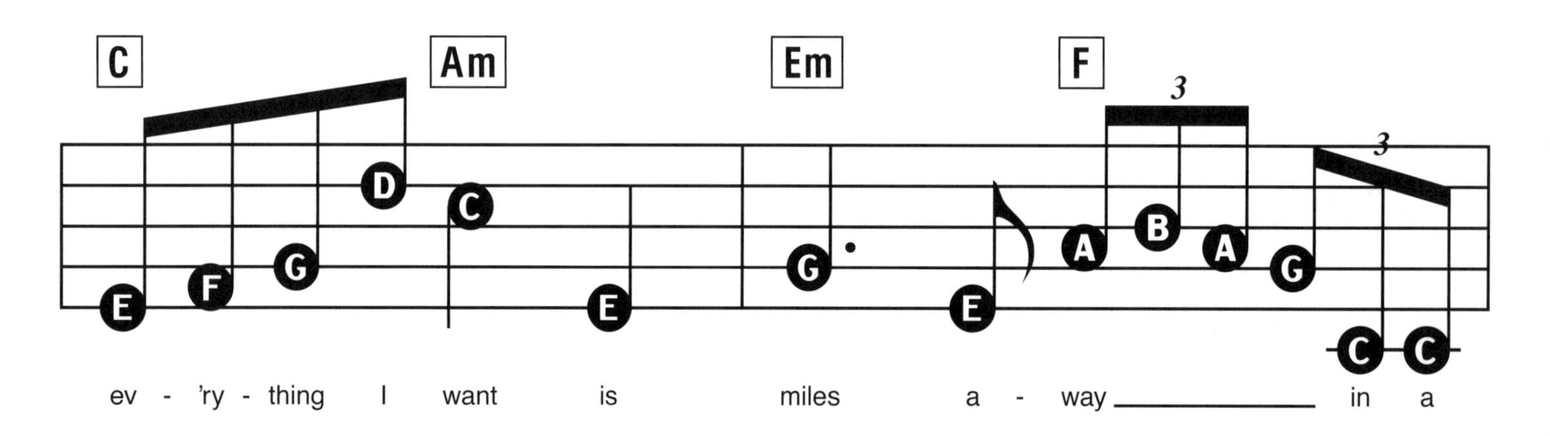

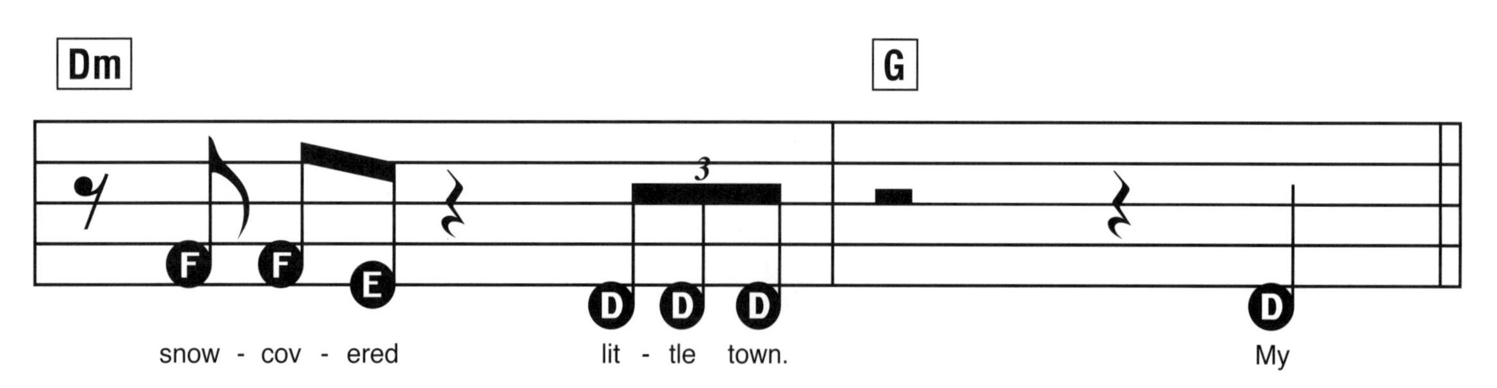

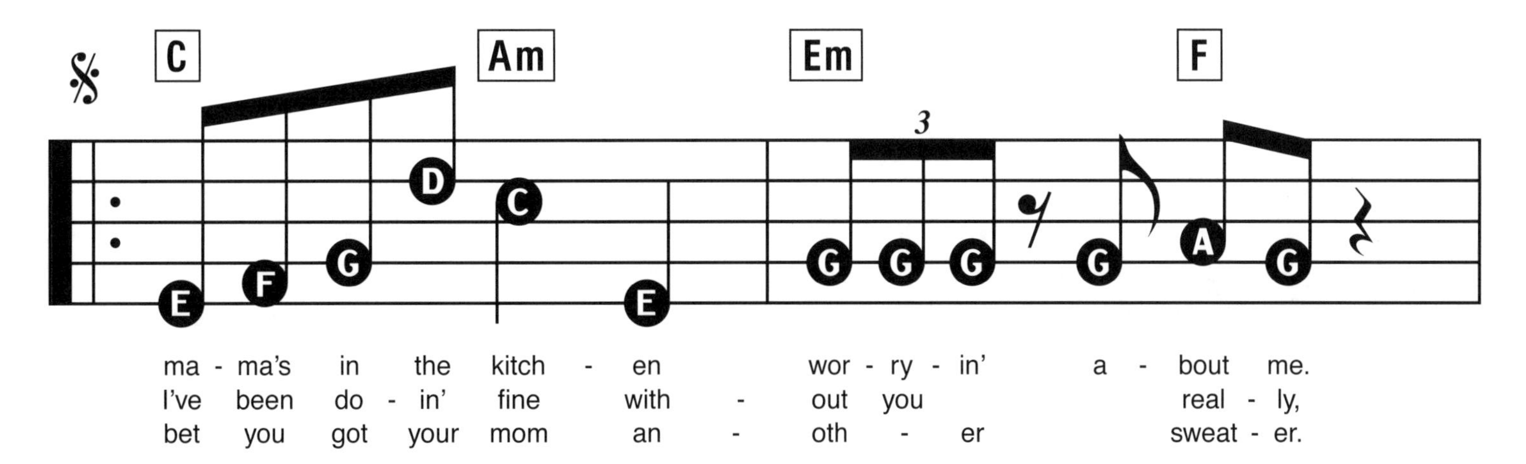
C Am Em F
E F G D C E G G G G A G
3
ma - ma's in the kitch - en wor - ry - in' a - bout me.
I've been do - in' fine with - out you real - ly,
bet you got your mom an - oth - er sweat - er.

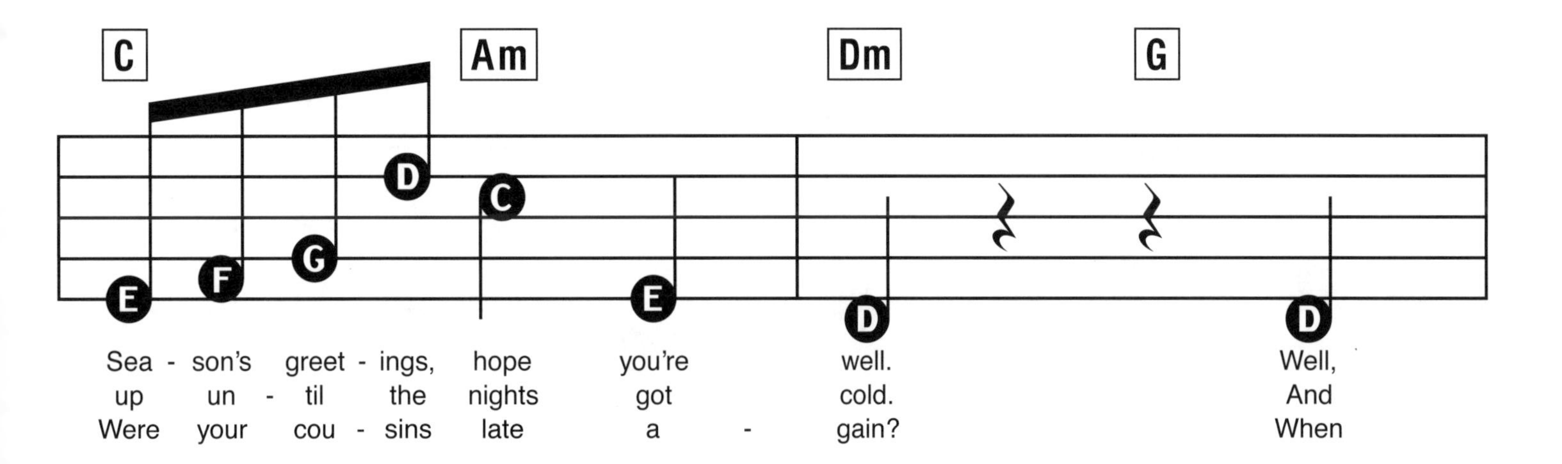
C Am Dm G
E F G D C E D D
Sea - son's greet - ings, hope you're well. Well,
up un - til the nights got cold. And
Were your cou - sins late a - gain? When

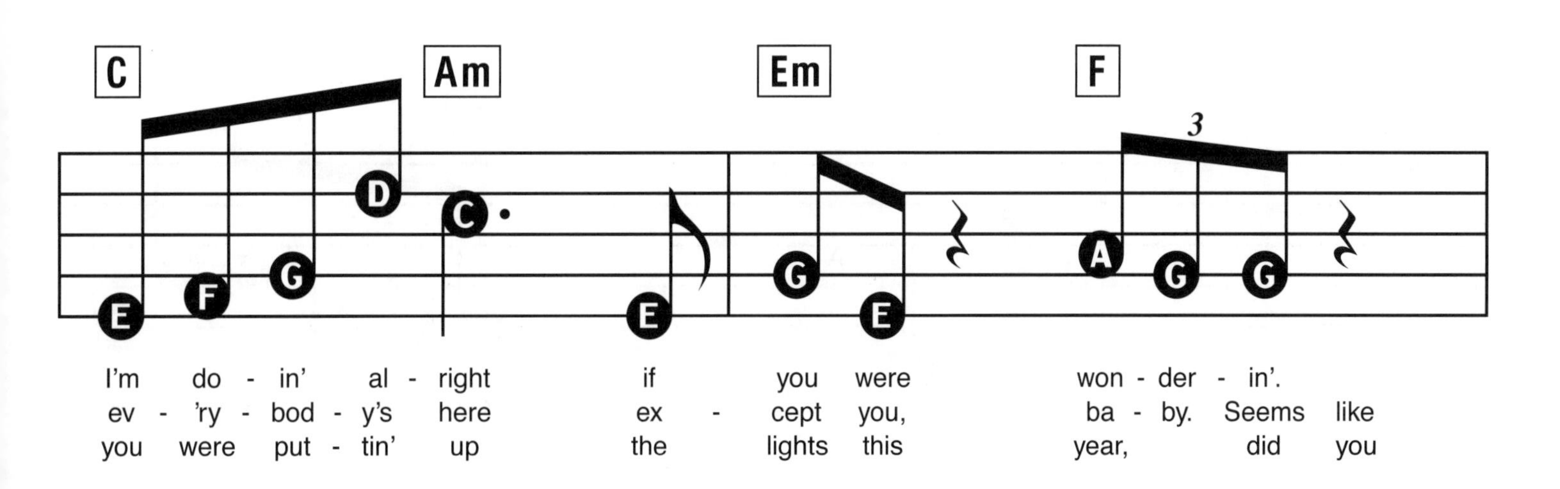
C Am Em F
E F G D C E G E A G G
3
I'm do - in' al - right if you were won - der - in'.
ev - 'ry - bod - y's here ex - cept you, ba - by. Seems like
you were put - tin' up the lights this year, did you

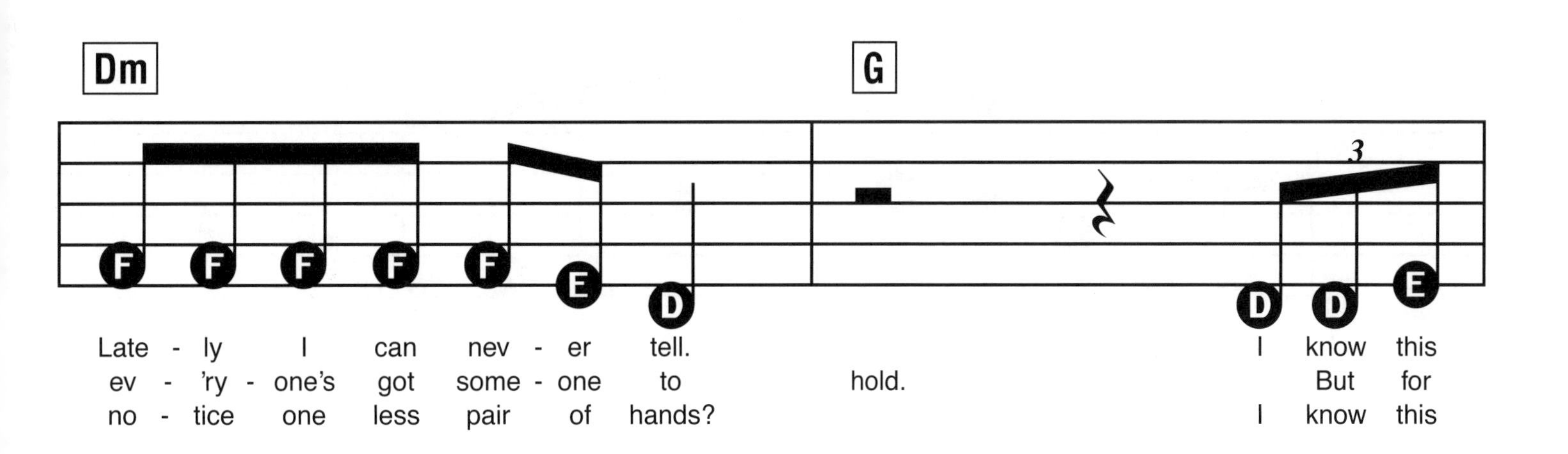
Dm G
F F F F F E D D D E
3
Late - ly I can nev - er tell. I know this
ev - 'ry - one's got some - one to hold. But for
no - tice one less pair of hands? I know this

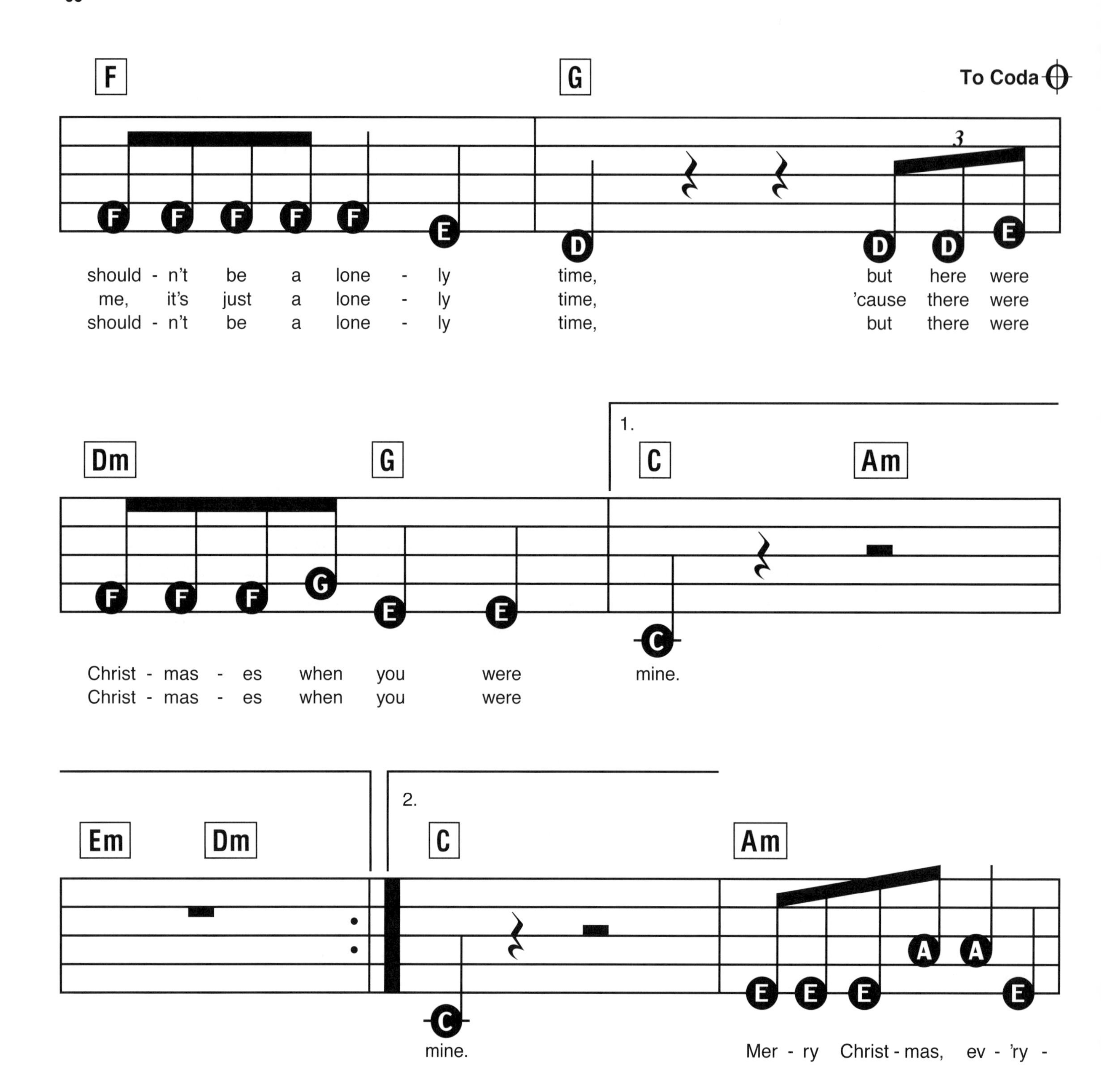
F
G
To Coda
3
should - n't be a lone - ly time, but here were
me, it's just a lone - ly time, 'cause there were
should - n't be a lone - ly time, but there were
Dm
G
1.
C
Am
Christ - mas - es when you were mine.
Christ - mas - es when you were
Em
Dm
2.
C
Am
mine.
Mer - ry Christ - mas, ev - 'ry -

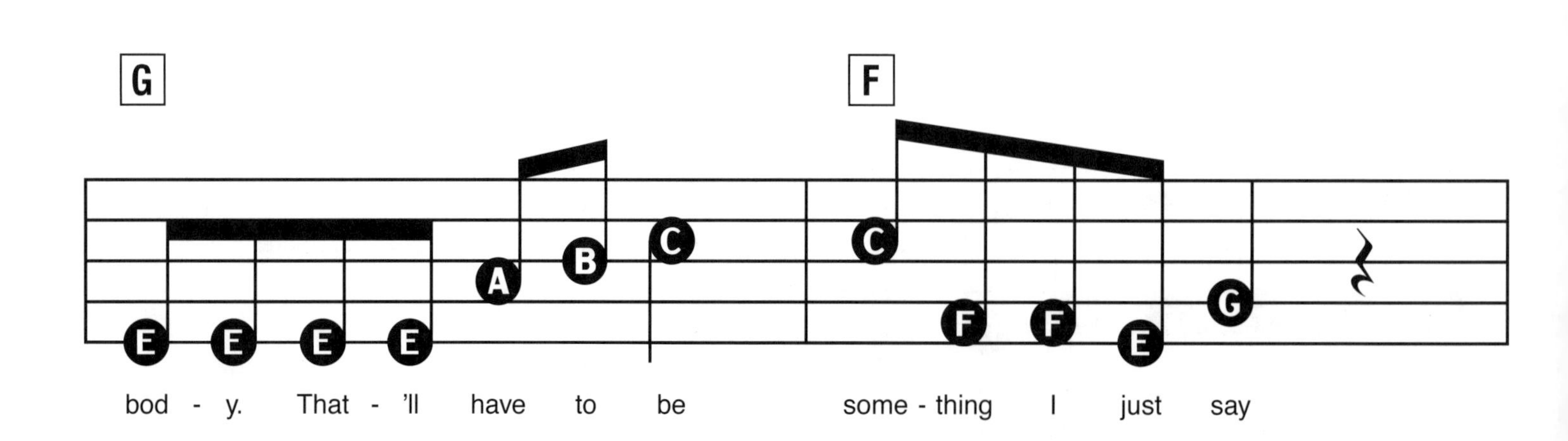
G
F
bod - y. That - 'll have to be some - thing I just say

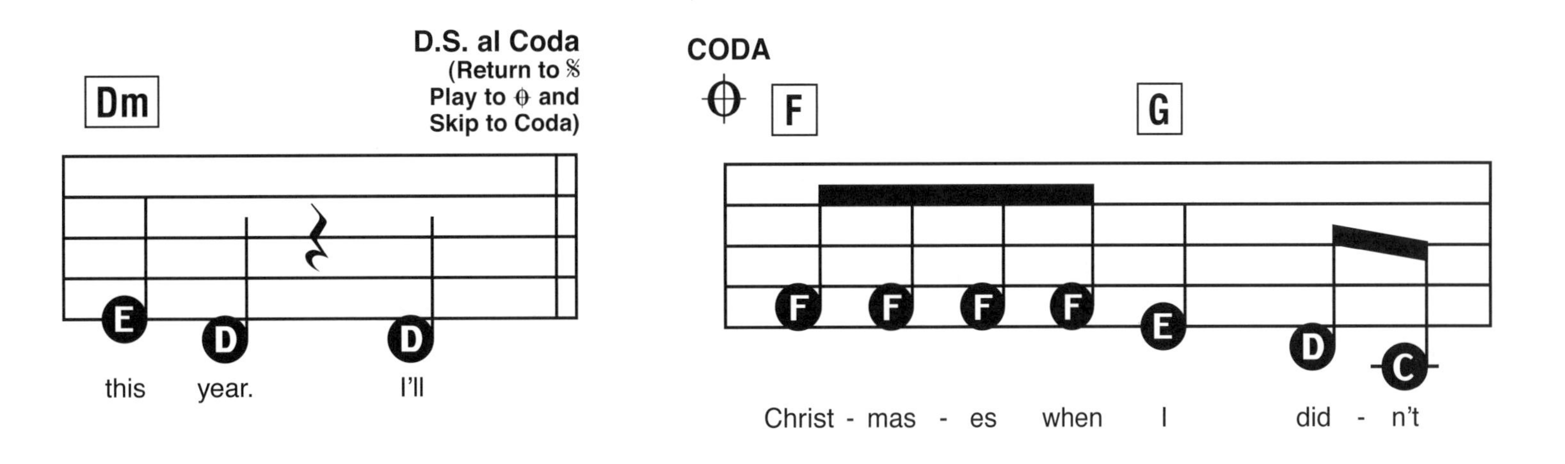
Dm
D.S. al Coda
(Return to 𝄋
Play to ⊕ and
Skip to Coda)
CODA
F
G
this year. I'll
Christ - mas - es when I did - n't

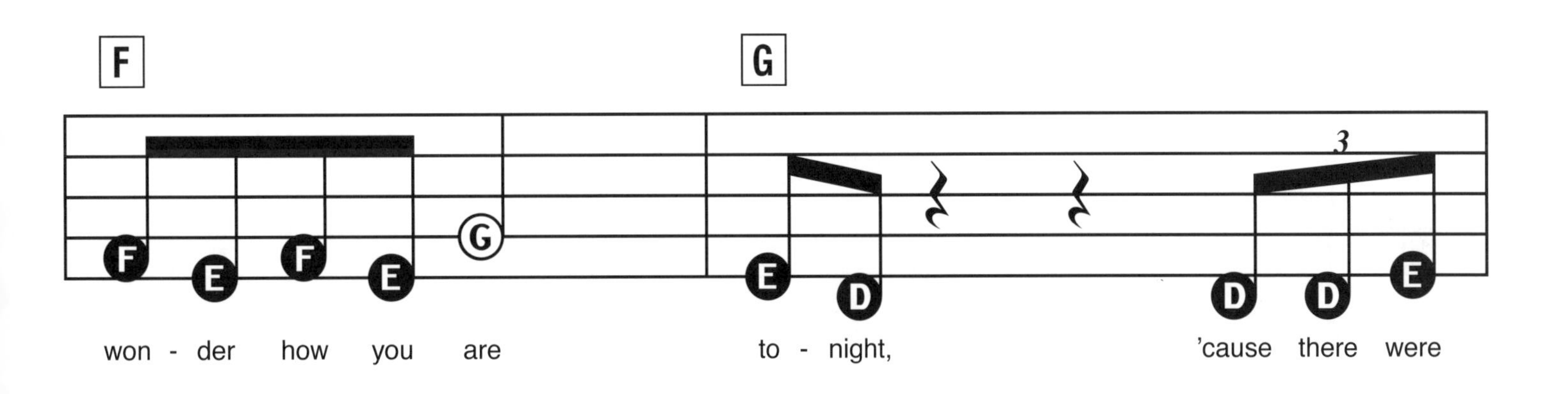
F
G
won - der how you are
to - night,
'cause there were

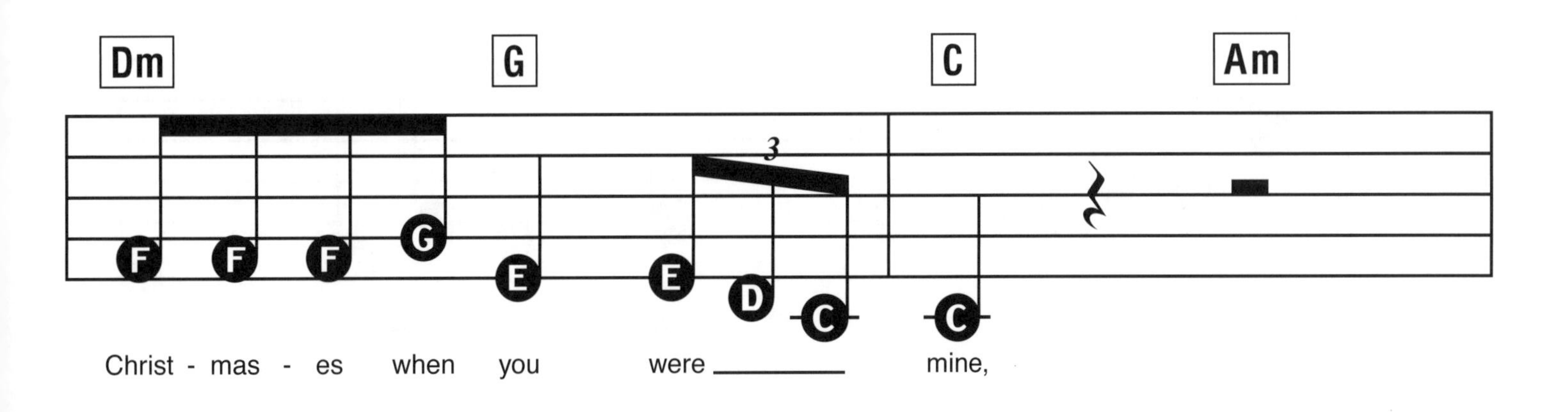
Dm
G
C
Am
Christ - mas - es when you were
mine,

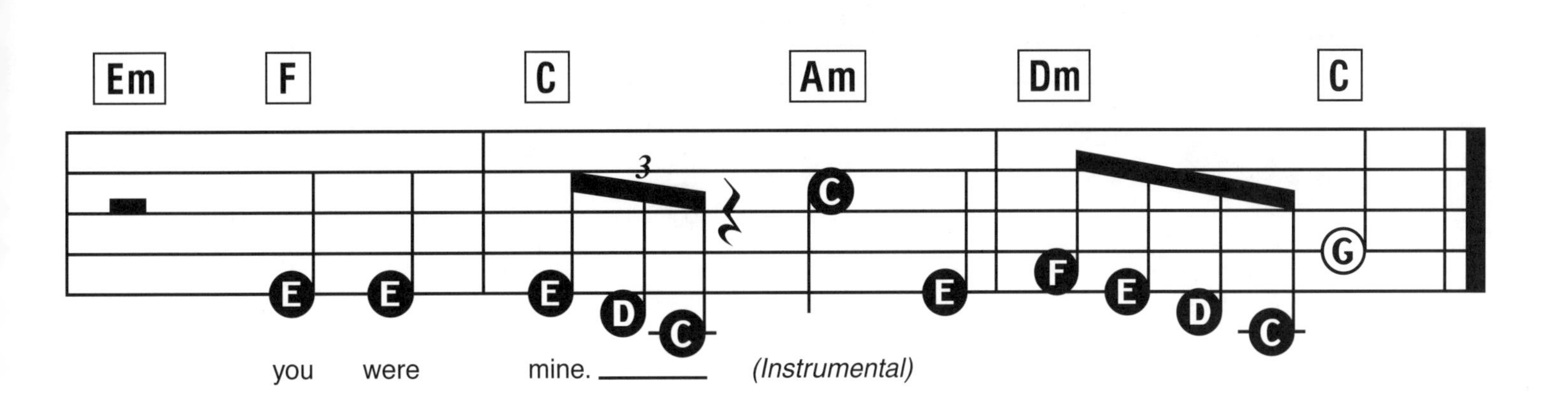
Em
F
C
Am
Dm
C
you were mine.
(Instrumental)

Grown-Up Christmas List

Registration 1
Rhythm: 4/4 Ballad

Words and Music by David Foster
and Linda Thompson-Jenner

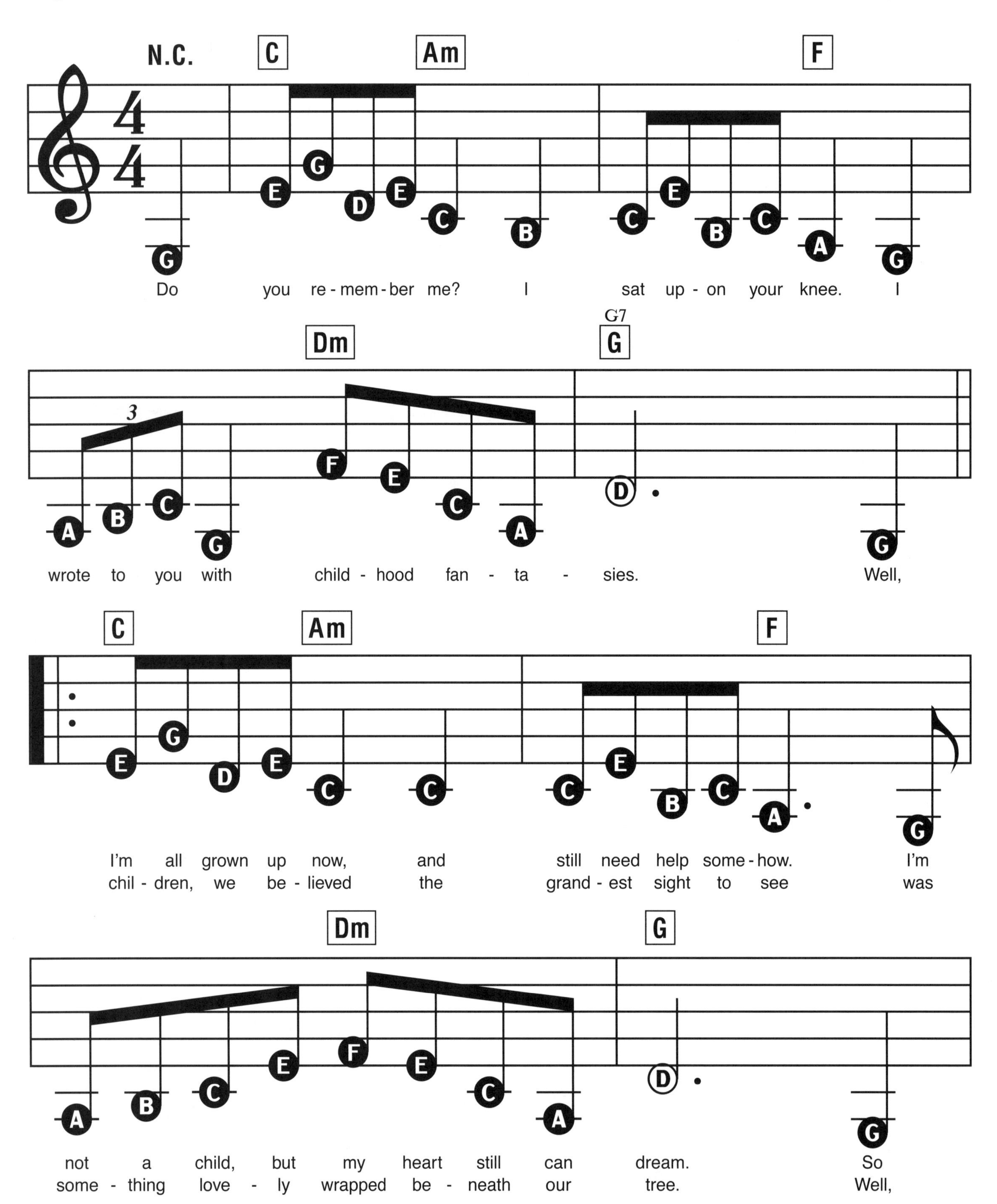

C
Am
F
E G D E C B C E B C A G
here's my life - long wish, my grown - up Christ - mas list, not
heav - en sure - ly knows that pack - ag - es and bows can
Dm
G
C
Am
A B C E F E C A D G E D C D E
for my - self, but for a world in need.
nev - er heal a hurt - ing hu - man soul.
No more lives torn a -
F
Dm
Em
Am
F
G7
G
A F E D E F B G E D E B C
part and wars would nev - er start and time would heal all hearts.
C
Am
F
Dm
C G E D C D C A F E D E F
And ev - 'ry - one would have a friend and right would al - ways
Em
Am
D7
D
B G E D E B C B A G
3
win and love would nev - er end.

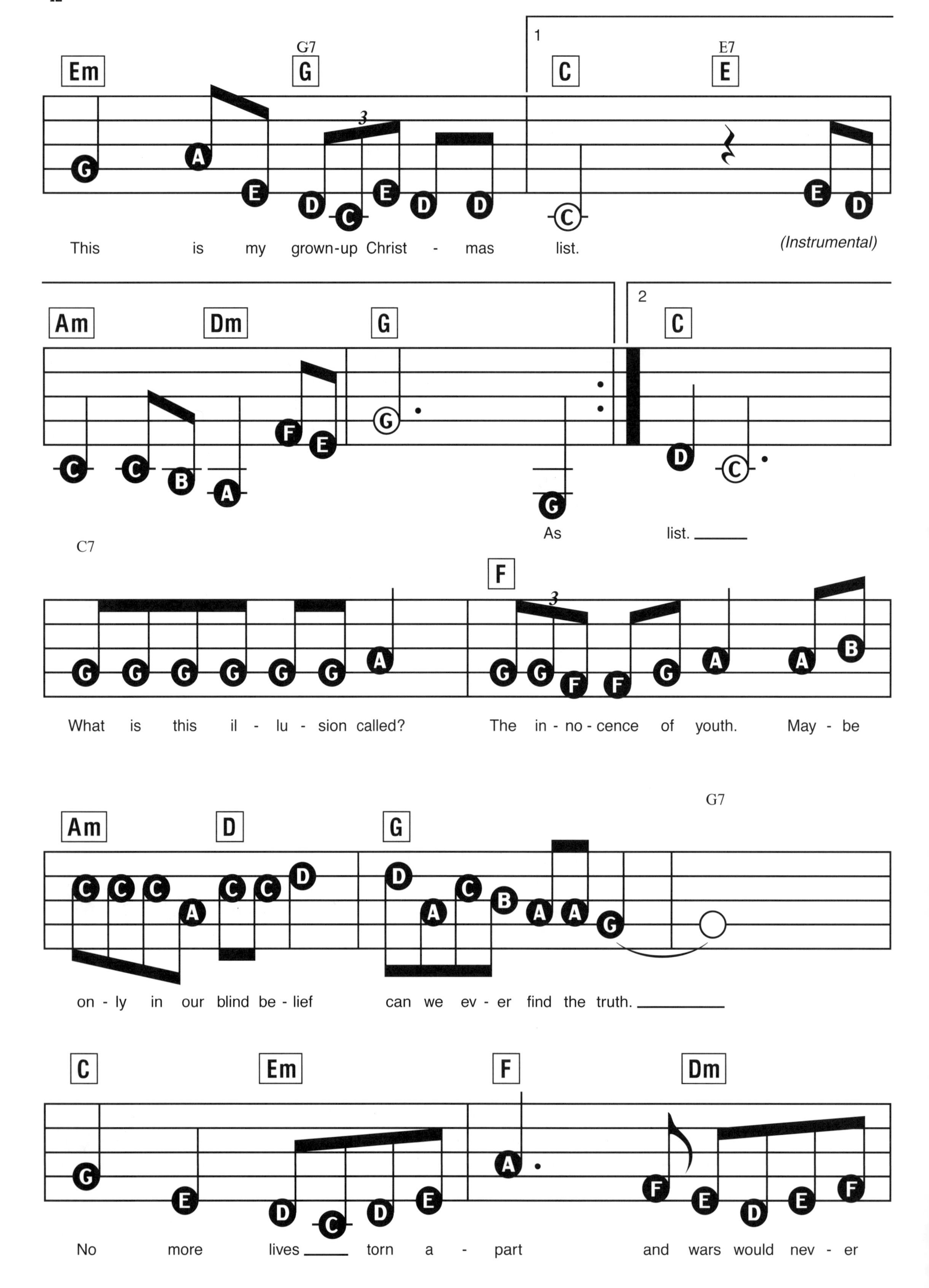
Em G7 G 1 C E7 E
This is my grown-up Christ - mas list.
(Instrumental)
Am Dm G 2 C
As list.
C7 F
What is this il - lu - sion called? The in - no - cence of youth. May - be
Am D G G7
on - ly in our blind be - lief can we ev - er find the truth.
C Em F Dm
No more lives torn a - part and wars would nev - er

Em
Am
F
B
G
E
D
E
B
C
start and time would heal all hearts.
C
Em
F
Dm
C
G
E
D
C
D
E
A
F
E
D
E
F
And ev - 'ry - one would have a friend and right would al - ways
Em
Am
Fm
B7
B
B
G
E
D
E
G
C
B
A
G
3
win and love would nev - er end, oh.
Em
G7
G
Em
G
A
E
D
C
E
D
G
G
E
G
A
C
D
B
A
G
3
This is my grown-up Christ - mas wish. This is my on - ly life-long
G7
G
C
G
E
G
E
D
C
E
D
C
D
D
C
3
wish. This is my grown-up Christ - mas list.

Happy Xmas
(War Is Over)

Registration 1
Rhythm: Slow Rock

Written by John Lennon and
Yoko Ono

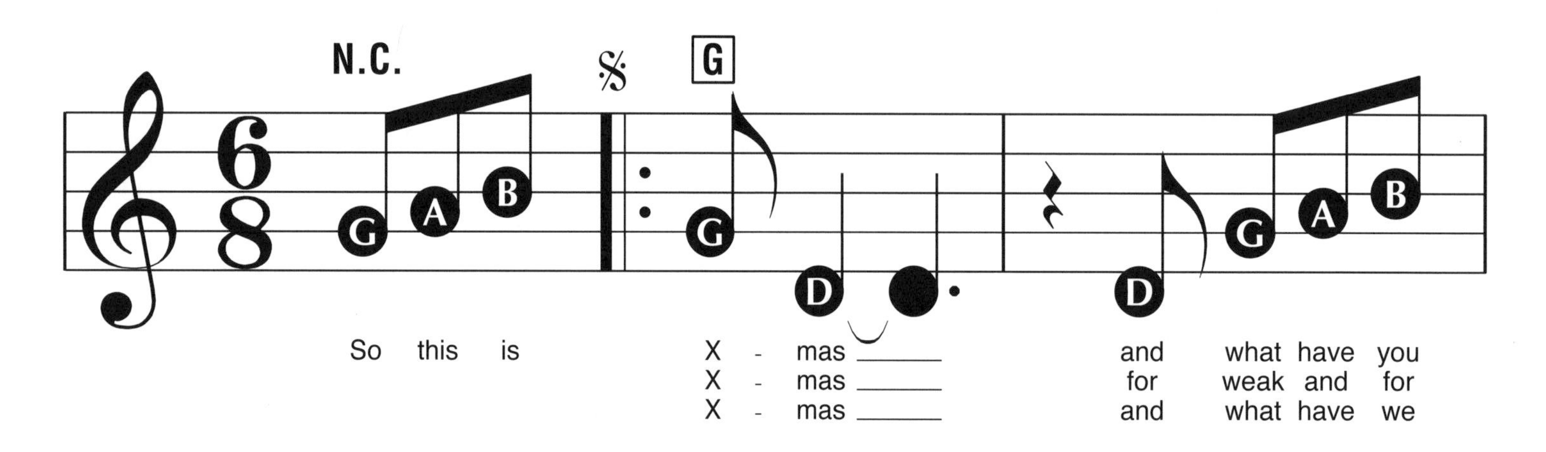

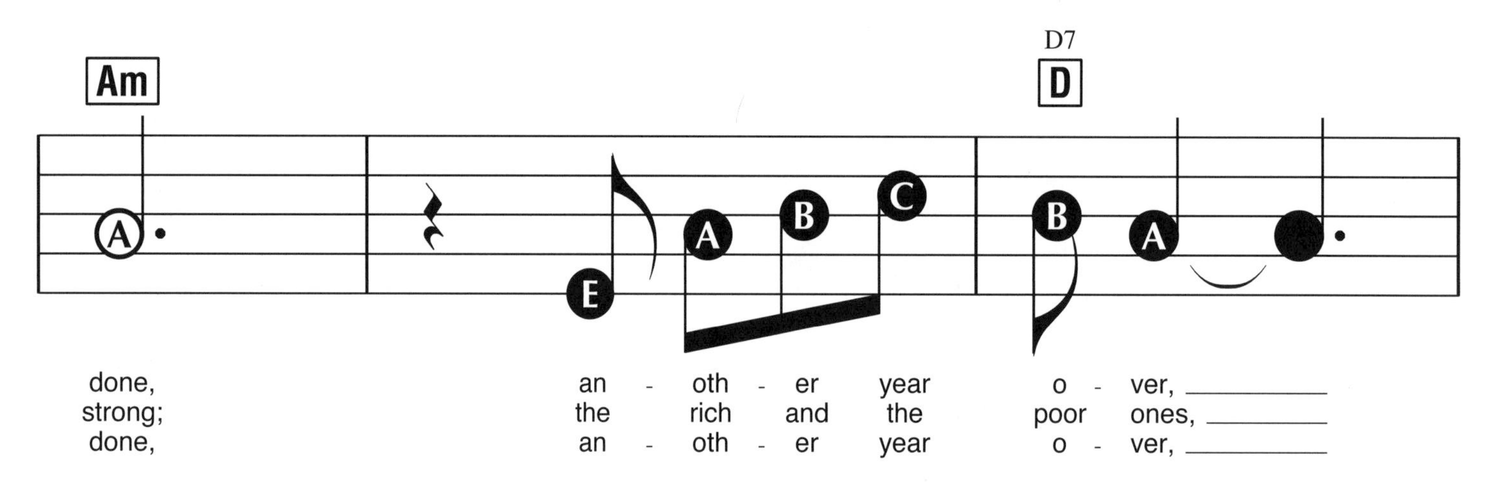

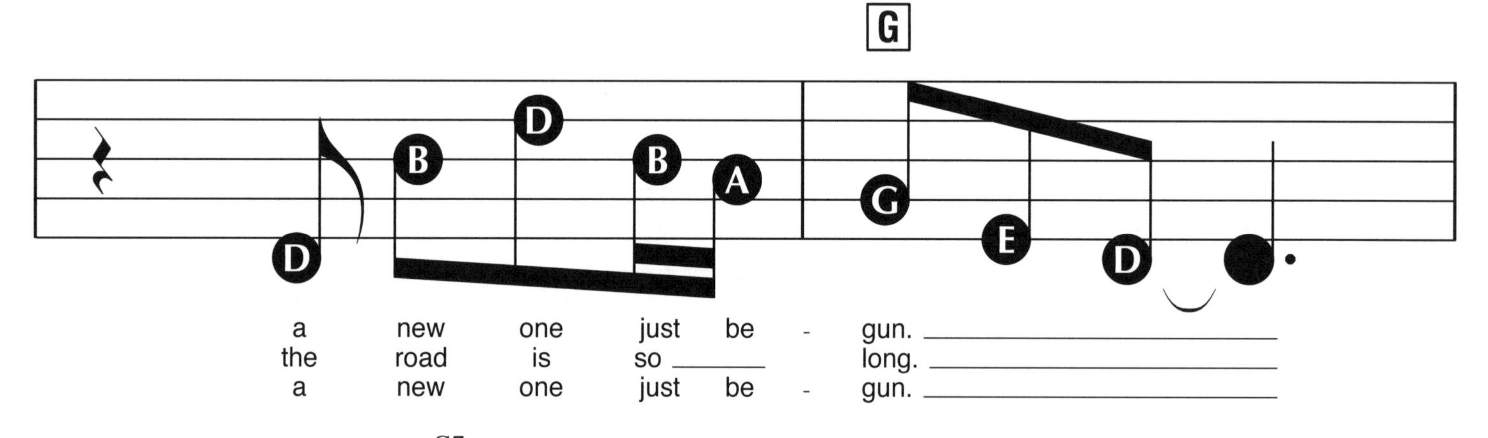

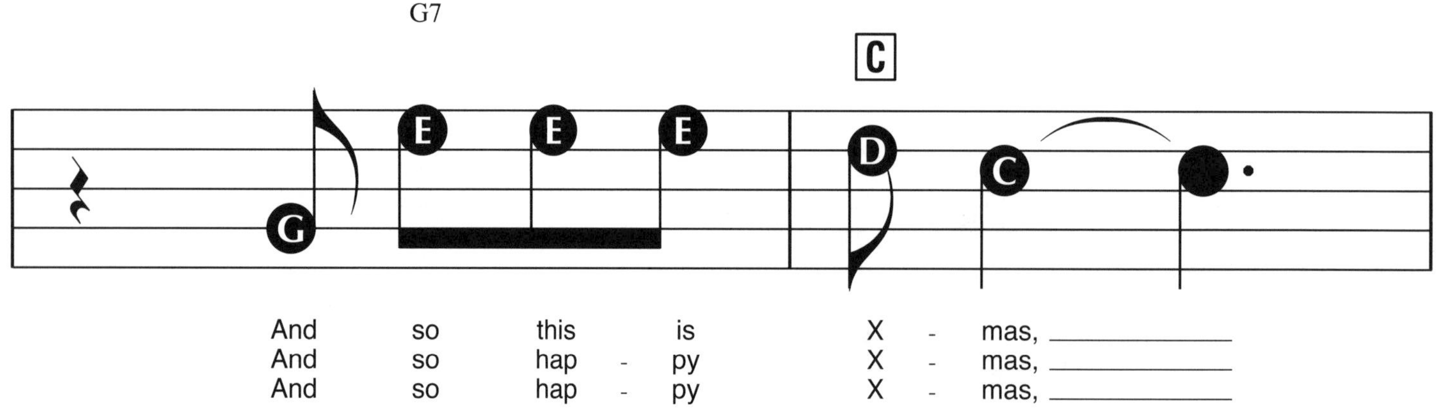

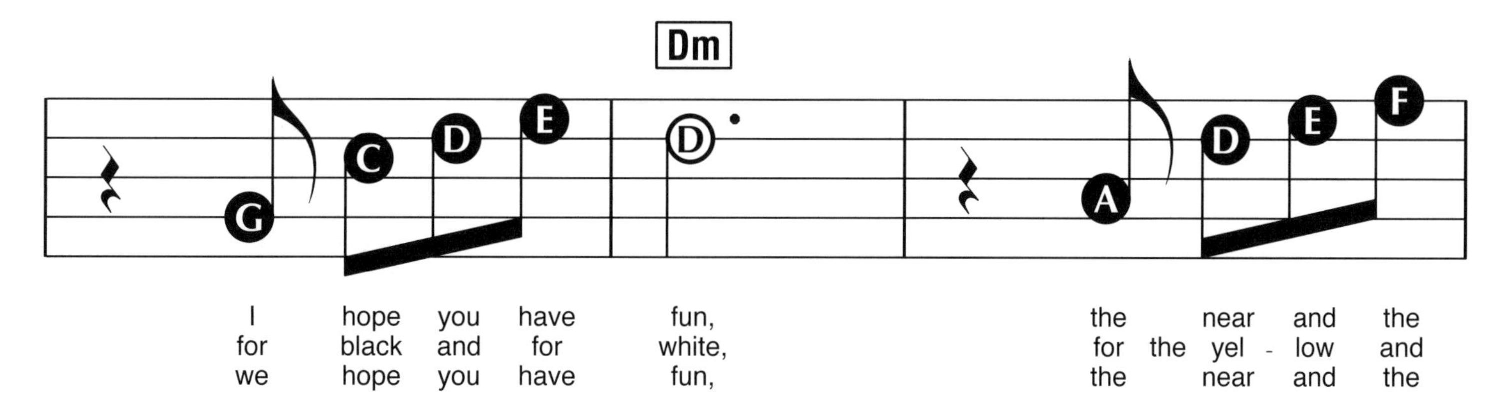
Dm
G
C
D
E
D
A
D
E
F
I hope you have fun, the near and the
for black and for white, for the yel - low and
we hope you have fun, the near and the

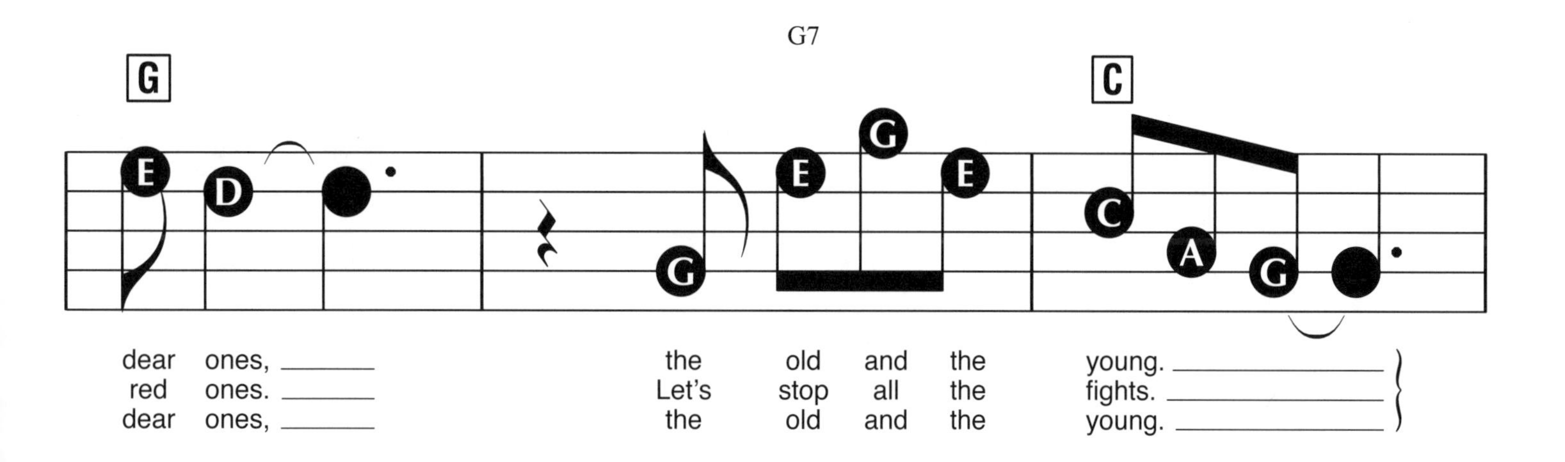
G
G7
C
E
D
G
E
G
E
C
A
G
dear ones, the old and the young.
red ones. Let's stop all the fights.
dear ones, the old and the young.

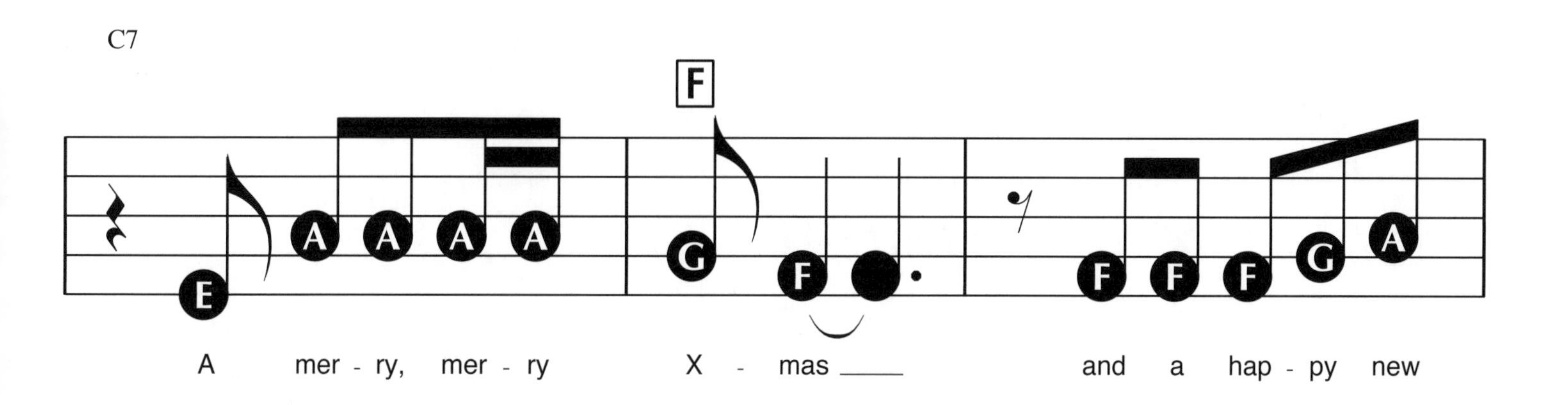
C7
F
E
A
A
A
A
G
F
F
F
F
G
A
A mer - ry, mer - ry X - mas and a hap - py new

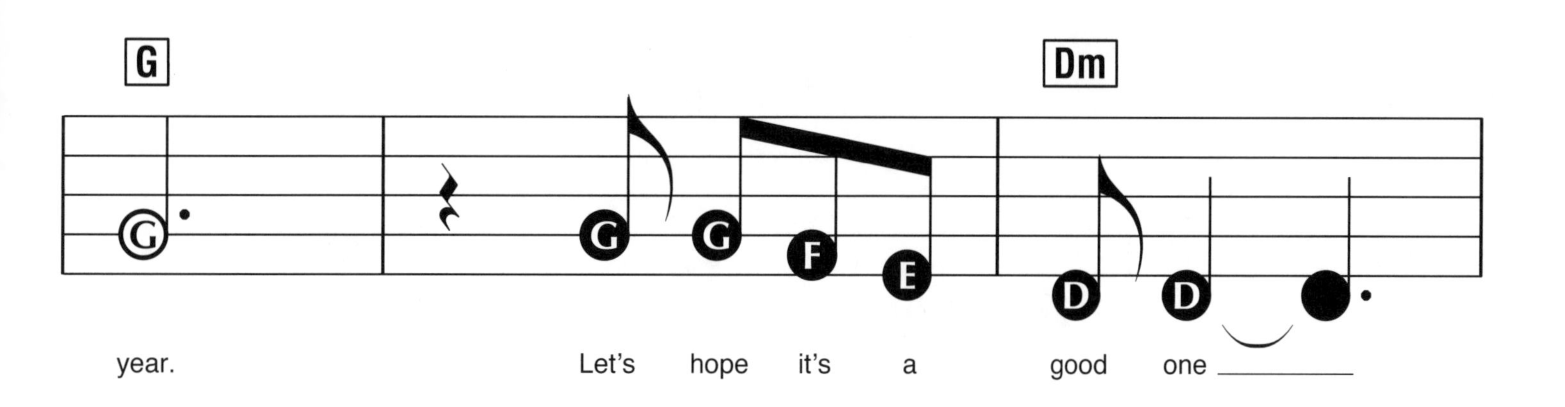
G
Dm
G
G
G
F
E
D
D
year. Let's hope it's a good one

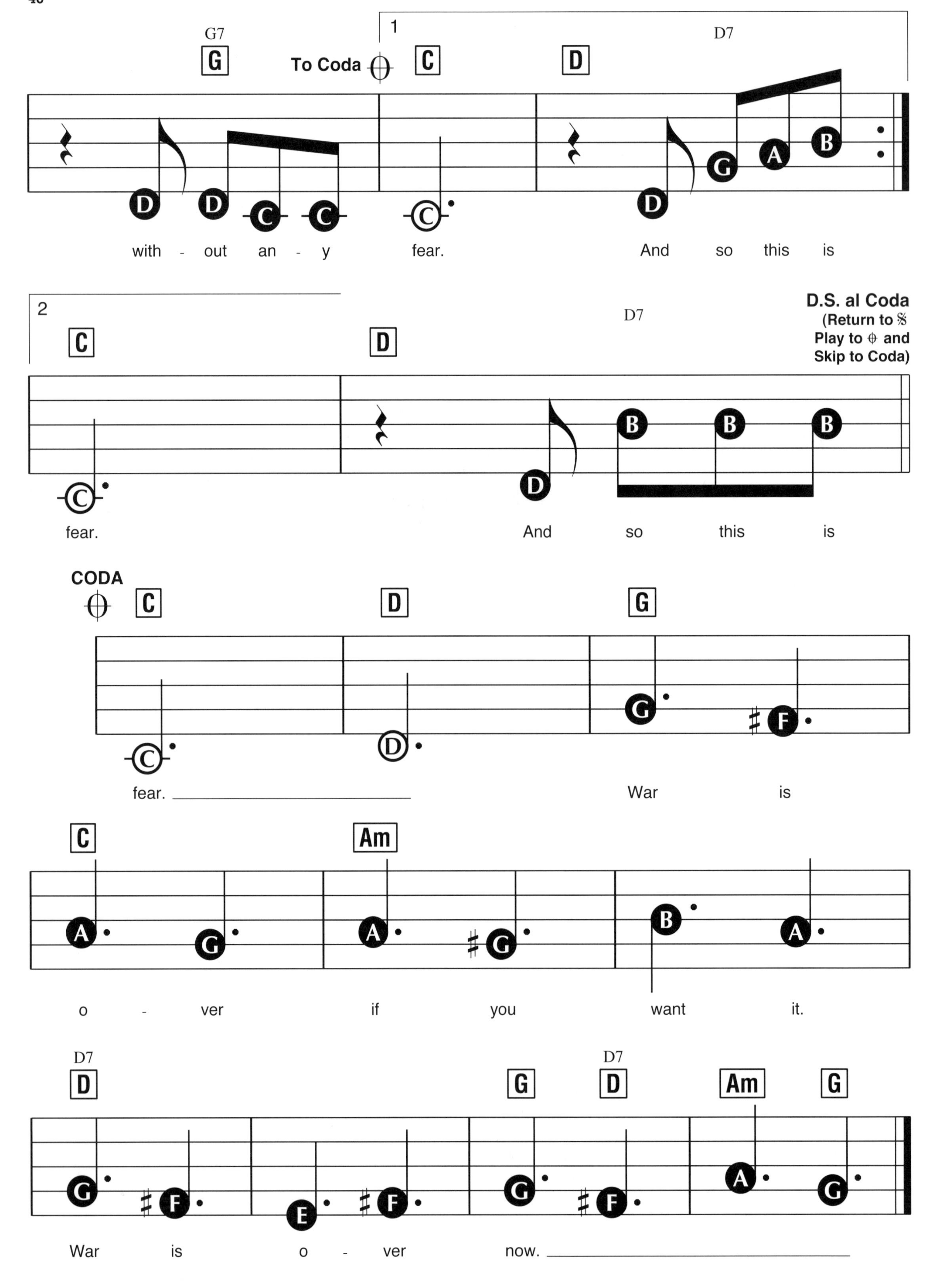
G7
G
To Coda
1
C
D
D7
D
D
C
C
C
D
G
A
B
with - out an - y
fear.
And so this is
2
C
D
D7
D.S. al Coda
(Return to 𝄋
Play to ⊕ and
Skip to Coda)
C
D
B
B
B
fear.
And so this is
CODA
C
D
G
C
D
G
F
fear.
War is
C
Am
A
G
A
G
B
A
o - ver
if you
want it.
D7
D
G
D7
D
Am
G
G
F
E
F
G
F
A
G
War is
o - ver
now.

Have Yourself a Merry Little Christmas

from MEET ME IN ST. LOUIS

Registration 1
Rhythm: Fox Trot or Ballad

Words and Music by Hugh Martin
and Ralph Blane

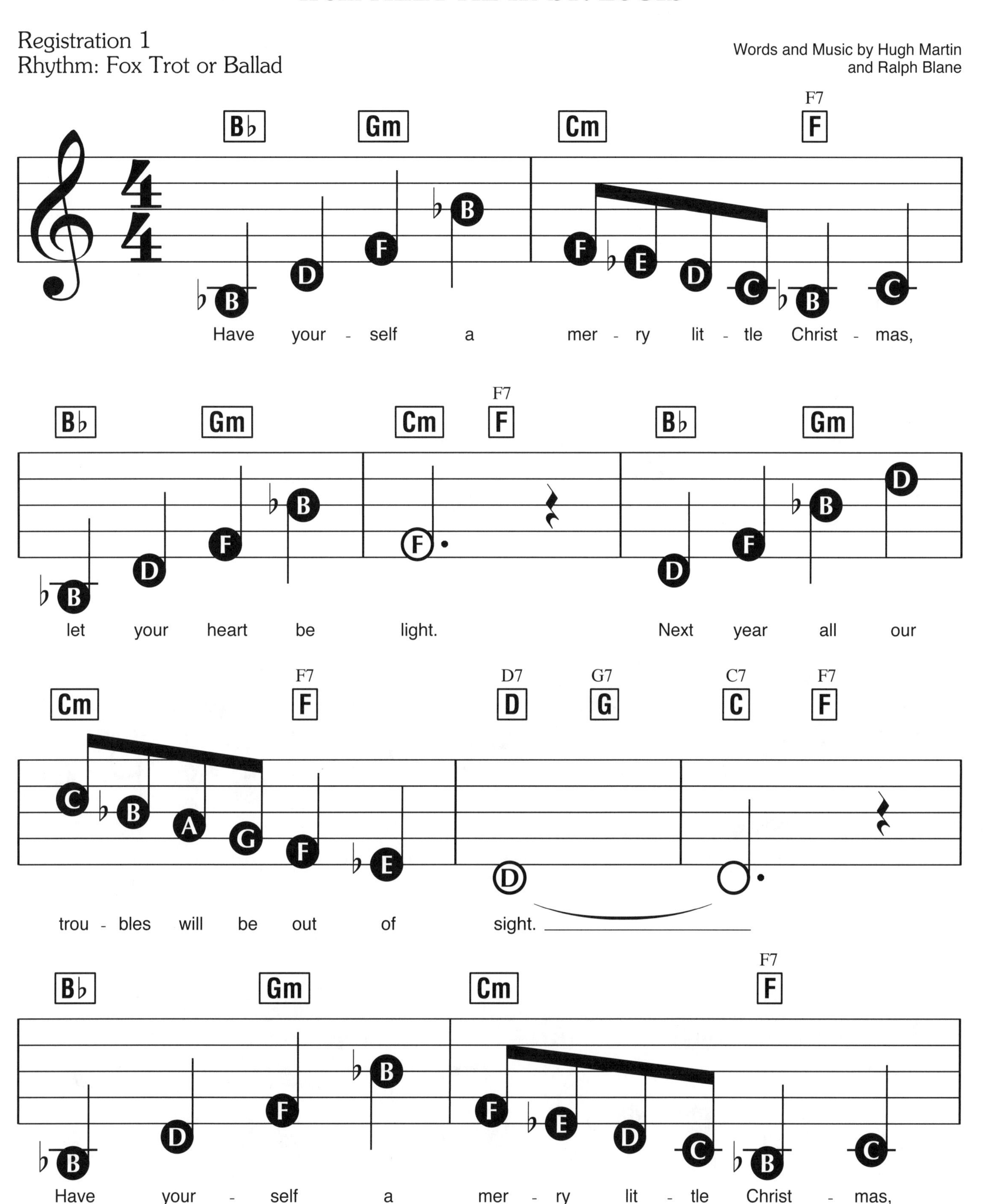

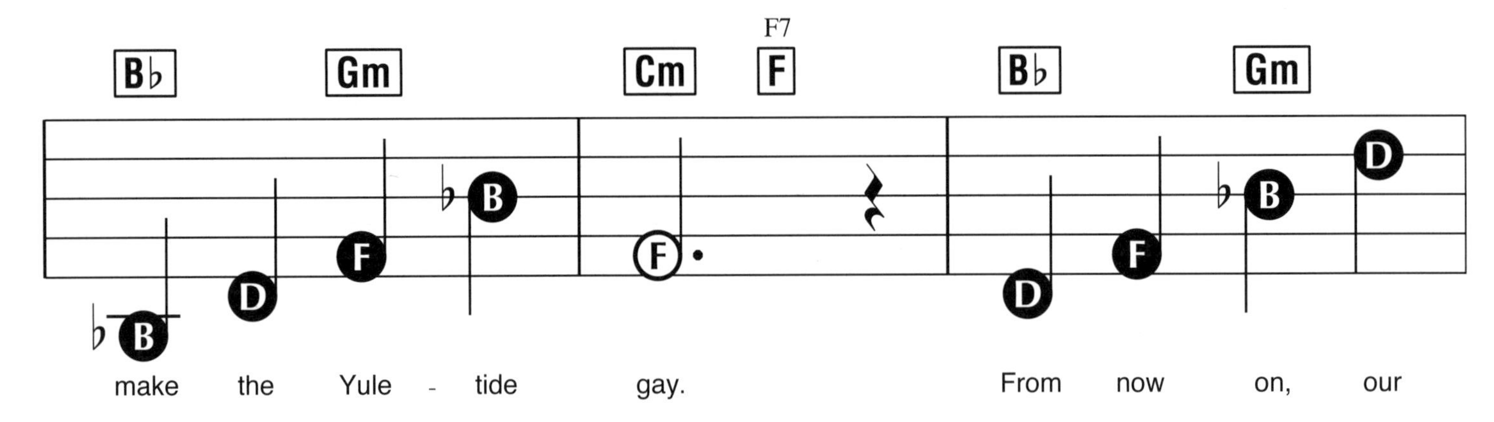
F7
B♭ Gm Cm F B♭ Gm
make the Yule - tide gay. From now on, our

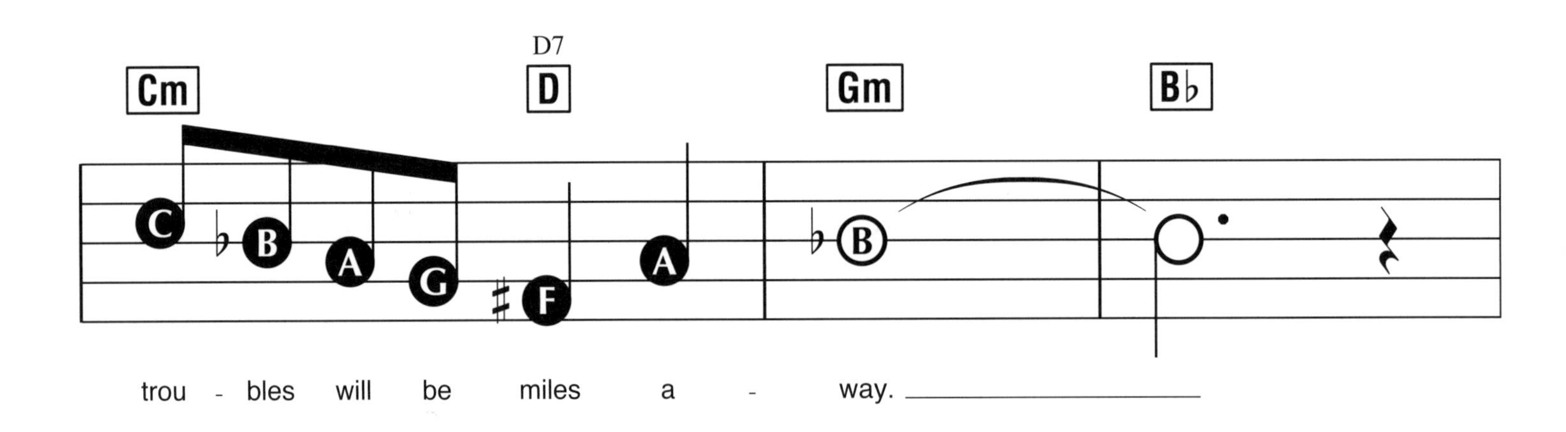
D7
Cm D Gm B♭
trou - bles will be miles a - way.

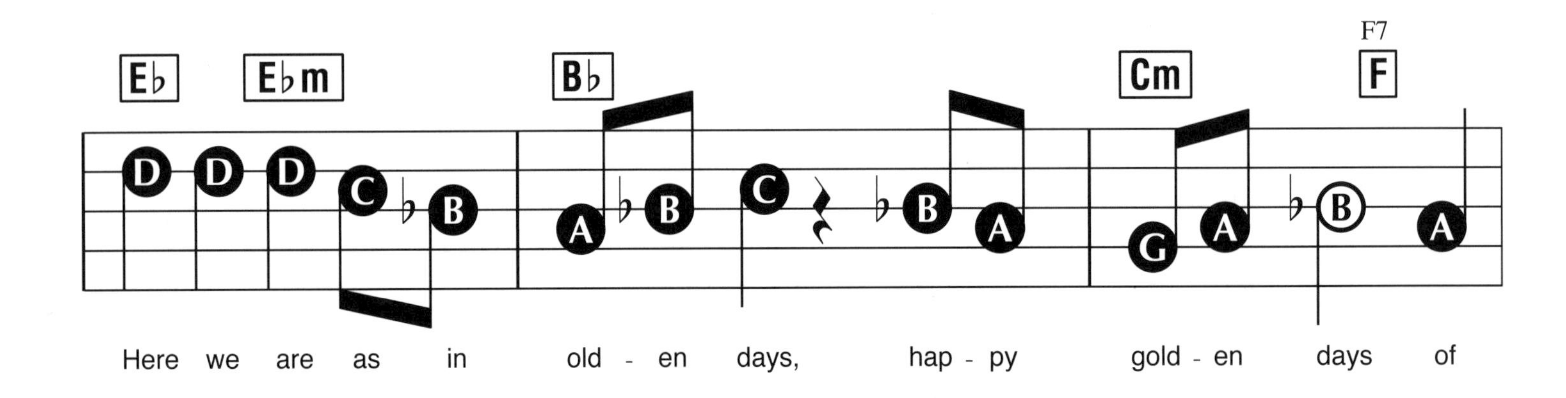
F7
E♭ E♭m B♭ Cm F
Here we are as in old - en days, hap - py gold - en days of

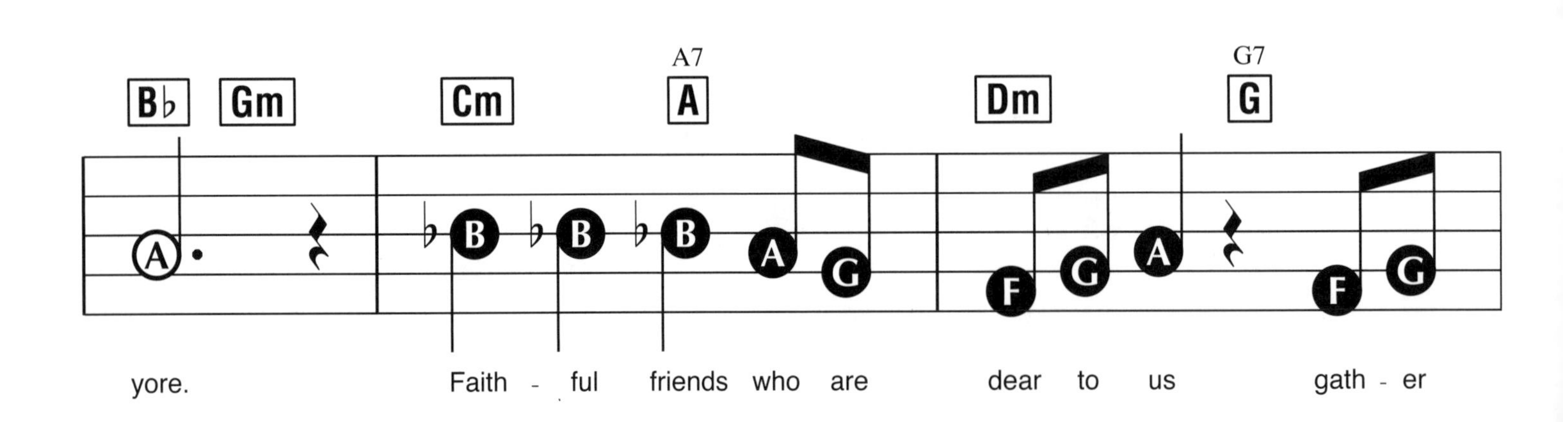
A7 G7
B♭ Gm Cm A Dm G
yore. Faith - ful friends who are dear to us gath - er

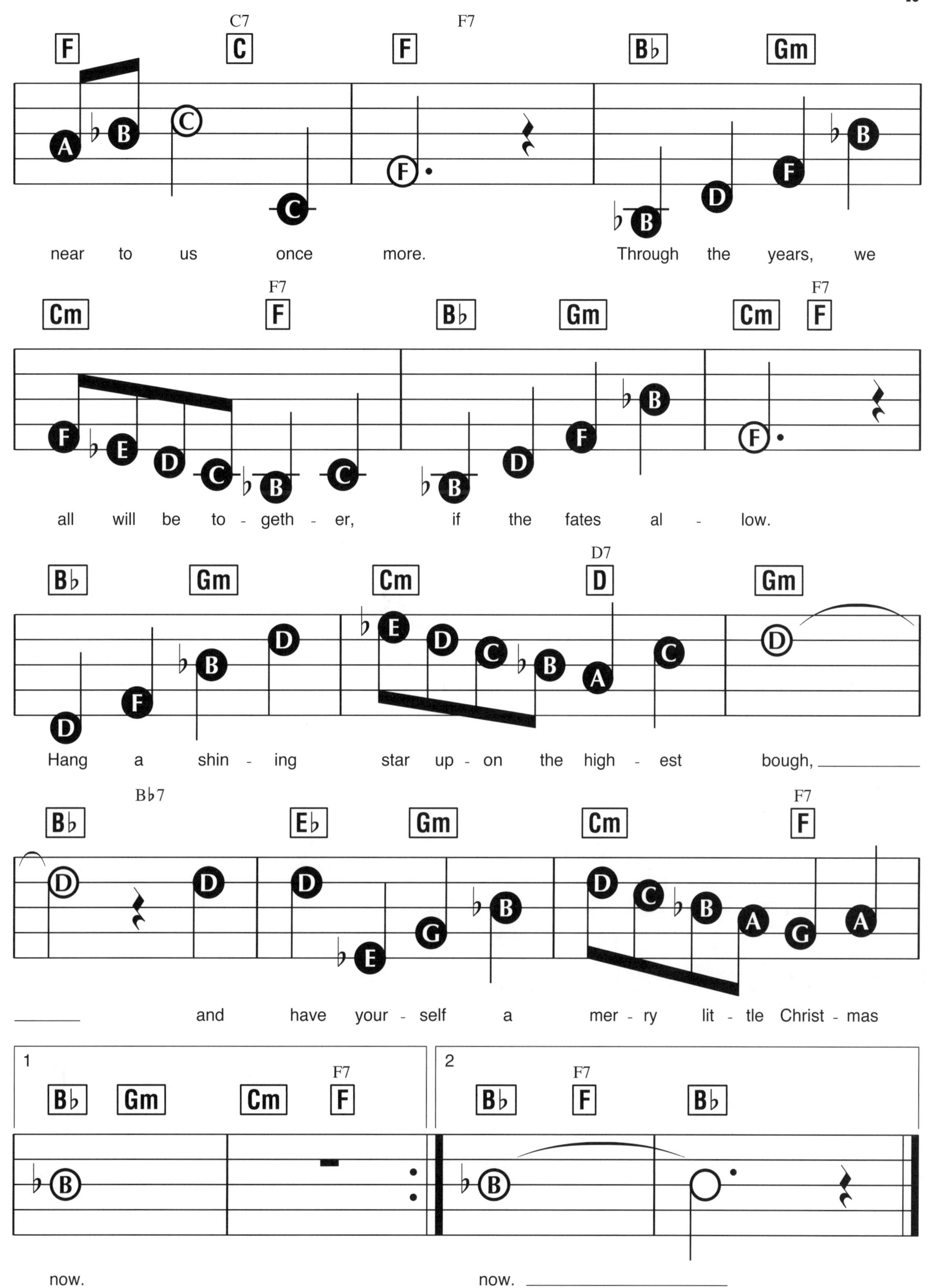
F C7 C F7 F B♭ Gm
near to us once more. Through the years, we
Cm F7 F B♭ Gm Cm F7 F
all will be to - geth - er, if the fates al - low.
B♭ Gm Cm D7 D Gm
Hang a shin - ing star up - on the high - est bough,
B♭ B♭7 E♭ Gm Cm F7 F
and have your - self a mer - ry lit - tle Christ - mas
1
B♭ Gm Cm F7 F
now.
2
B♭ F7 F B♭
now.

(There's No Place Like)

Home for the Holidays

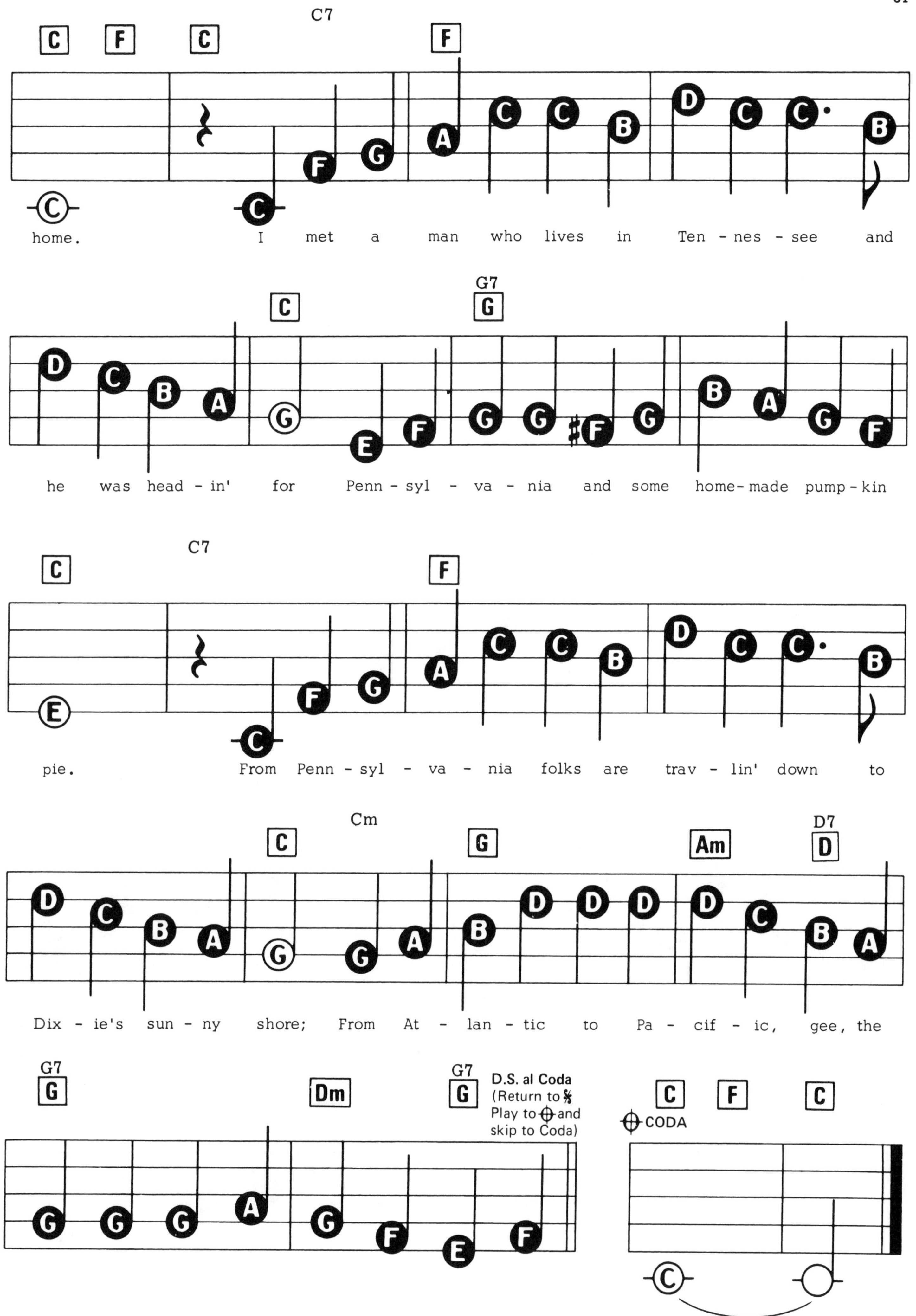
C F C
C7
F
home.
I met a man who lives in Ten - nes - see and
C
G7
G
he was head - in' for Penn - syl - va - nia and some home- made pump - kin
C
C7
F
pie.
From Penn - syl - va - nia folks are trav - lin' down to
C
Cm
G
Am
D7
D
Dix - ie's sun - ny shore; From At - lan - tic to Pa - cif - ic, gee, the
G7
G
Dm
G7
G
D.S. al Coda
(Return to 𝄋
Play to ⊕ and
skip to Coda)
⊕ CODA
C F C
traf - fic is ter - rif - ic! Oh, There's
home.

I Heard the Bells on Christmas Day

Registration 9
Rhythm: Ballad

Words by Henry Wadsworth Longfellow
Adapted by Johnny Marks
Music by Johnny Marks

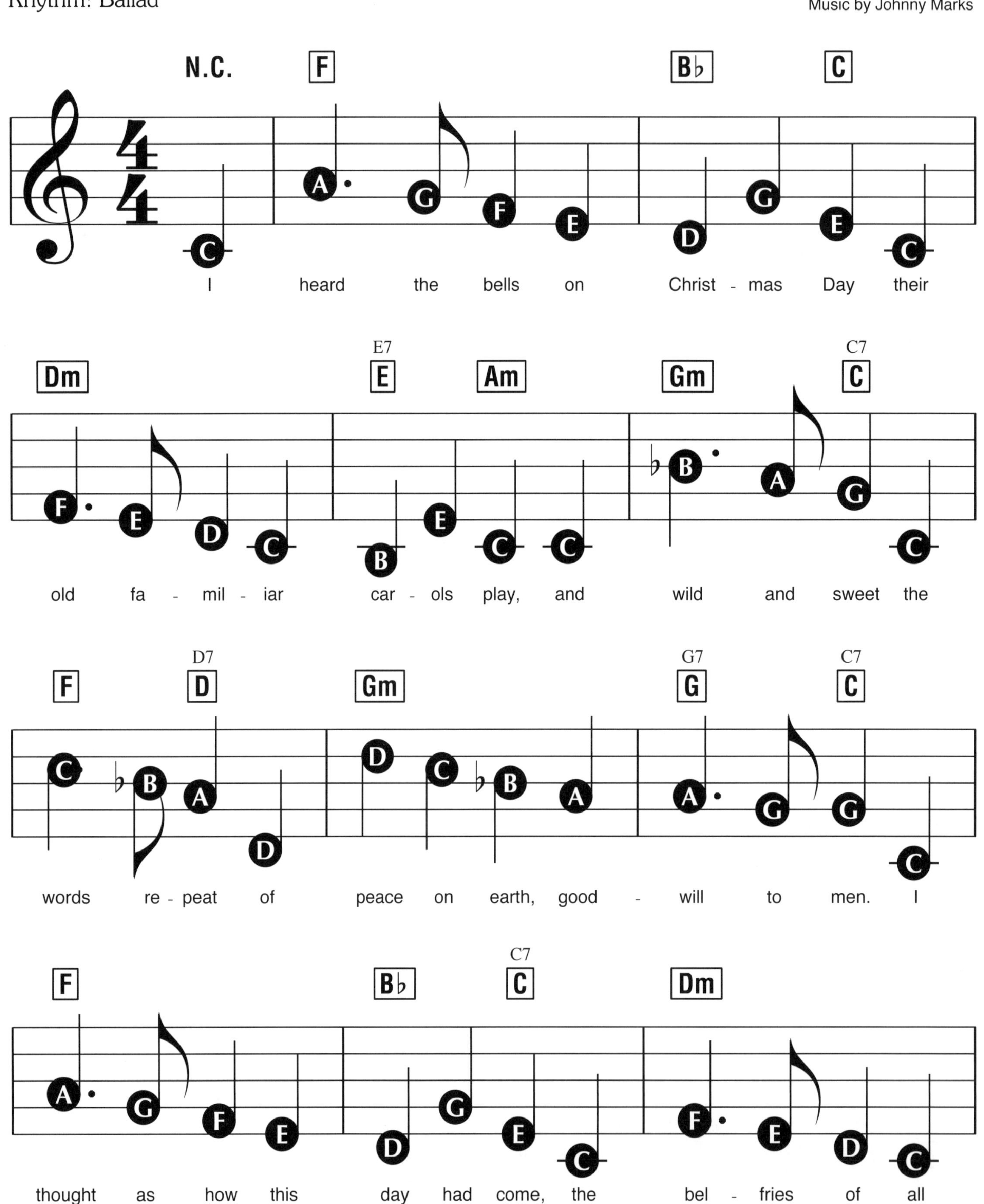

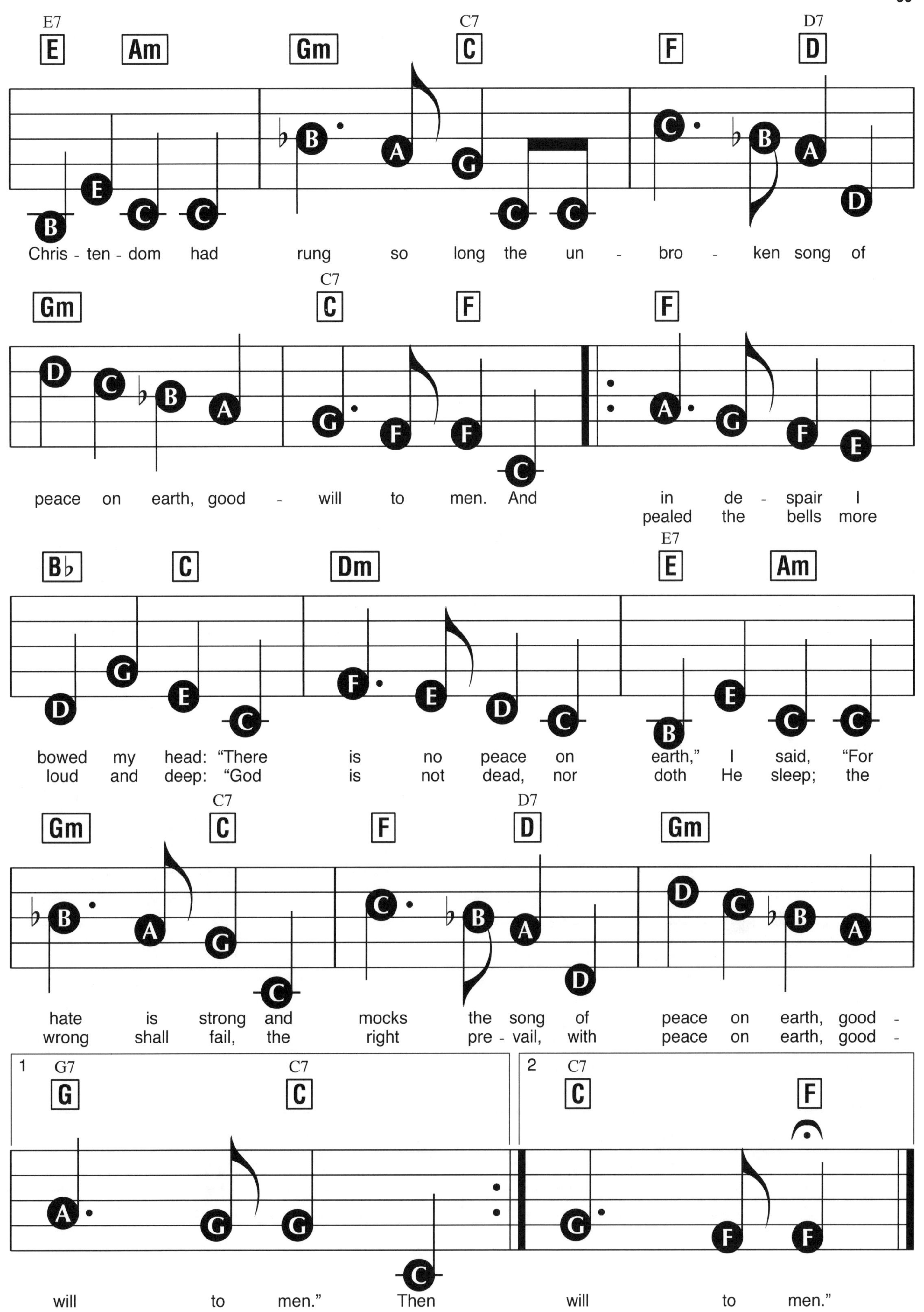
E7 E Am Gm C7 C F D7 D
Chris - ten - dom had rung so long the un - bro - ken song of
Gm C7 C F F
peace on earth, good - will to men. And
in de - spair I
pealed the bells more
B♭ C Dm E7 E Am
bowed my head: "There is no peace on earth," I said, "For
loud and deep: "God is not dead, nor doth He sleep; the
Gm C7 C F D7 D Gm
hate is strong and mocks the song of peace on earth, good -
wrong shall fail, the right pre - vail, with peace on earth, good -
1 G7 G C7 C
will to men." Then
2 C7 C F
will to men."

I Wish It Could Be Christmas All Year Long

Registration 2
Rhythm: Fox Trot

Words and Music by
Phil Baron

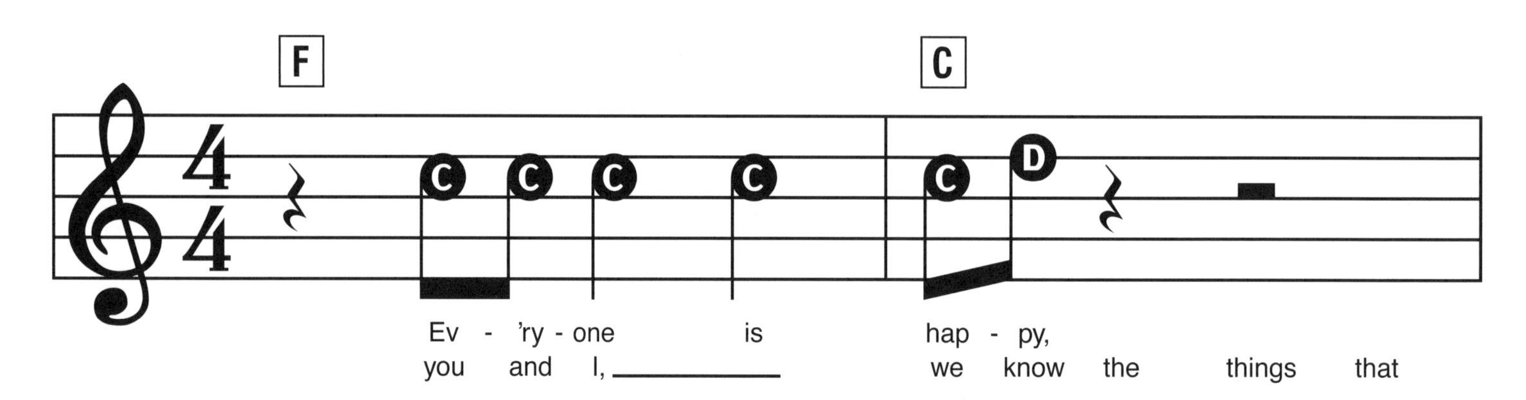

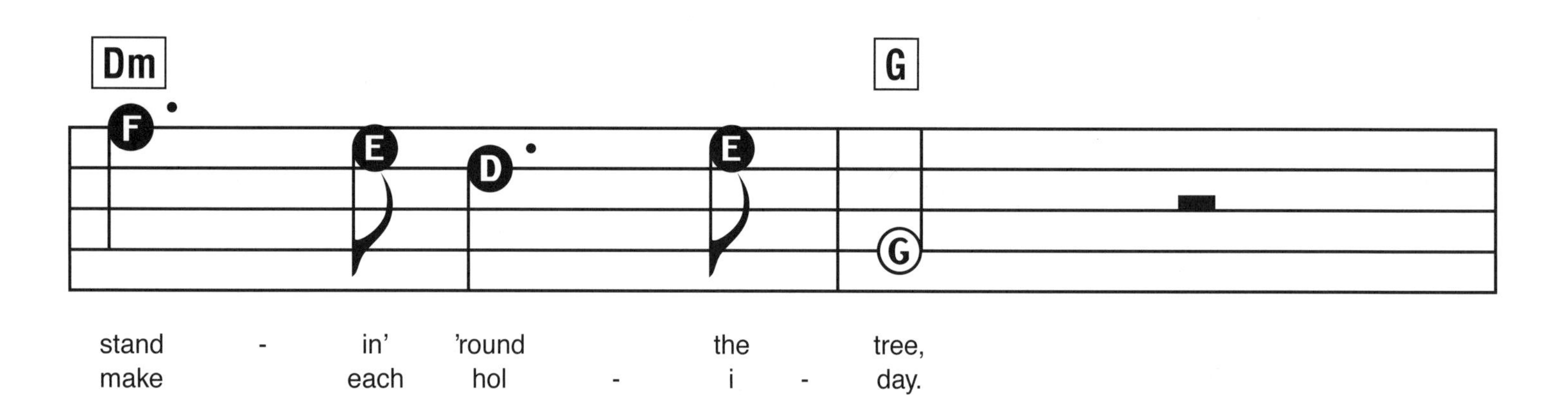

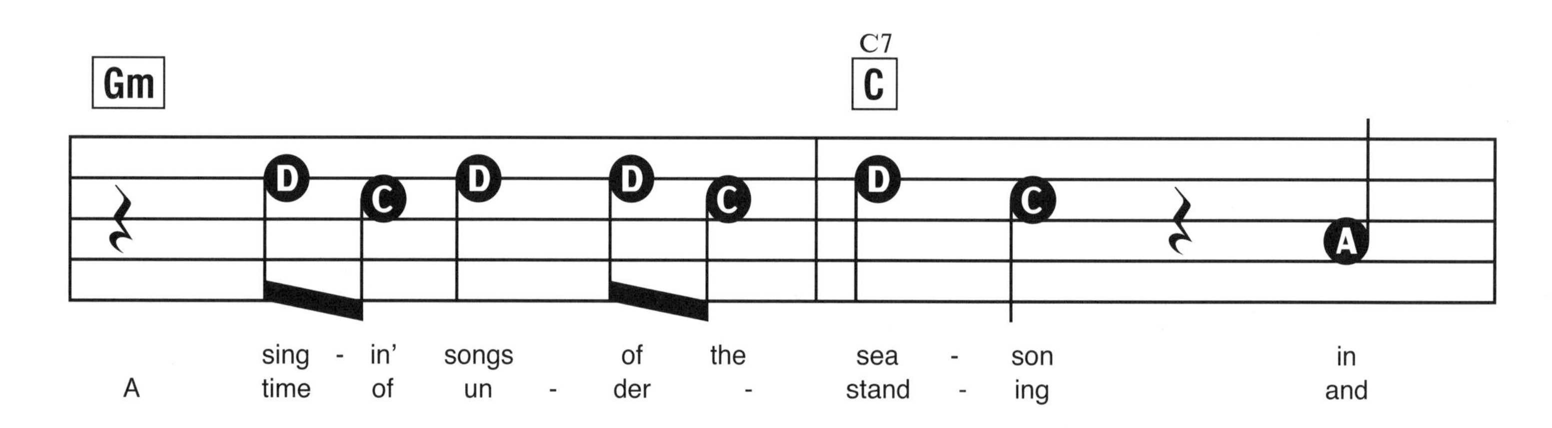

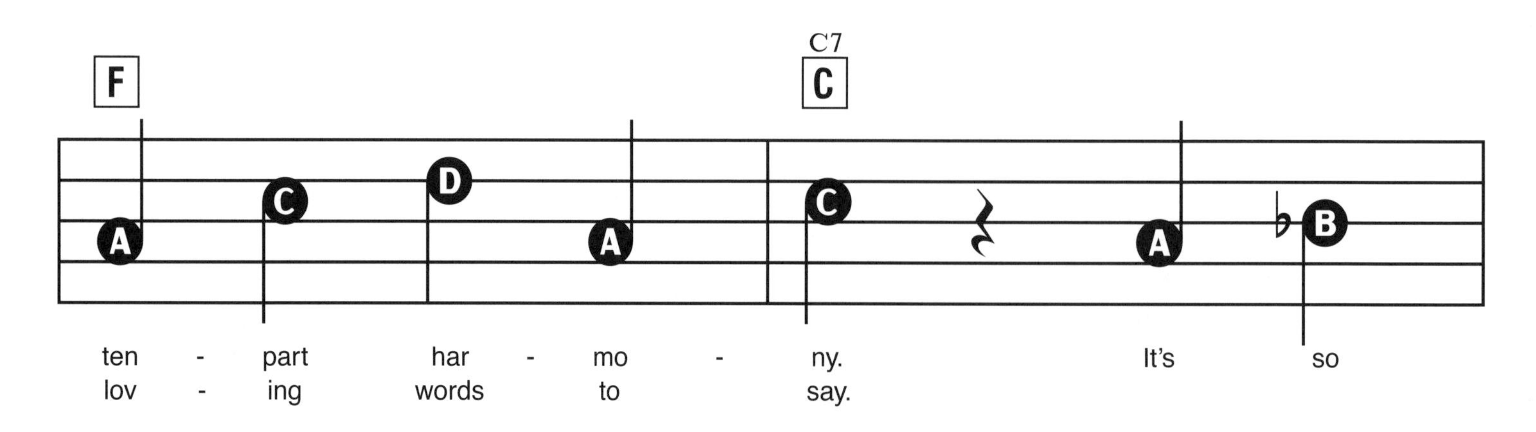

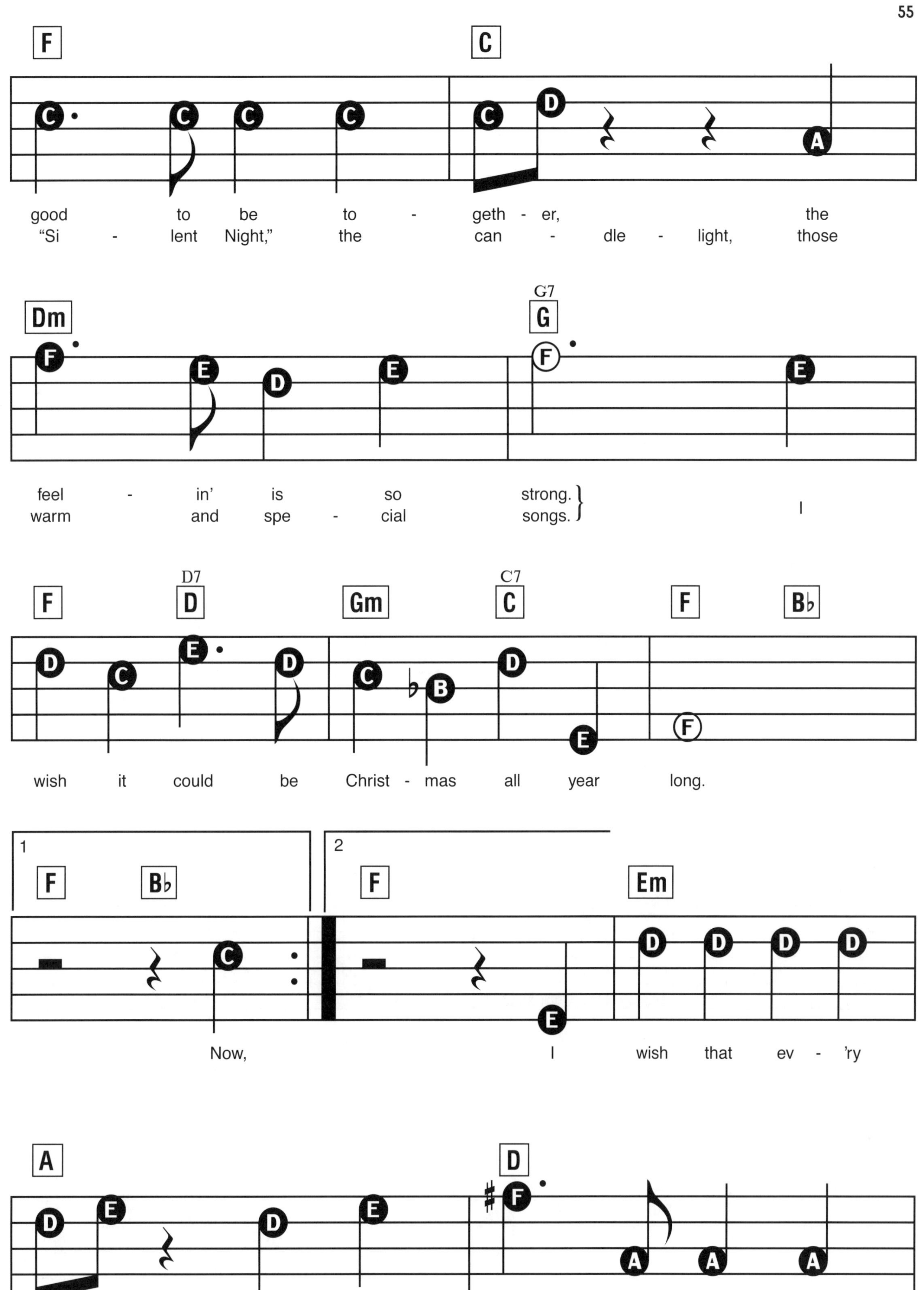
F
C
good to be to - geth - er, the
"Si - lent Night," the can - dle - light, those
Dm
G7
G
feel - in' is so strong.
warm and spe - cial songs.
I
F
D7
D
Gm
C7
C
F
B♭
wish it could be Christ - mas all year long.
1
F
B♭
Now,
2
F
Em
I wish that ev - 'ry
A
D
spir - it in the world could feel the

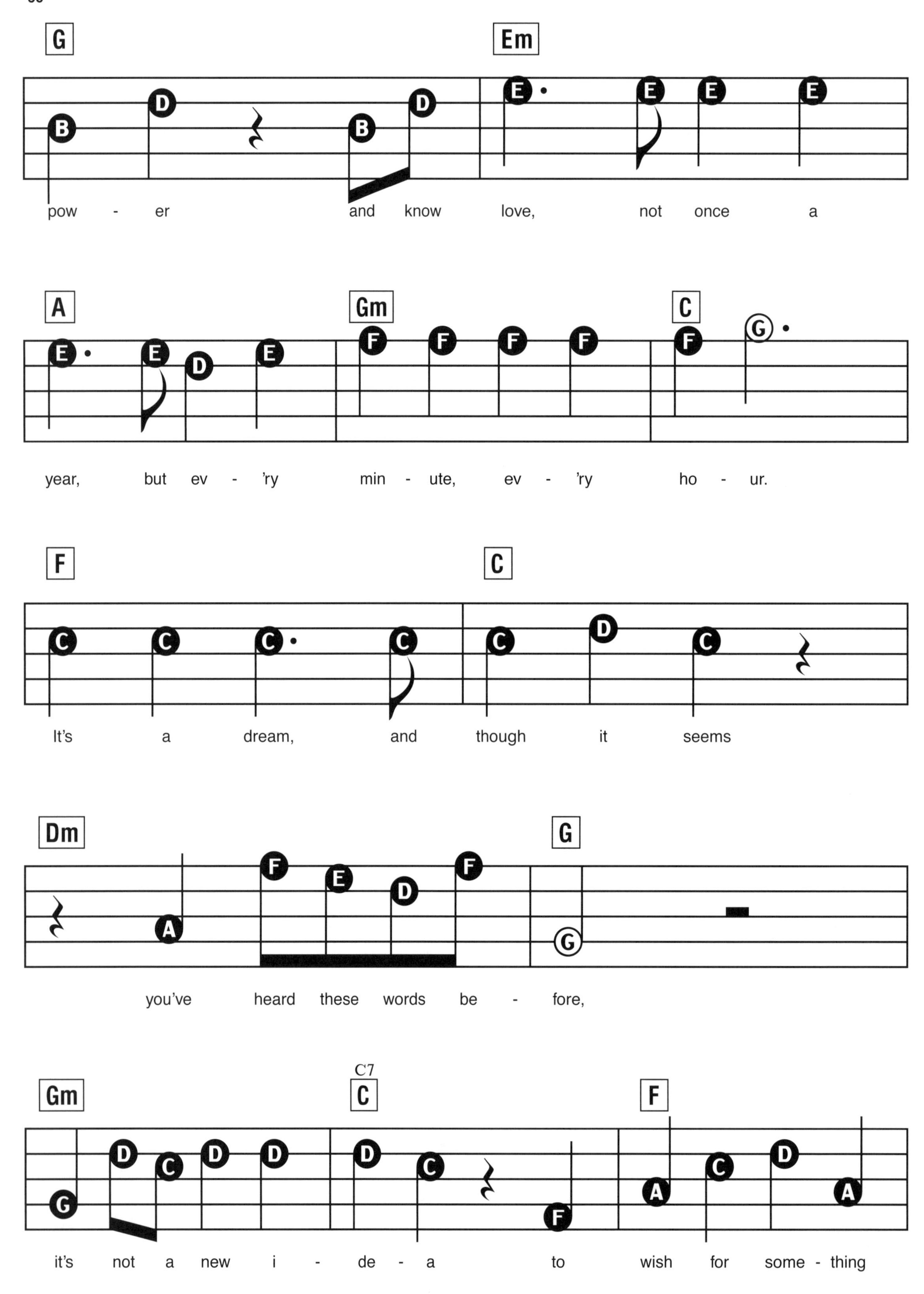
G
B D B D
pow - er and know
Em
E E E E
love, not once a
A
E E D E
year, but ev - 'ry
Gm
F F F F
min - ute, ev - 'ry
C
F G
ho - ur.
F
C C C C
It's a dream, and
C
C D C
though it seems
Dm
A F E D F
you've heard these words be -
G
G
fore,
Gm
G D C D D
it's not a new i -
C7
C
D C F
de - a to
F
A C D A
wish for some - thing

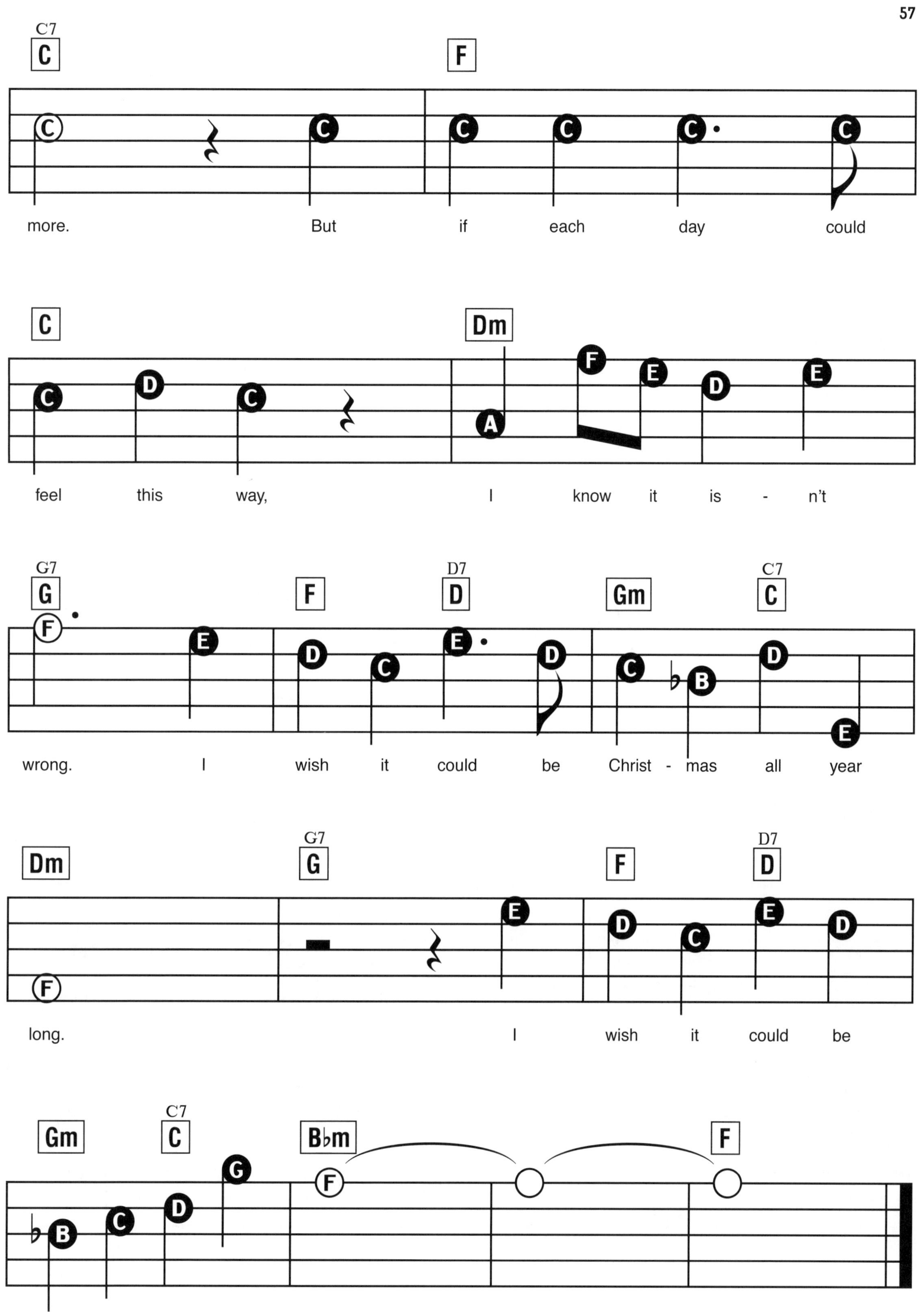
C7
C
F
more. But if each day could
C
Dm
feel this way, I know it is - n't
G7
G
F
D7
D
Gm
C7
C
wrong. I wish it could be Christ - mas all year
Dm
G7
G
F
D7
D
long. I wish it could be
Gm
C7
C
B♭m
F
Christ - mas all year long.

I'll Be Home for Christmas

Registration 1
Rhythm: Fox Trot

Words and Music by Kim Gannon
and Walter Kent

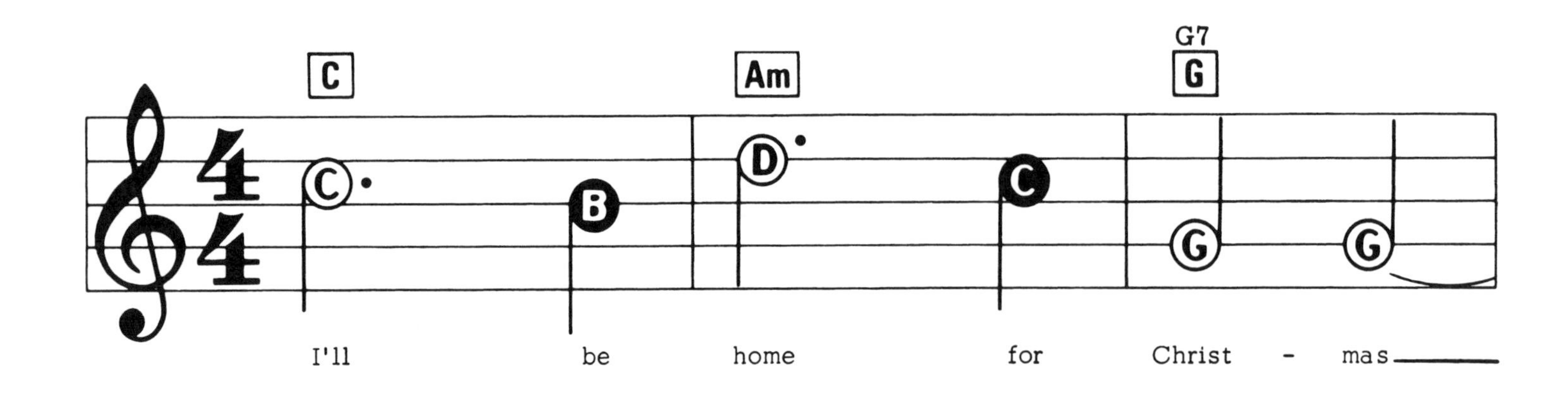

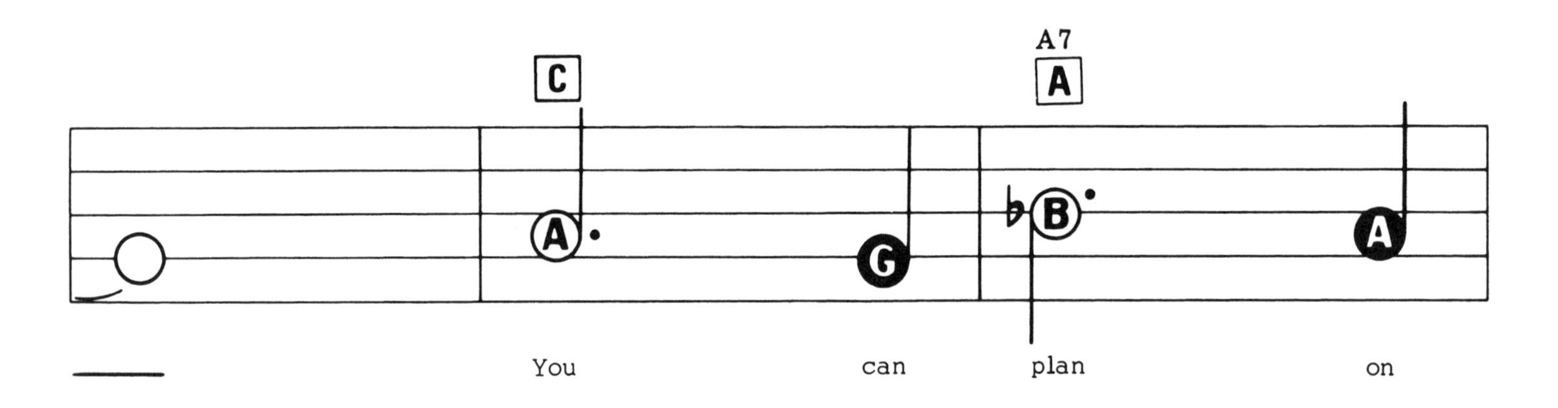

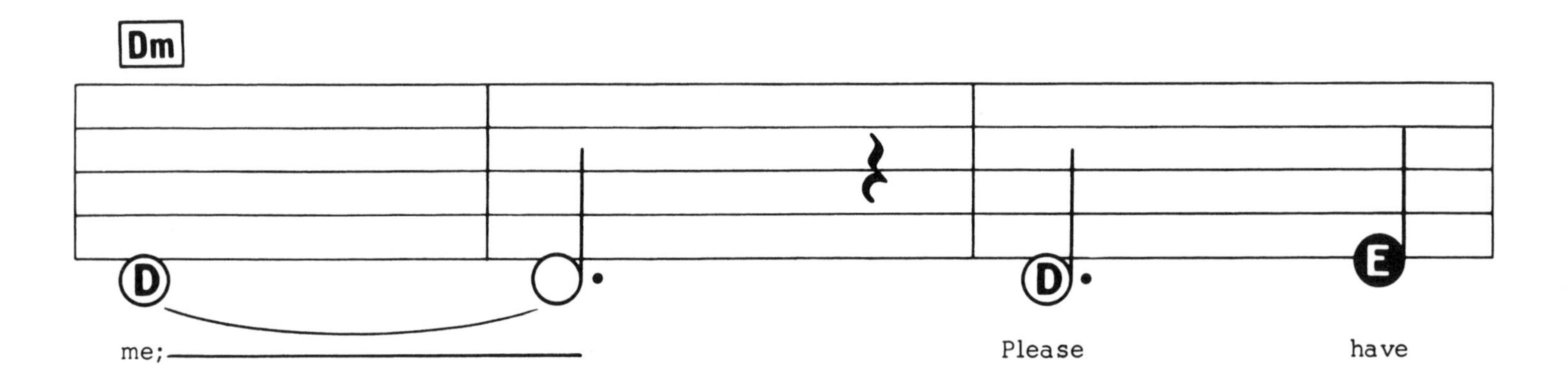

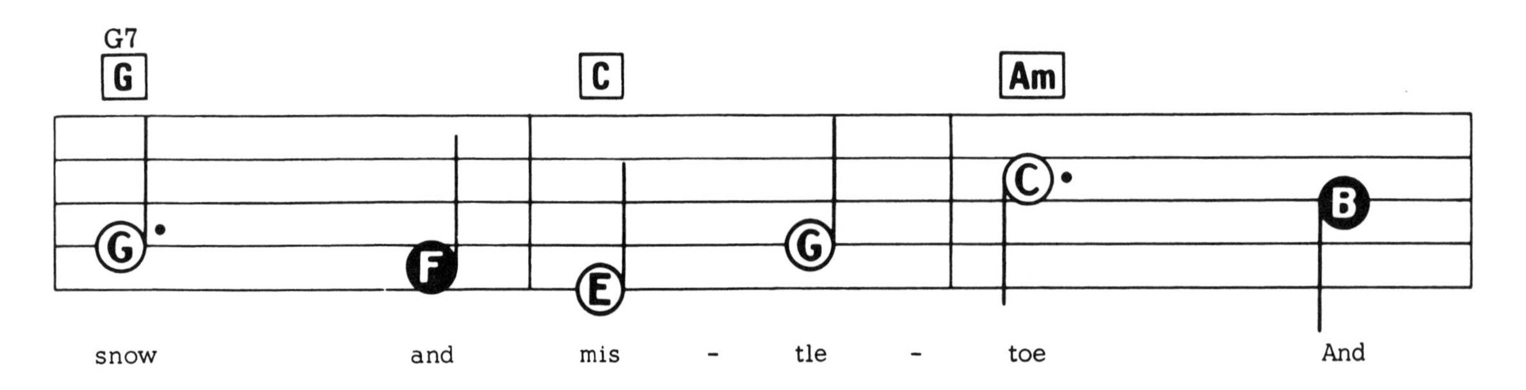

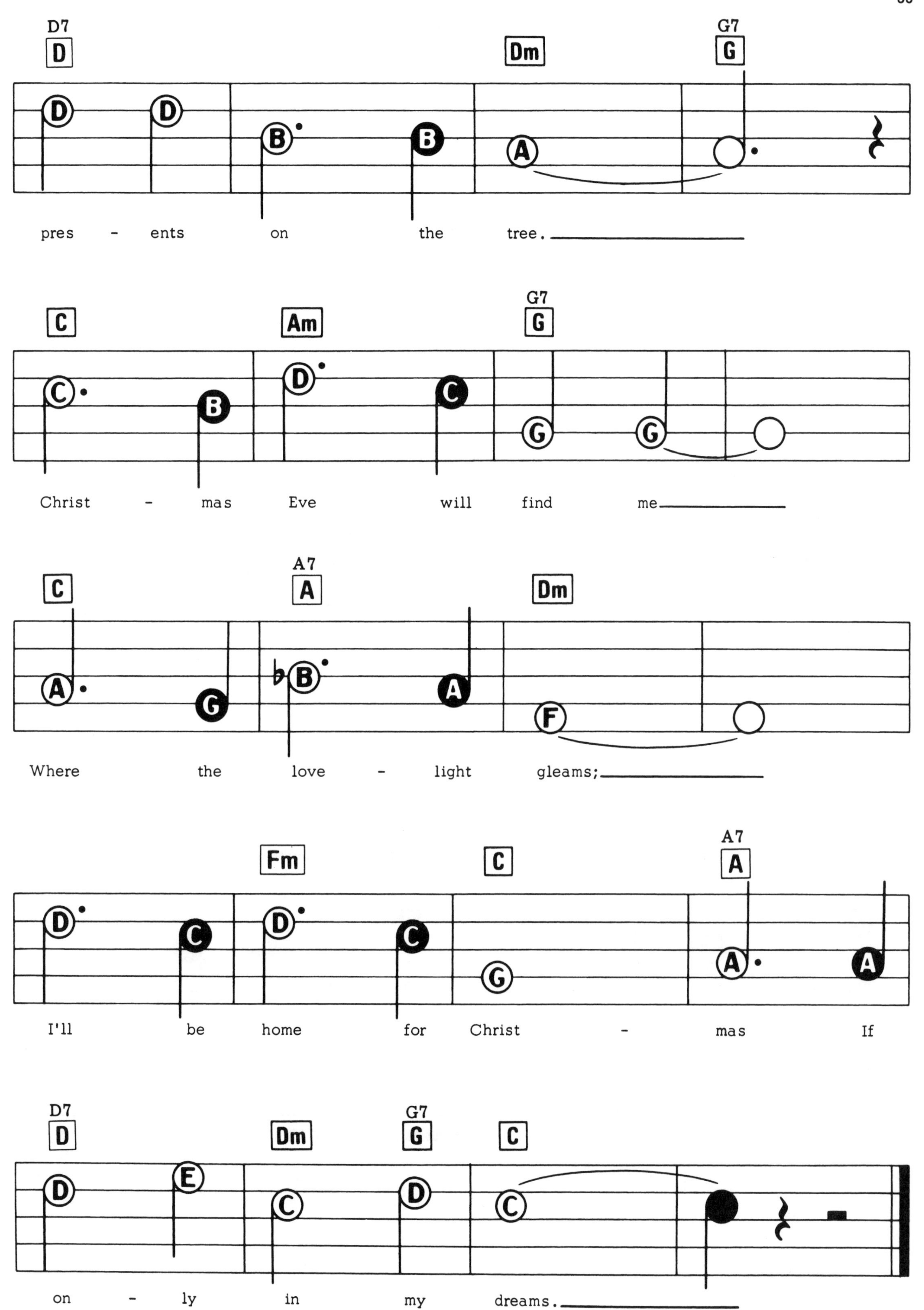
D7
D
Dm
G7
G
pres - ents on the tree.
C
Am
G7
G
Christ - mas Eve will find me
C
A7
A
Dm
Where the love - light gleams;
Fm
C
A7
A
I'll be home for Christ - mas If
D7
D
Dm
G7
G
C
on - ly in my dreams.

It Must Have Been the Mistletoe
(Our First Christmas)

Registration 1
Rhythm: 6/8 or Waltz

Words and Music by Justin Wilde
and Doug Konecky

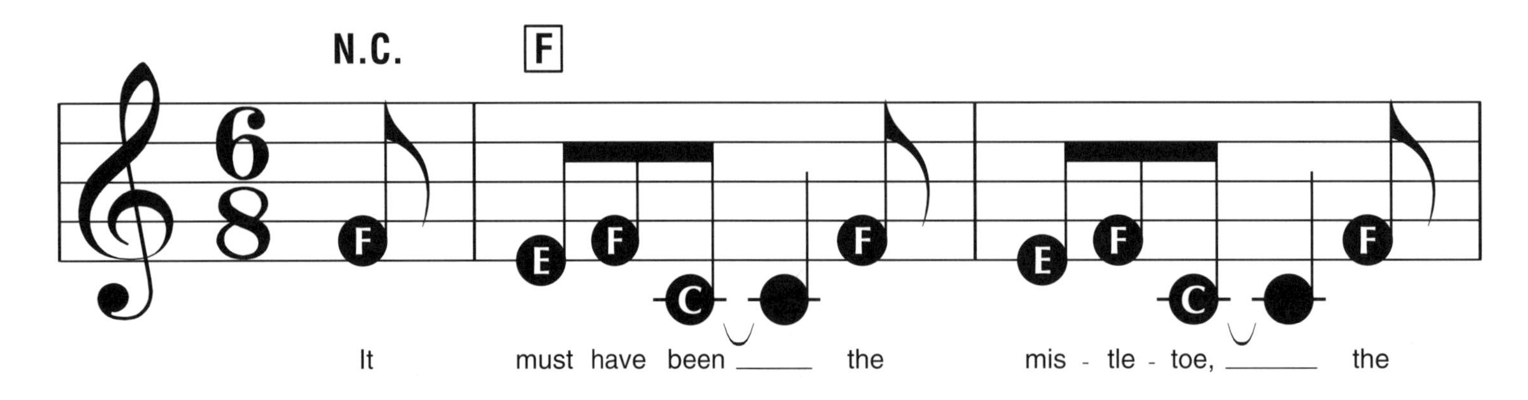

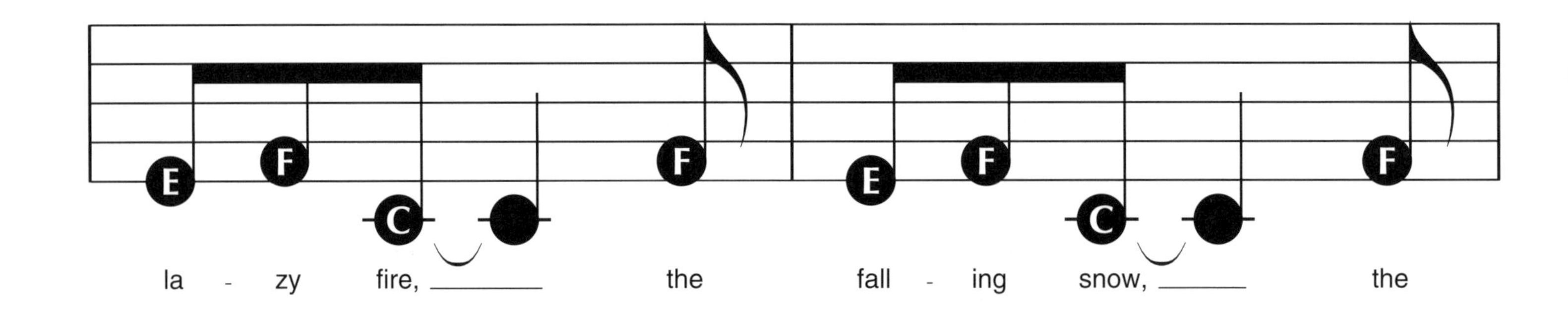

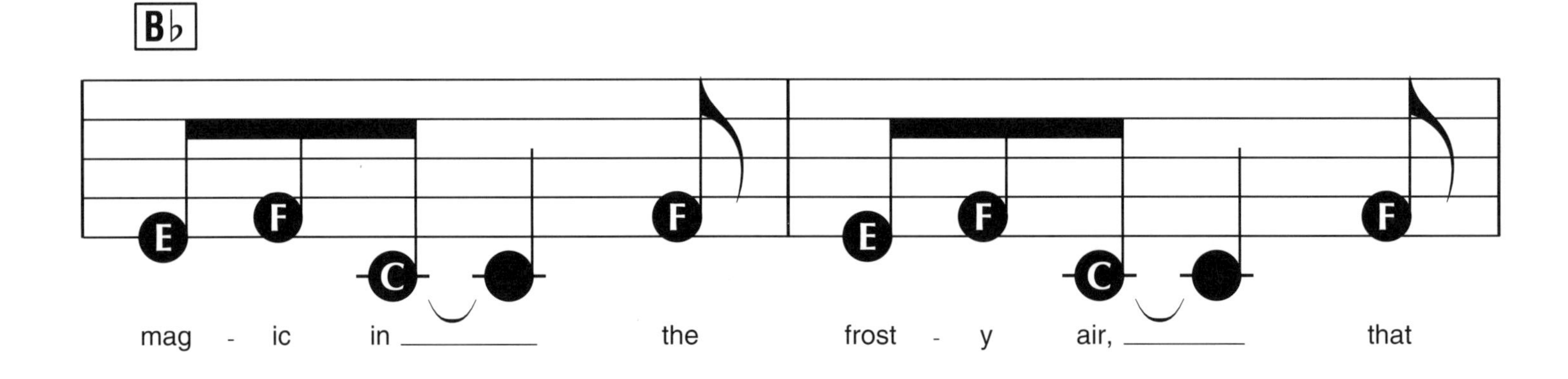

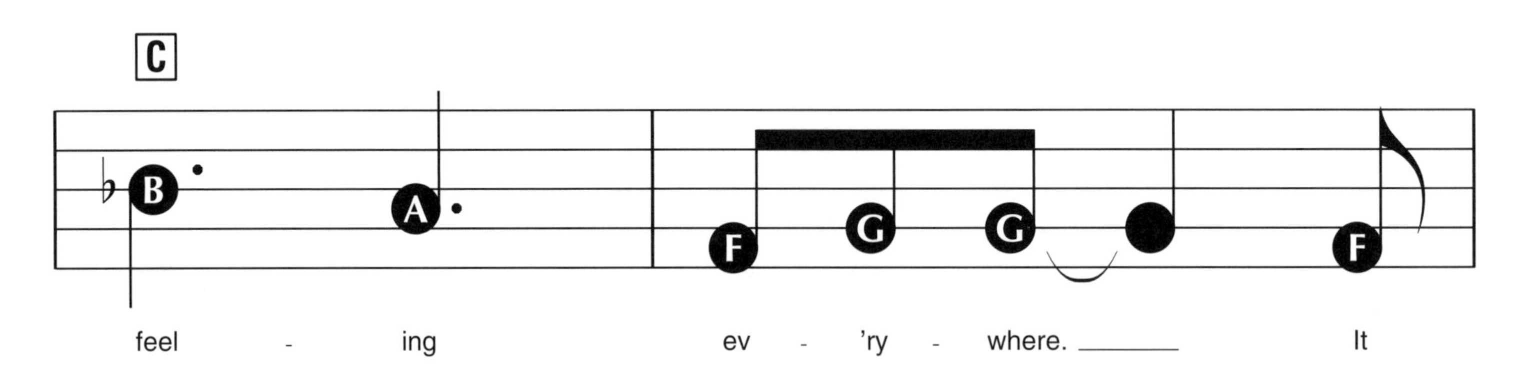

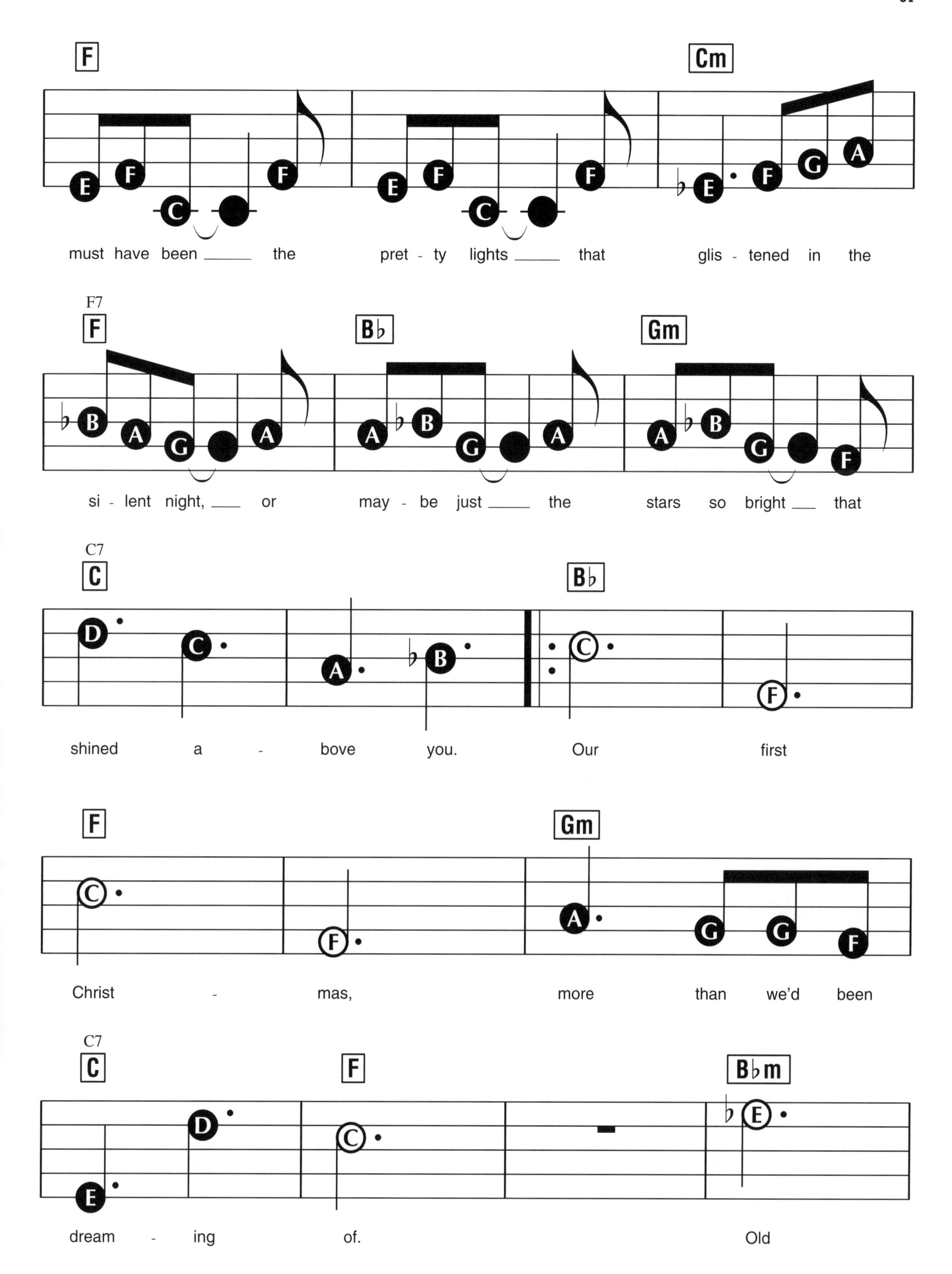
F
Cm
must have been ___ the pret - ty lights ___ that glis - tened in the
F7
F
B♭
Gm
si - lent night, ___ or may - be just ___ the stars so bright ___ that
C7
C
B♭
shined a - bove you. Our first
F
Gm
Christ - mas, more than we'd been
C7
C
F
B♭m
dream - ing of. Old

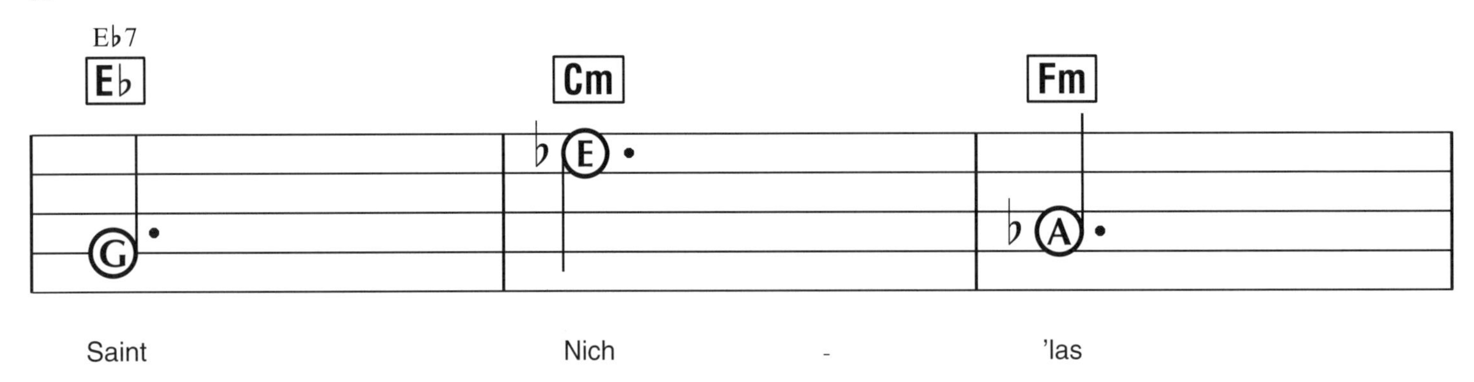
E♭7
E♭
Cm
Fm
G E A
Saint Nich - 'las

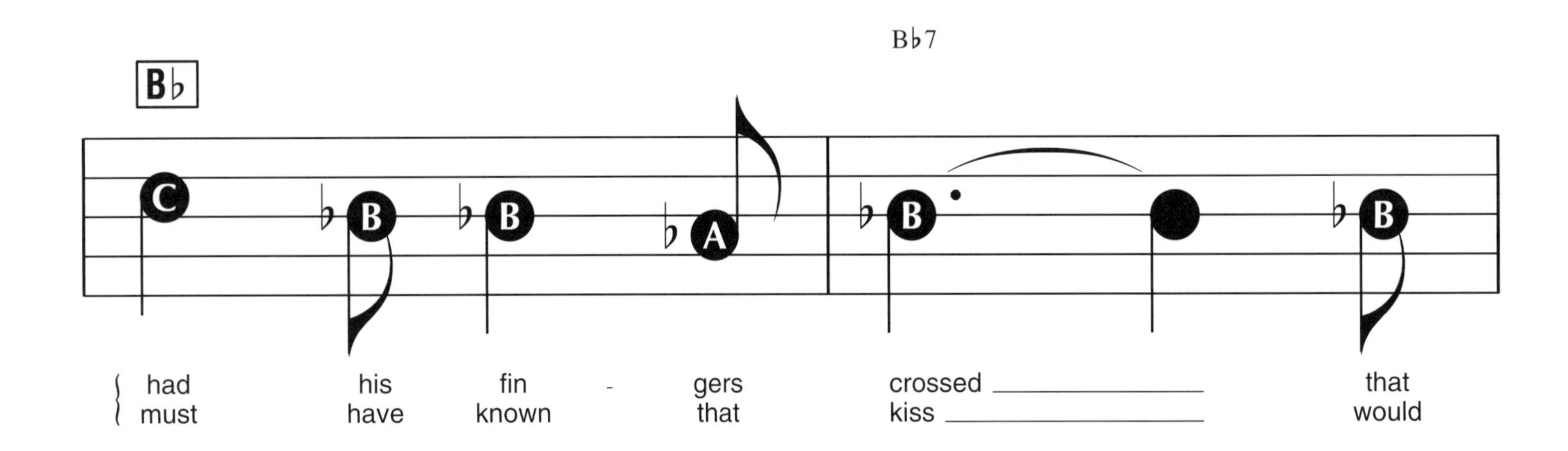
B♭7
B♭
C B B A B B
had his fin - gers crossed that
must have known that kiss would

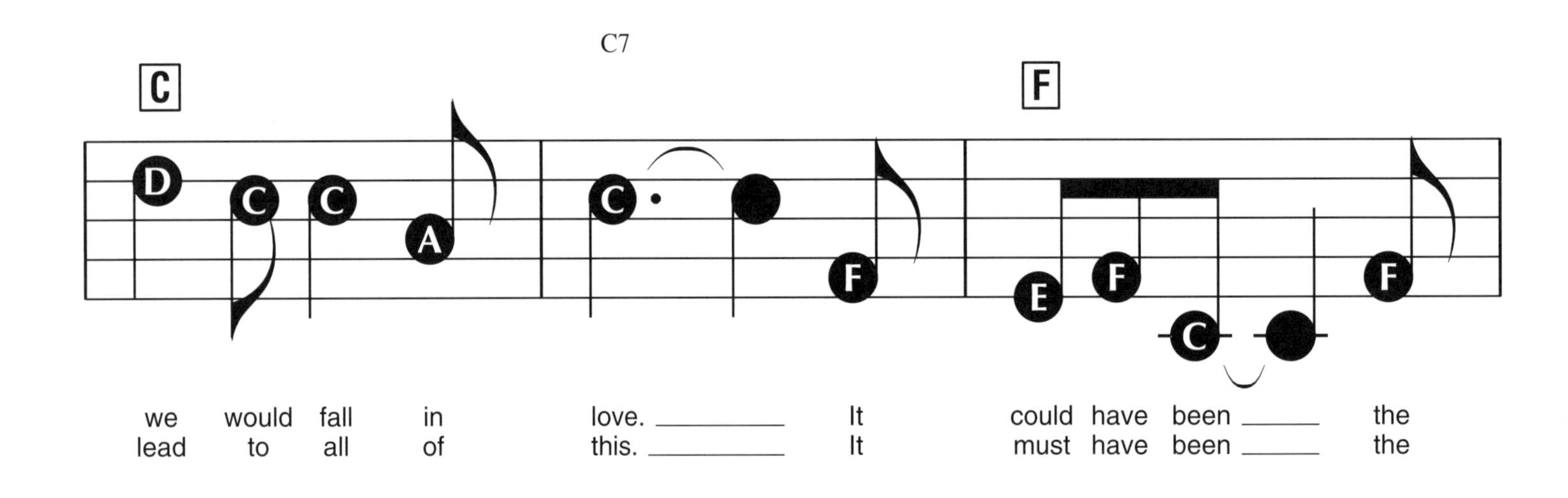
C7
C
F
D C C A C F E F C F
we would fall in love. It could have been the
lead to all of this. It must have been the

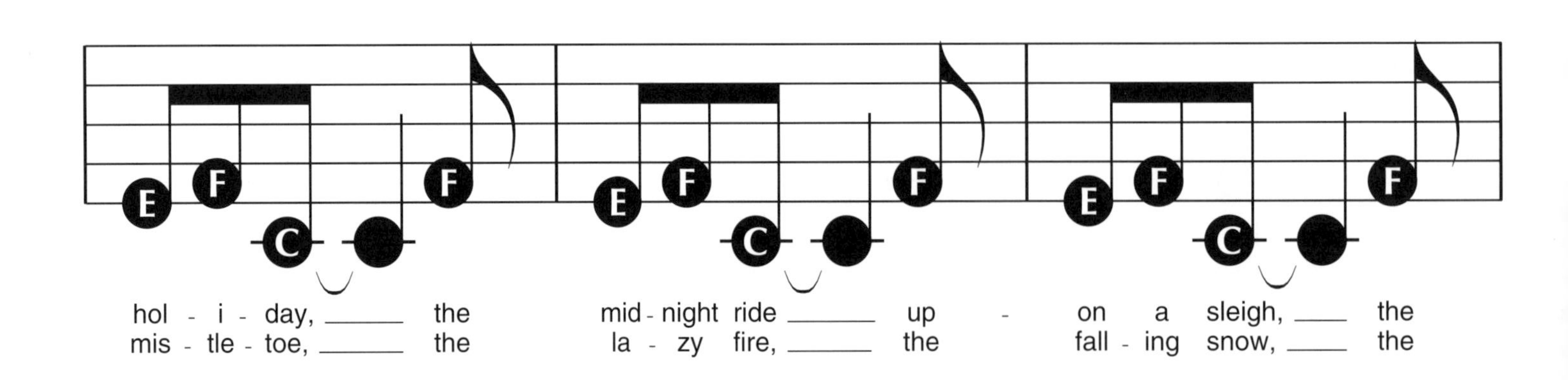
E F C F E F C F E F C F
hol - i - day, the mid - night ride up - on a sleigh, the
mis - tle - toe, the la - zy fire, the fall - ing snow, the

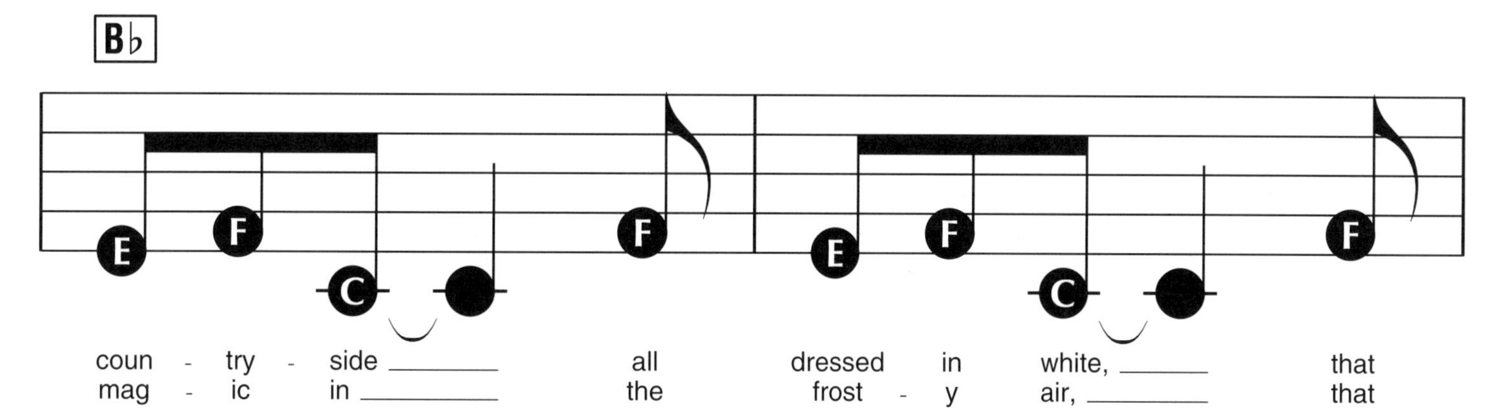
B♭
coun - try - side all dressed in white, that
mag - ic in the frost - y air, that

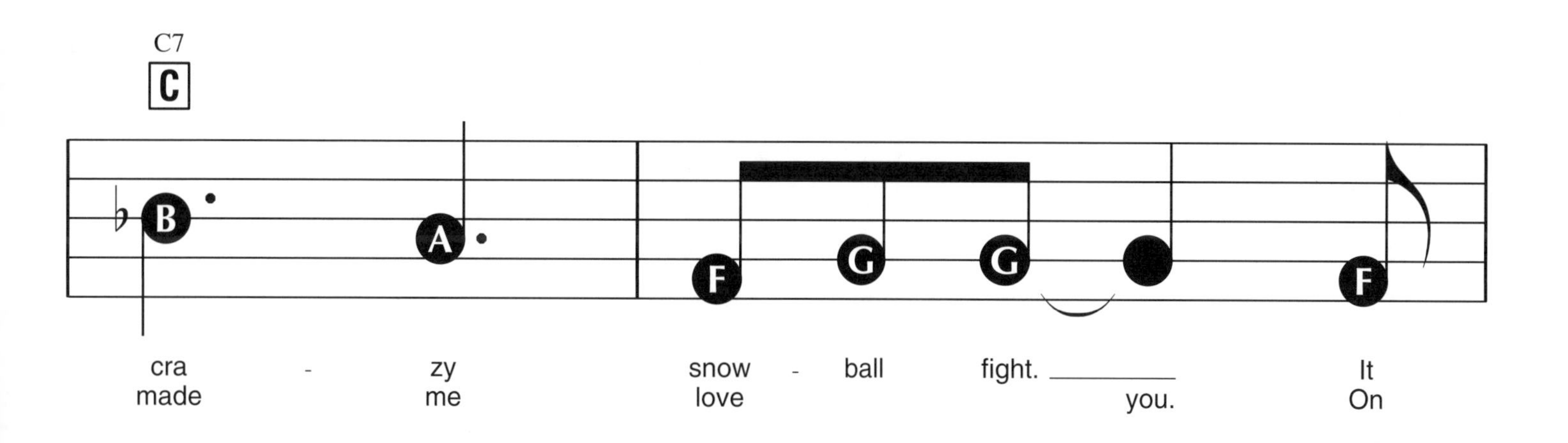
C7
C
cra - zy snow - ball fight. It
made me love you. On

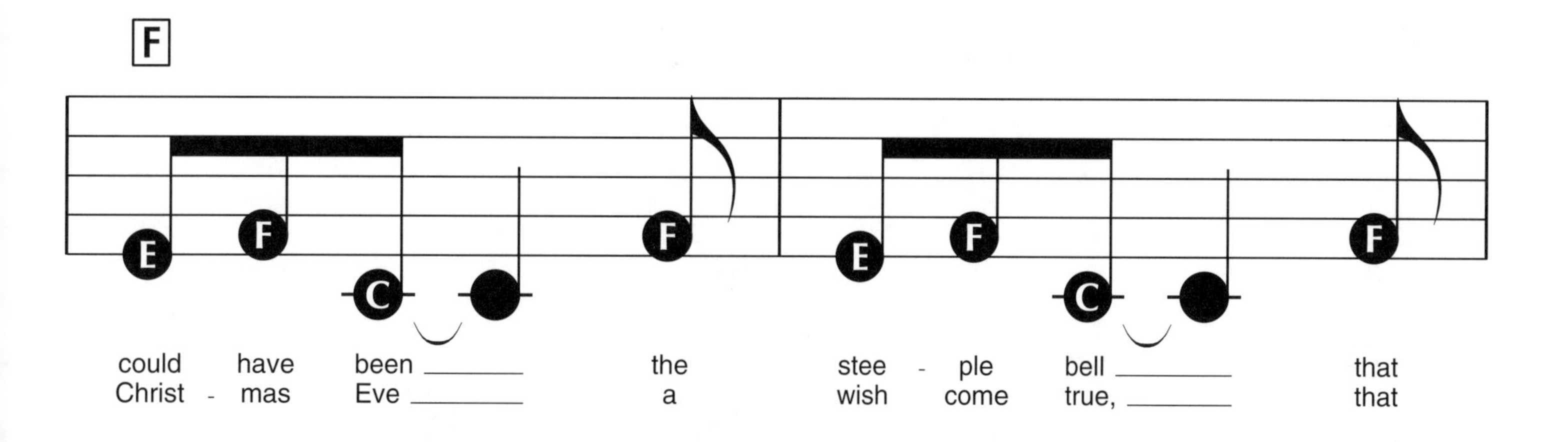
F
could have been the stee - ple bell that
Christ - mas Eve a wish come true, that

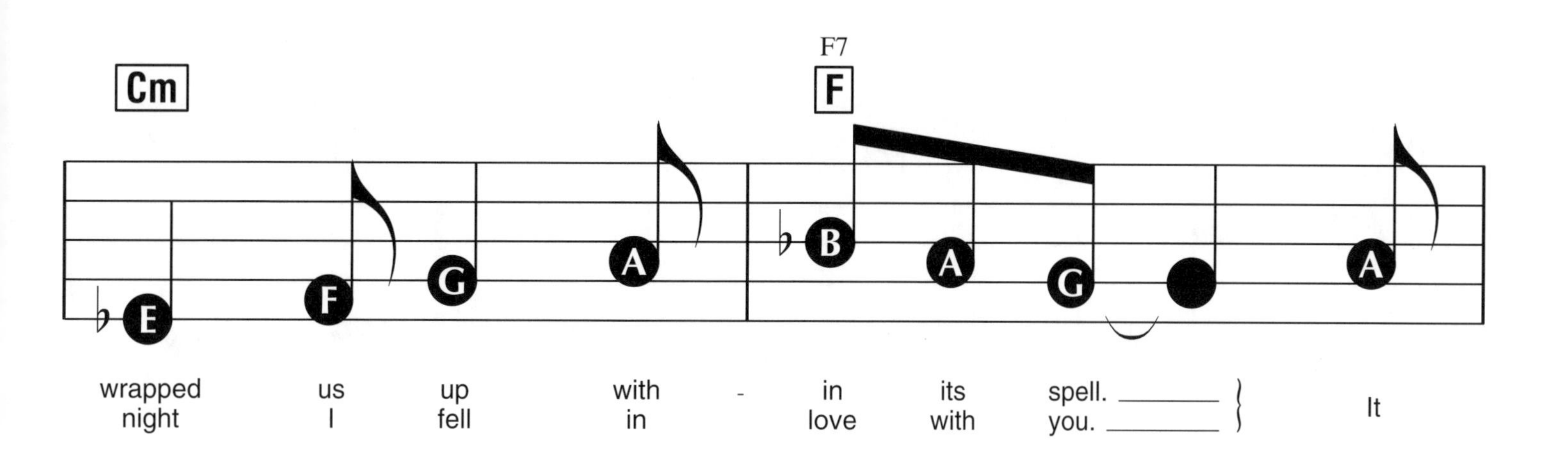
Cm
F7
F
wrapped us up with - in its spell. It
night I fell in love with you.

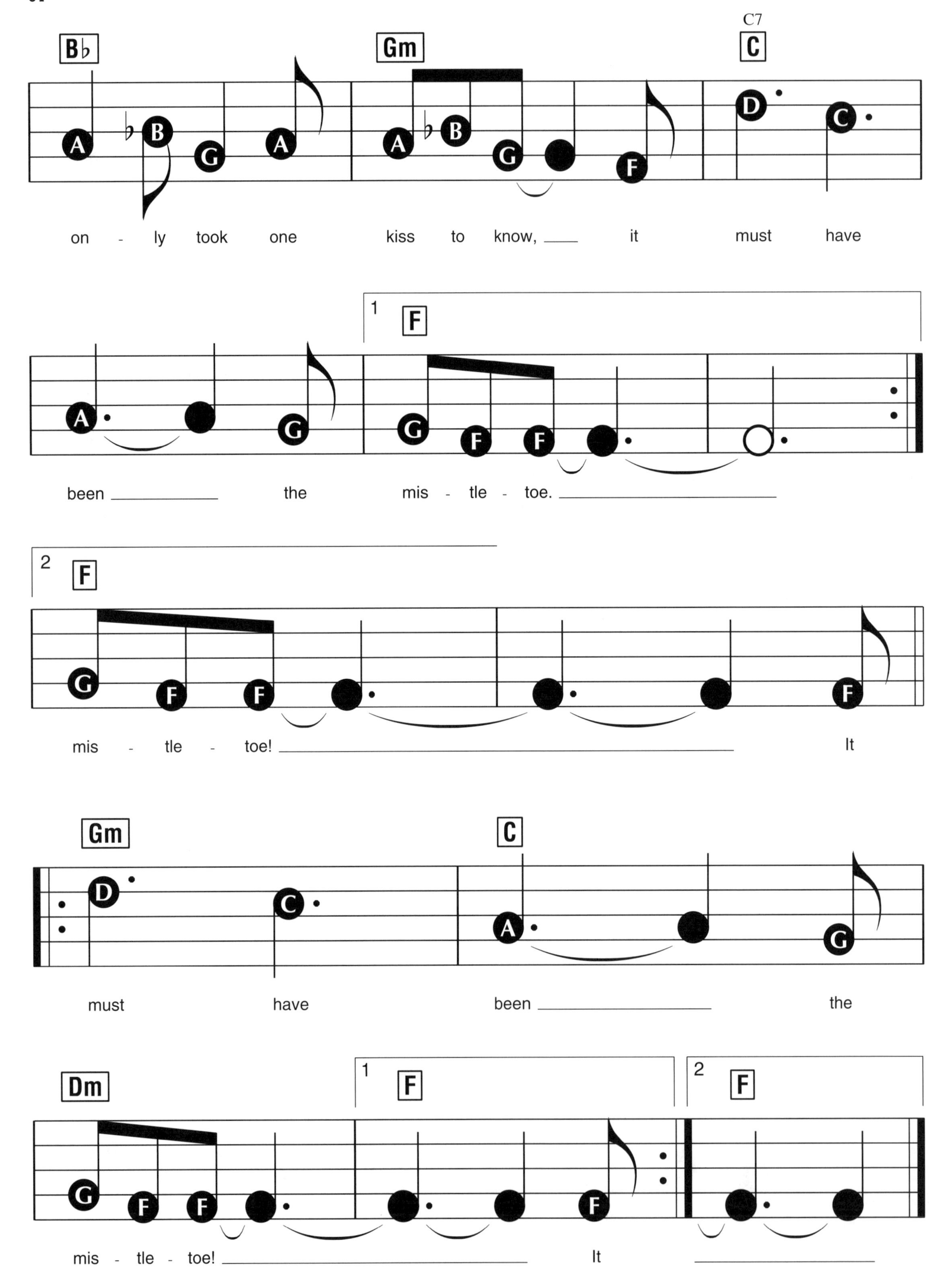

C7
B♭ Gm C
A B G A A B G F D C
on - ly took one kiss to know, it must have
1 F
A G G F F
been the mis - tle - toe.
2 F
G F F F
mis - tle - toe! It
Gm C
D C A G
must have been the
Dm
1 F
2 F
G F F F
mis - tle - toe! It

Merry Christmas, Darling

Registration 1
Rhythm: Ballad

Words and Music by Richard Carpenter
and Frank Pooler

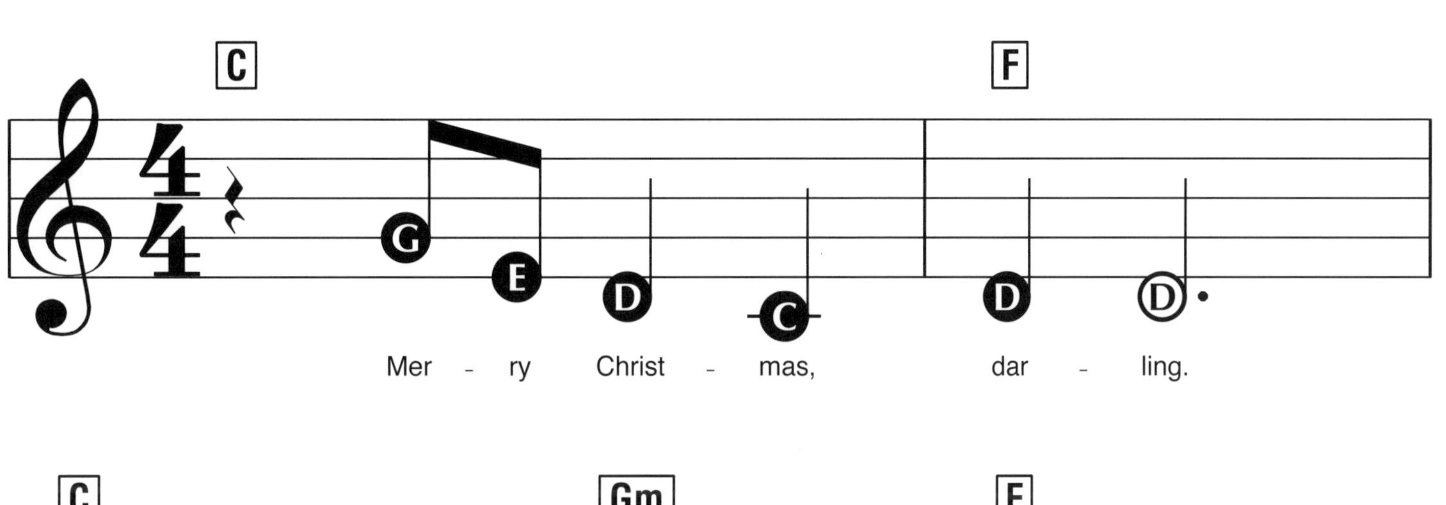

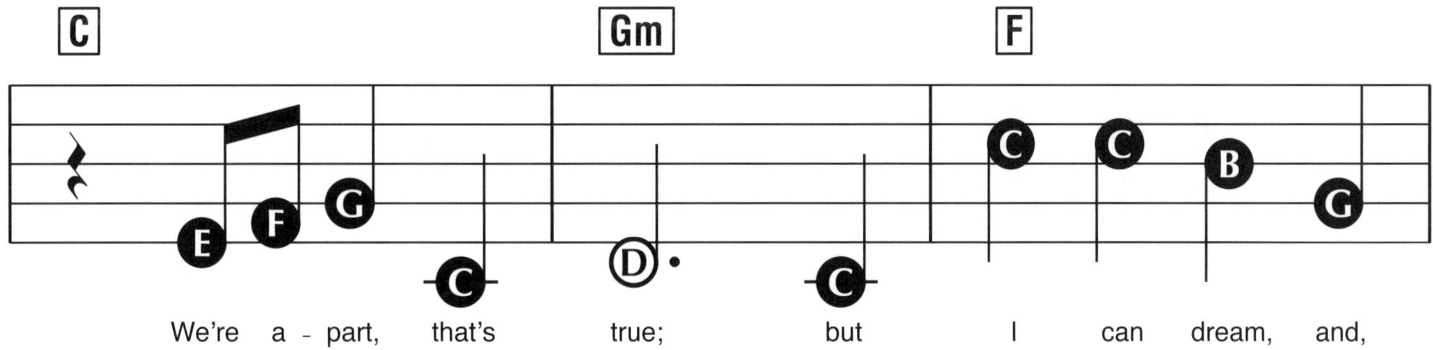

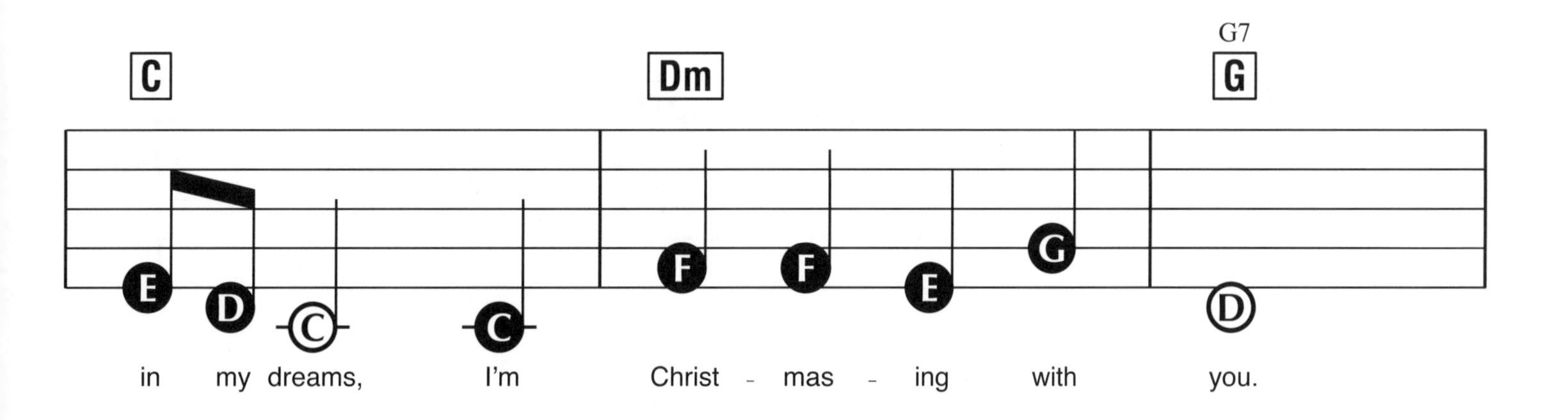

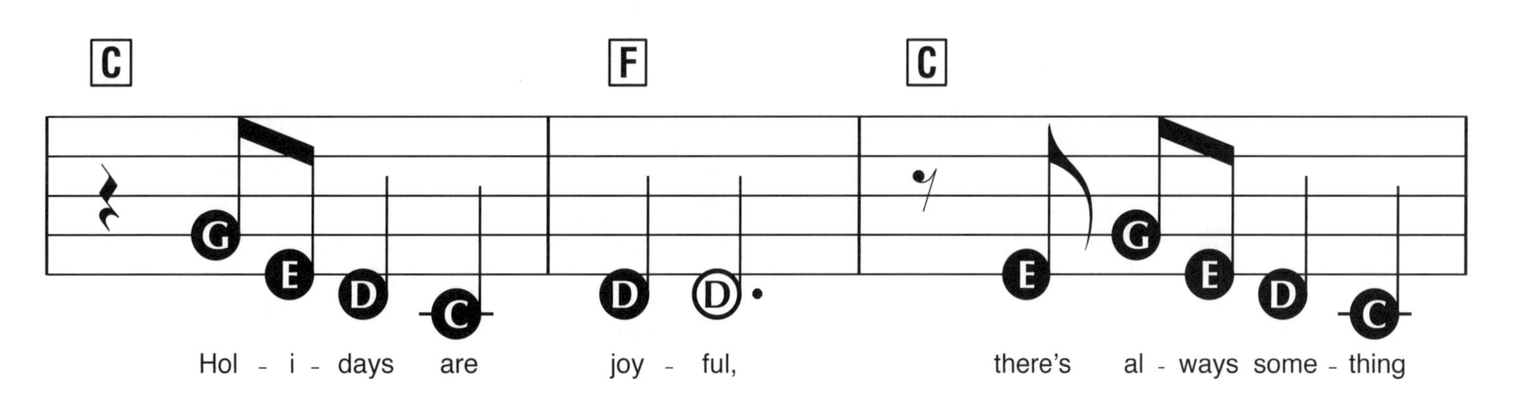

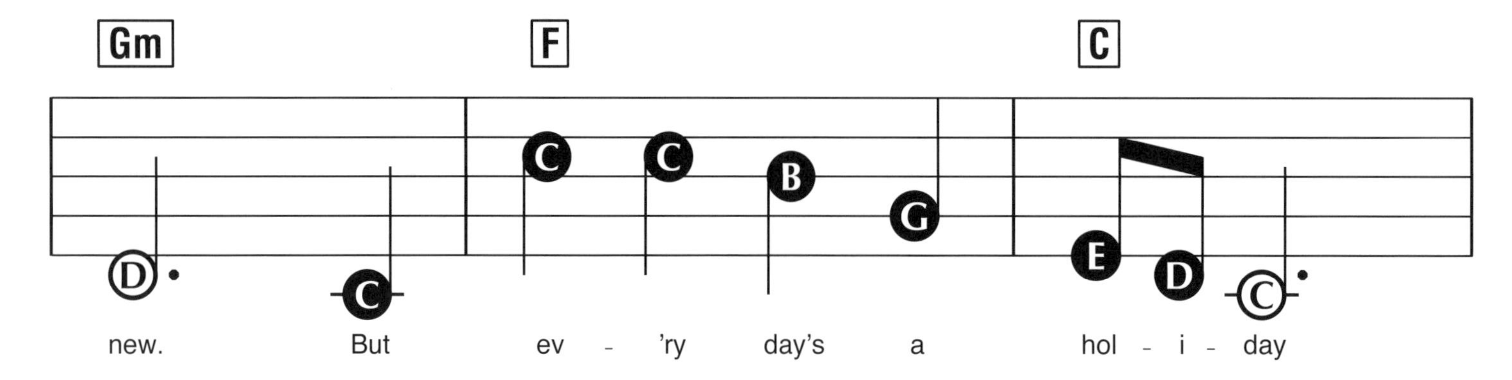
Gm F C
D C C C B G E D C
new. But ev - 'ry day's a hol - i - day

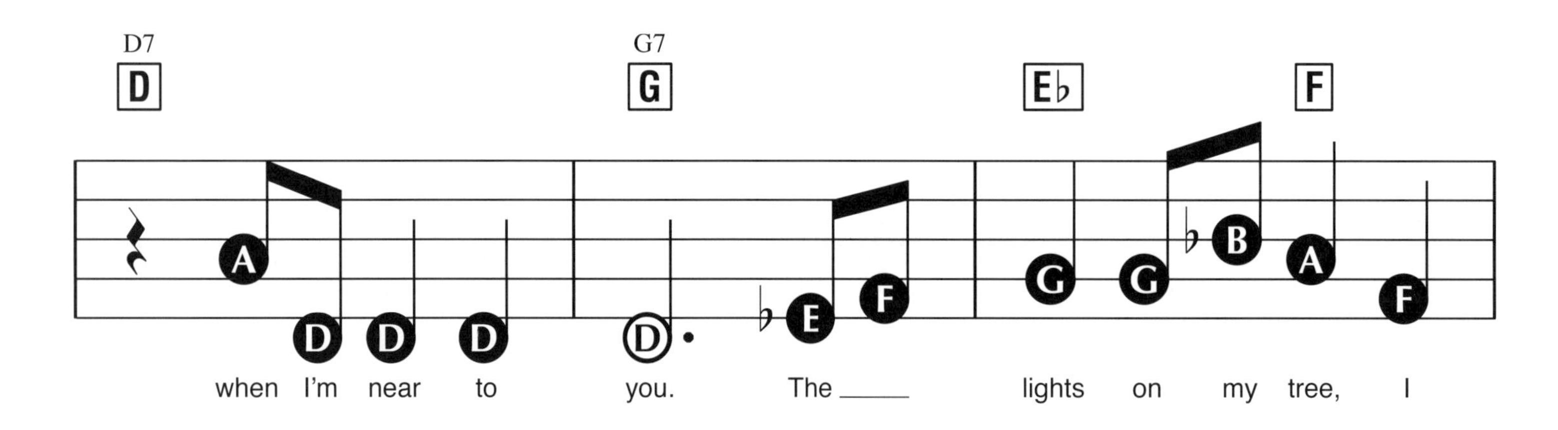
D7 G7
D G E♭ F
A D D D D E F G G B A F
when I'm near to you. The lights on my tree, I

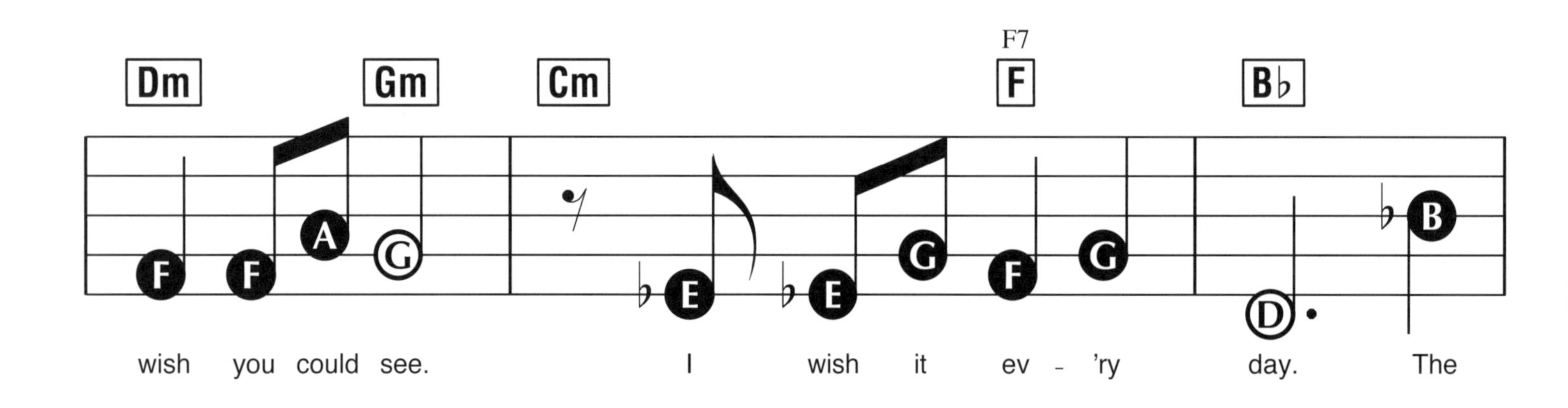
F7
Dm Gm Cm F B♭
F F A G E E G F G D B
wish you could see. I wish it ev - 'ry day. The

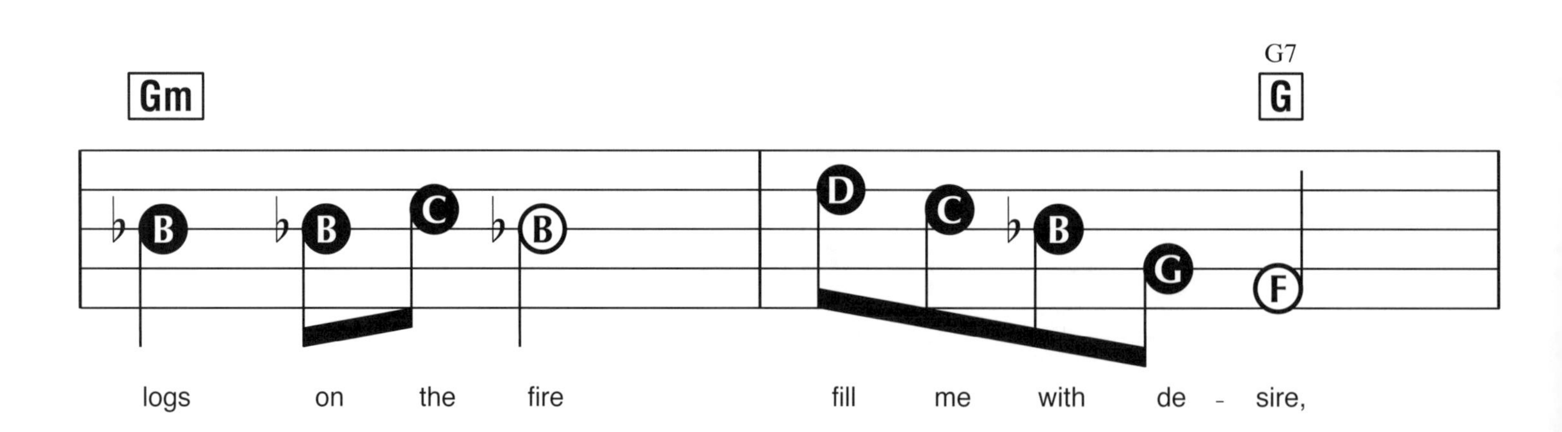
G7
Gm G
B B C B D C B G F
logs on the fire fill me with de - sire,

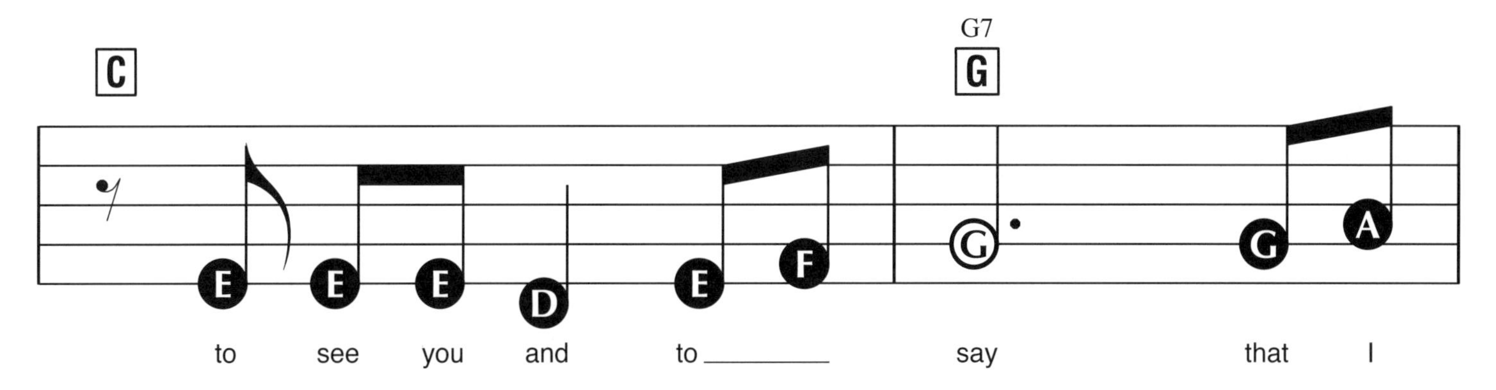
G7
C
G
E
E
E
D
E
F
G
G
A
to see you and to
say that I

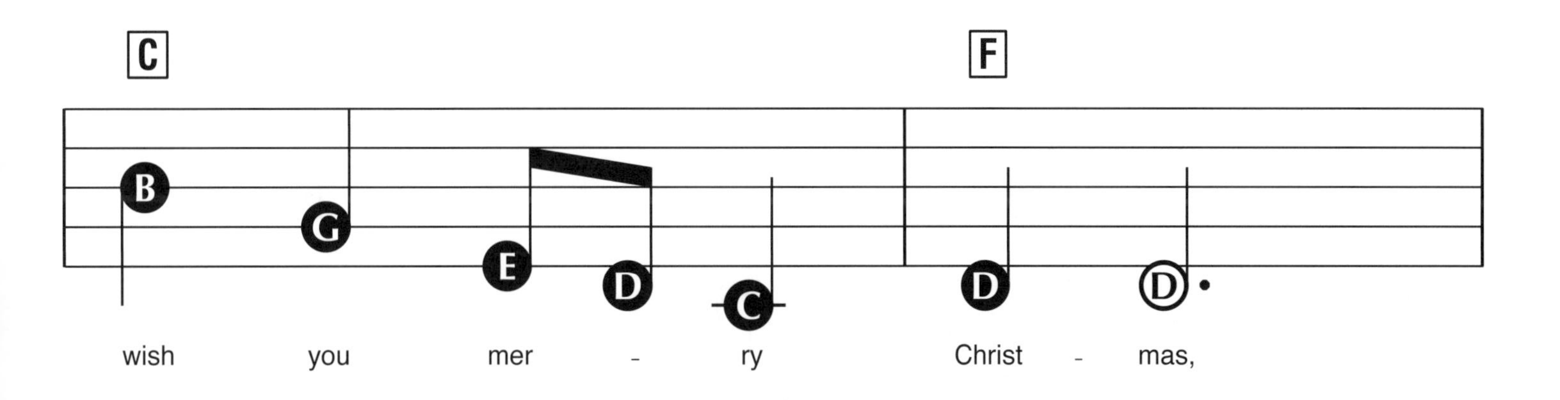
C
F
B
G
E
D
C
D
D
wish you mer - ry
Christ - mas,

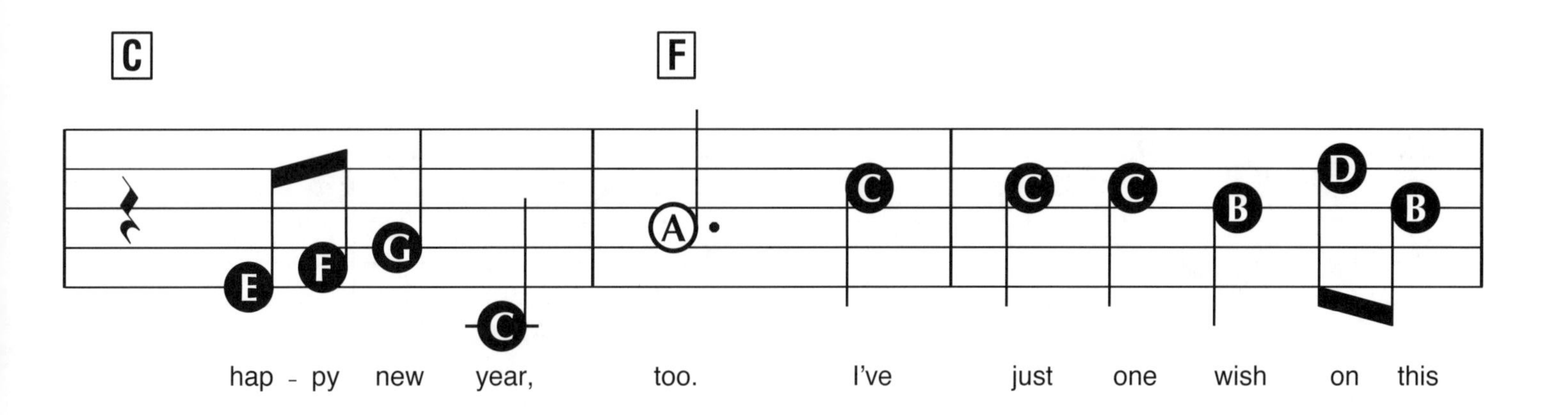
C
F
E
F
G
C
A
C
C
C
B
D
B
hap - py new year,
too. I've
just one wish on this

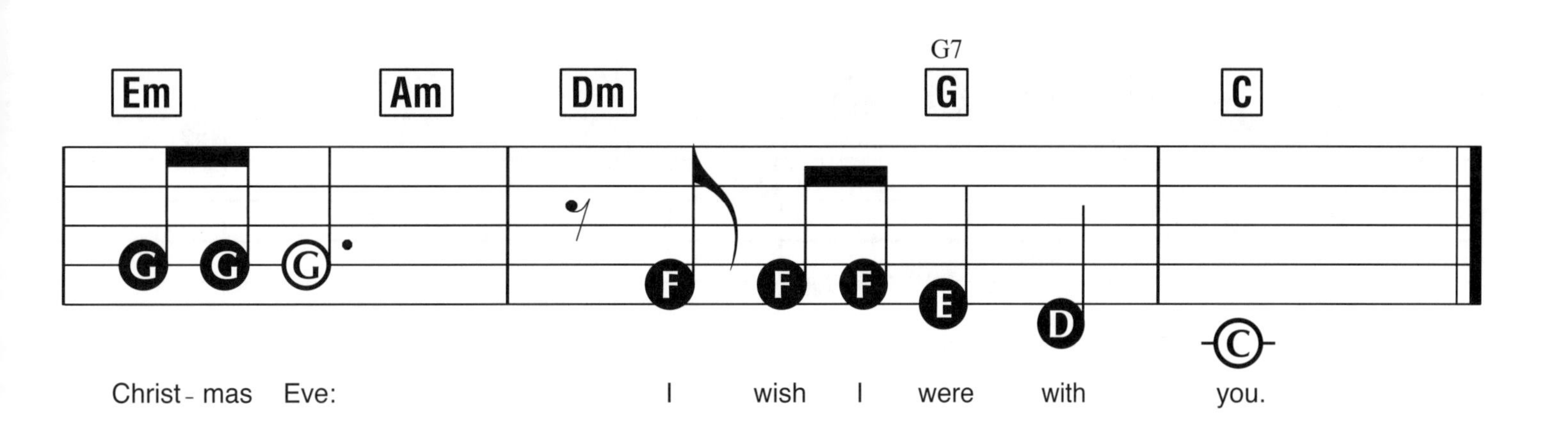
Em
Am
Dm
G7
G
C
G
G
G
F
F
F
E
D
C
Christ - mas Eve:
I wish I were with
you.

One Little Christmas Tree

Registration 1
Rhythm: 4/4 Ballad or Fox Trot

Words and Music by Ronald N. Miller
and Bryan Wells

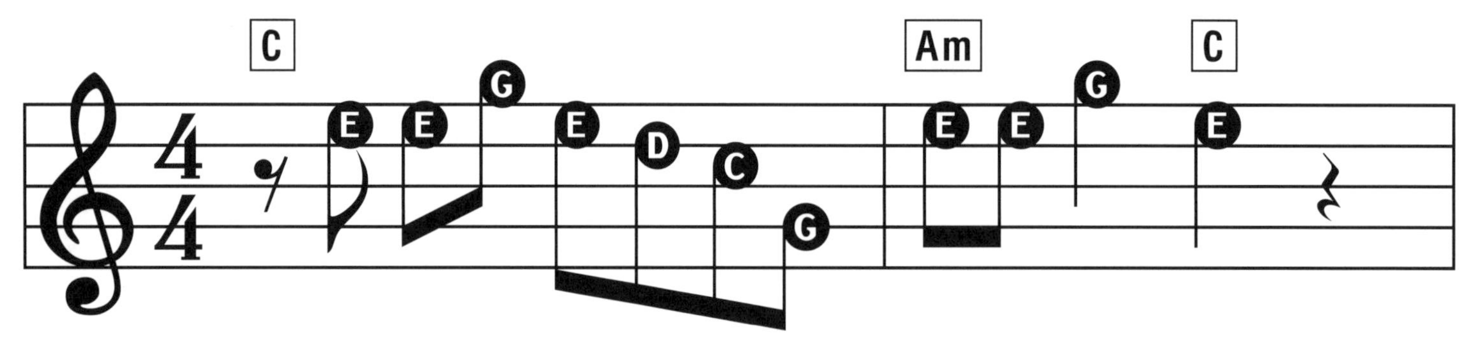

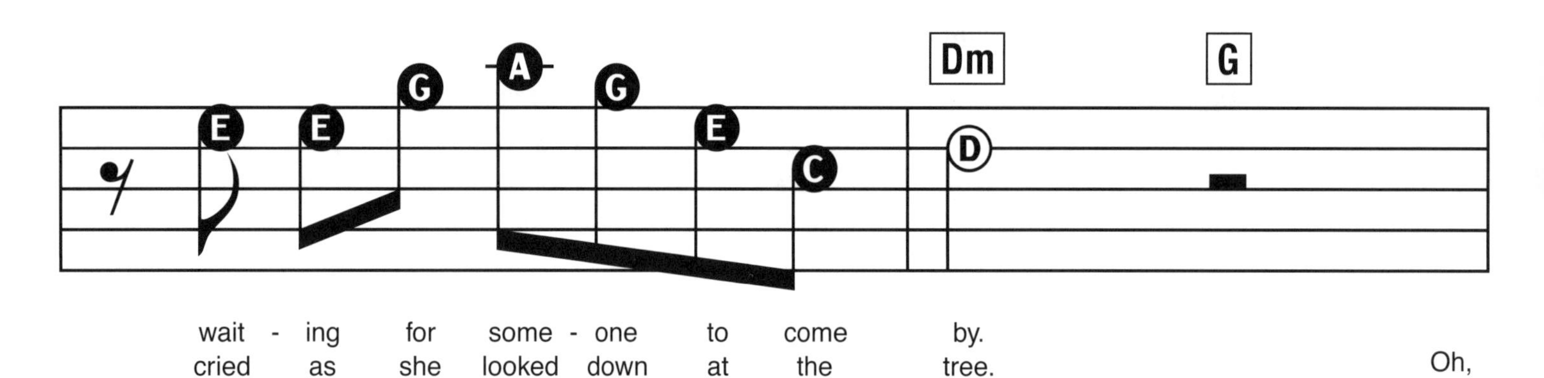

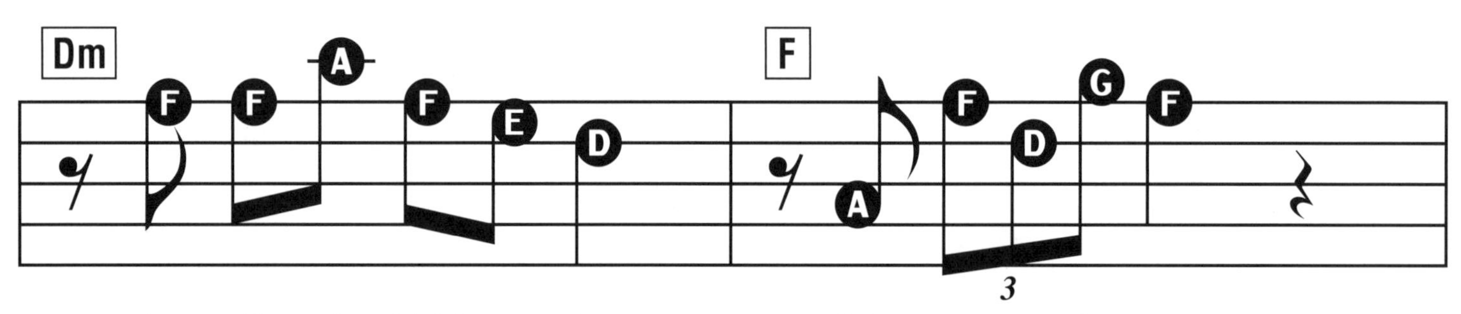

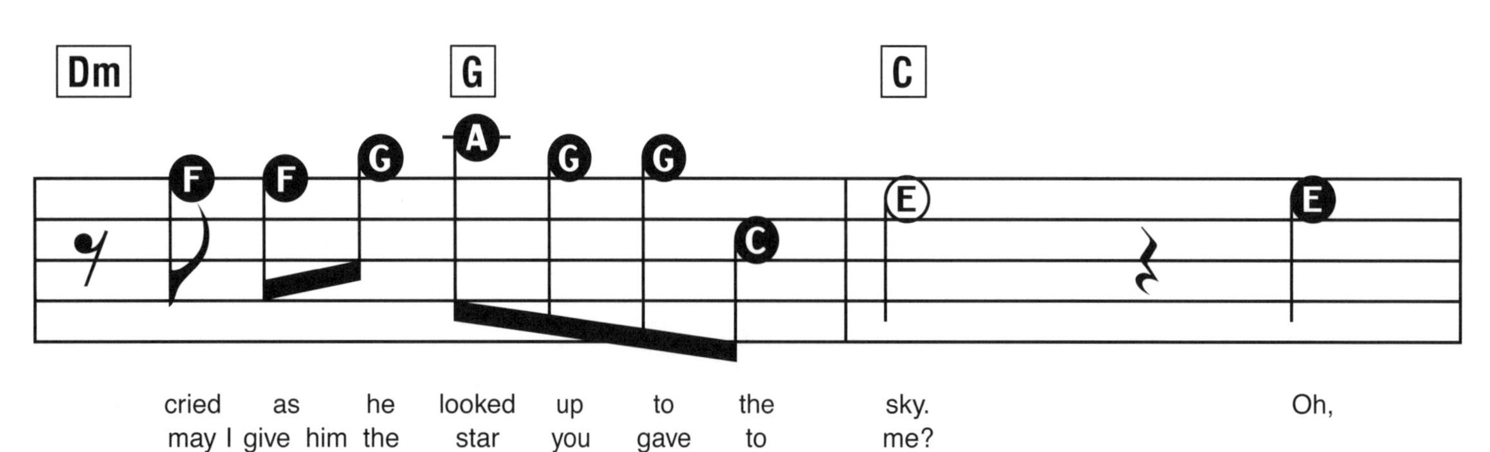

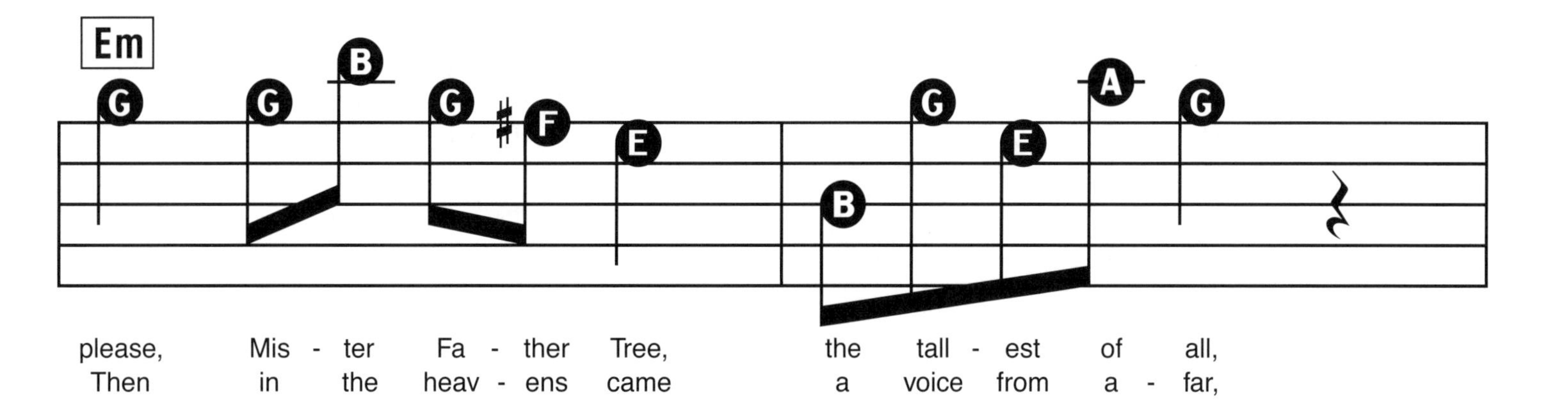
Em
please, Mis - ter Fa - ther Tree, the tall - est of all,
Then in the heav - ens came a voice from a - far,

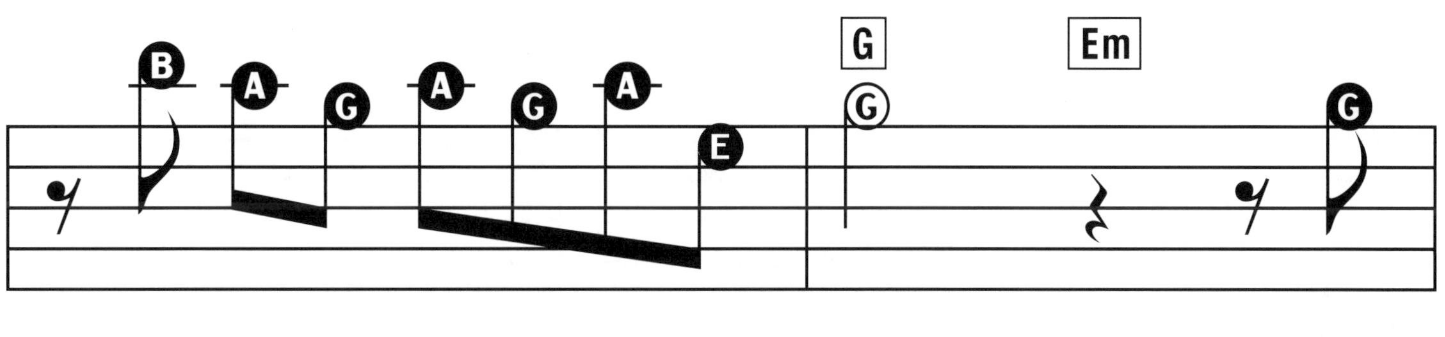
G
Em
I'm so a - fraid and so a - lone. Could
a voice that was heard through - out the world. Go

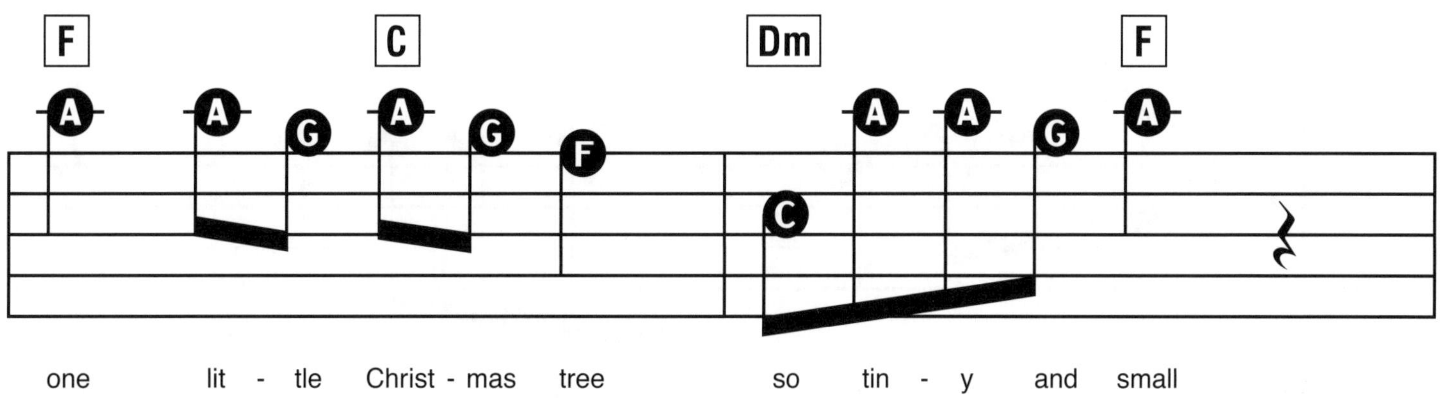
F
C
Dm
F
one lit - tle Christ - mas tree so tin - y and small
down, lit - tle an - gel girl, and give him your star. To -

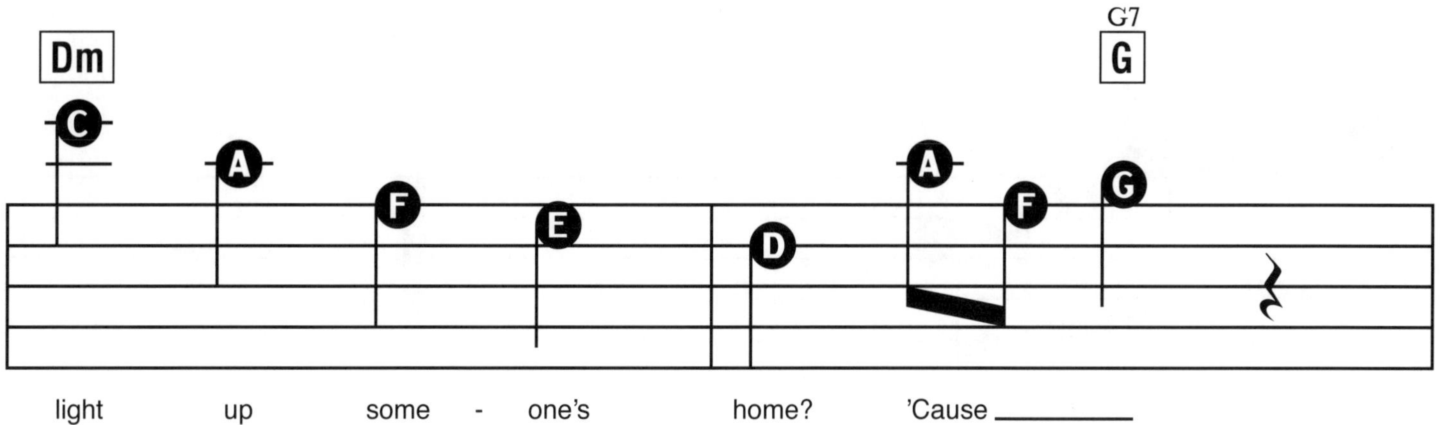
Dm
G7
G
light up some - one's home? 'Cause
night he'll light the world. 'Cause

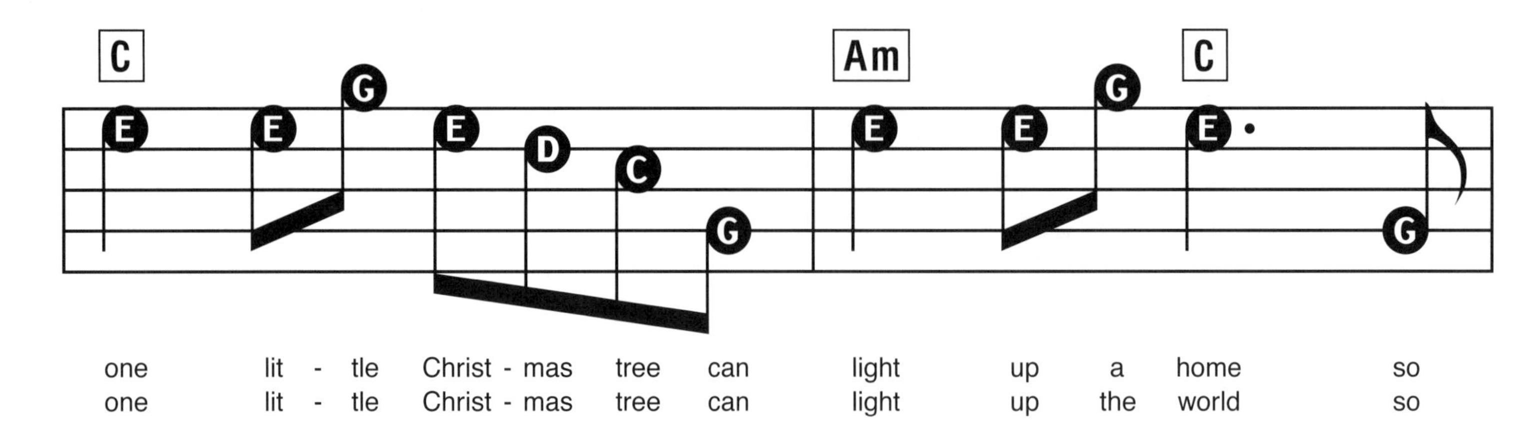
C
Am
C
one lit - tle Christ - mas tree can light up a home so
one lit - tle Christ - mas tree can light up the world so

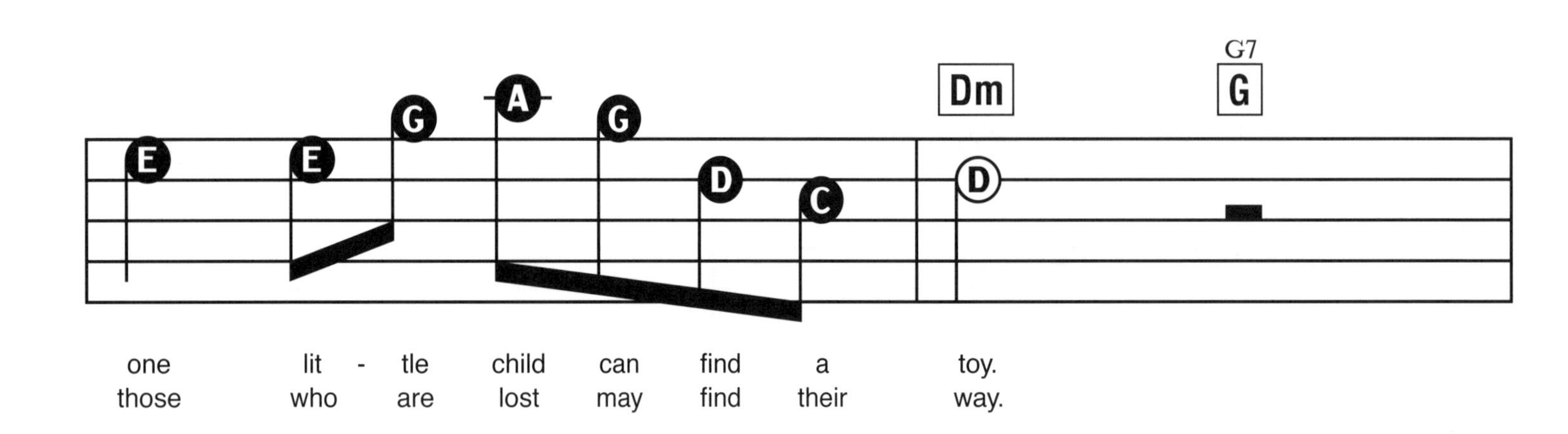
Dm
G7
G
one lit - tle child can find a toy.
those who are lost may find their way.

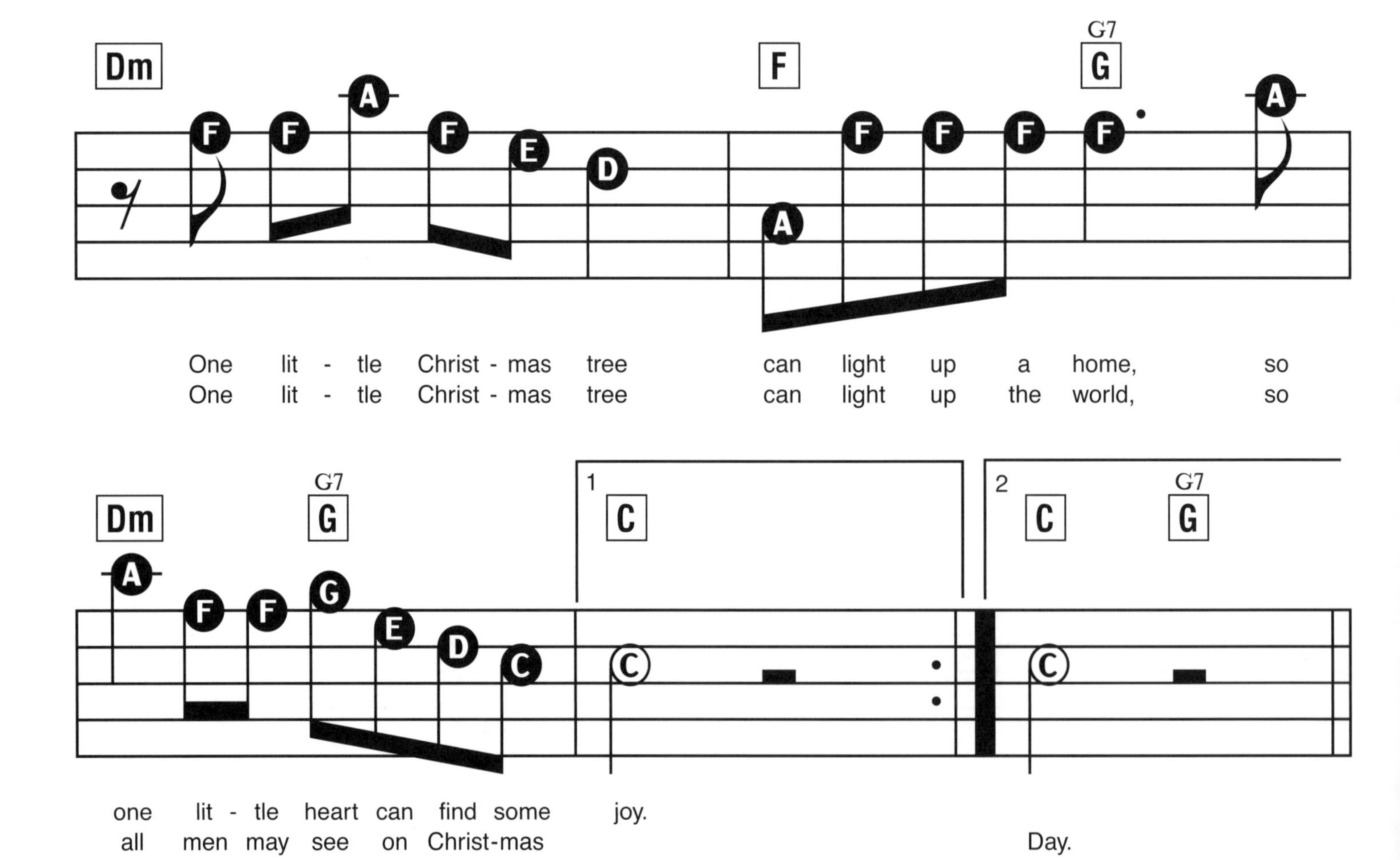
Dm
F
G7
G
One lit - tle Christ - mas tree can light up a home, so
One lit - tle Christ - mas tree can light up the world, so
Dm
G7
G
1
C
2
C
G7
G
one lit - tle heart can find some joy.
all men may see on Christ-mas Day.

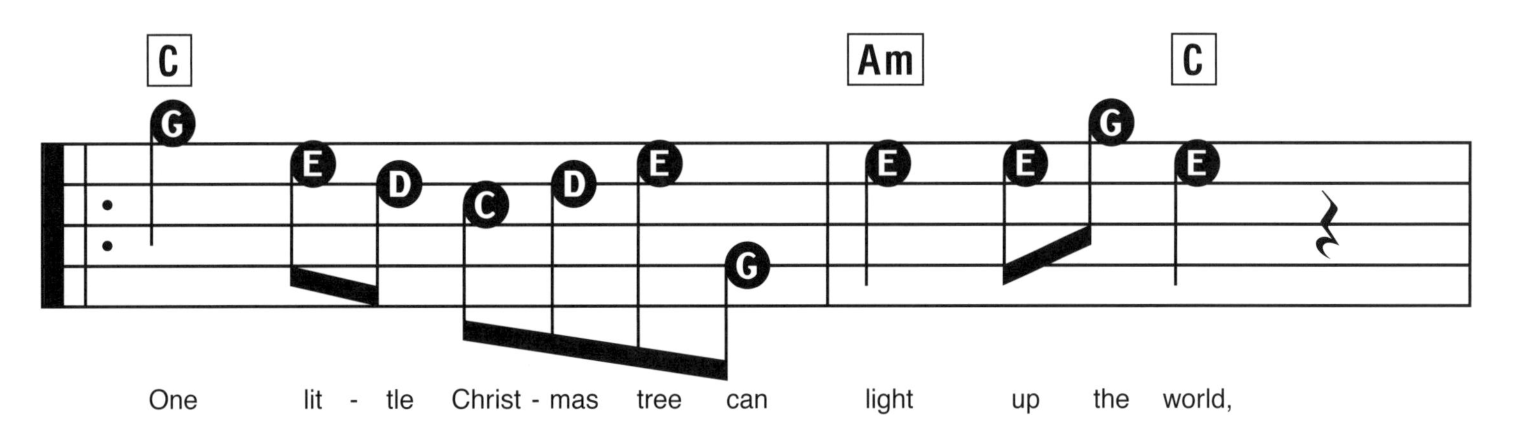
C
Am
C
One lit - tle Christ - mas tree can light up the world,

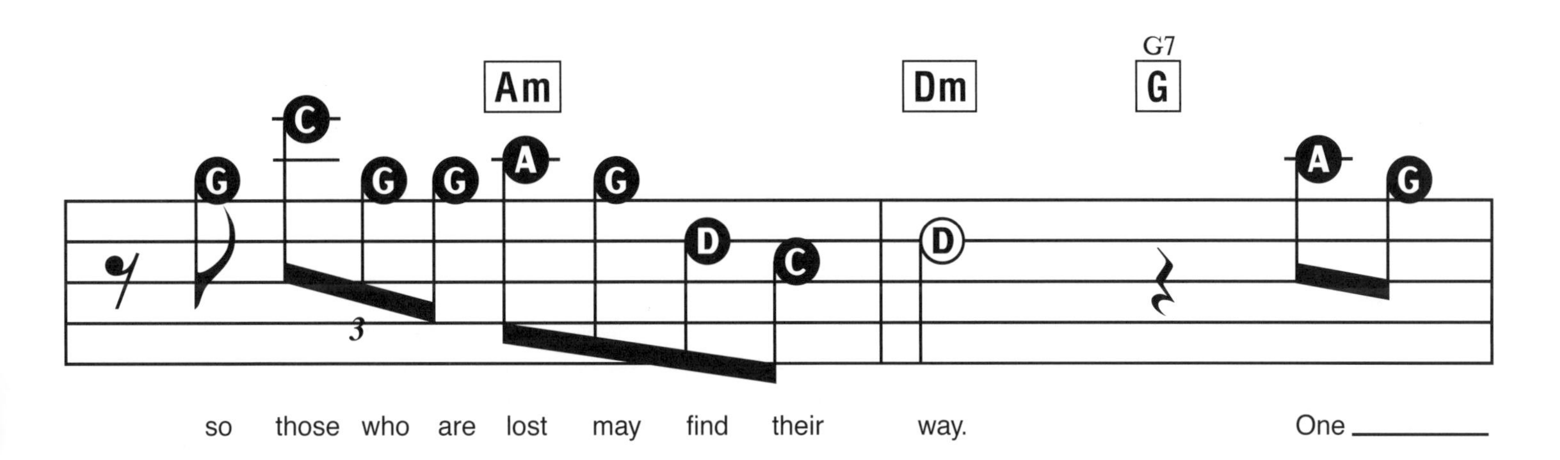
Am
Dm
G7
G
so those who are lost may find their way. One

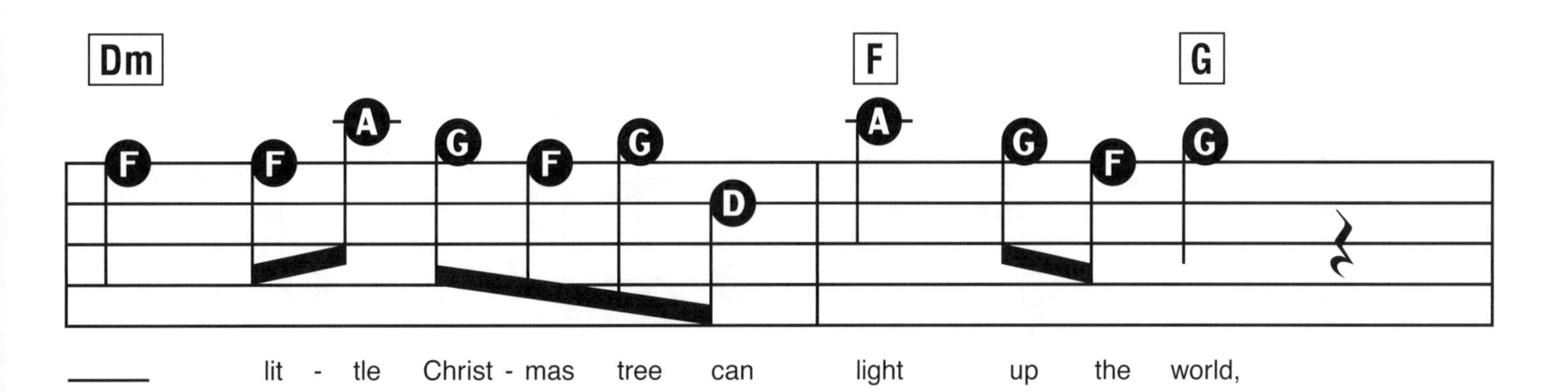
Dm
F
G
lit - tle Christ - mas tree can light up the world,

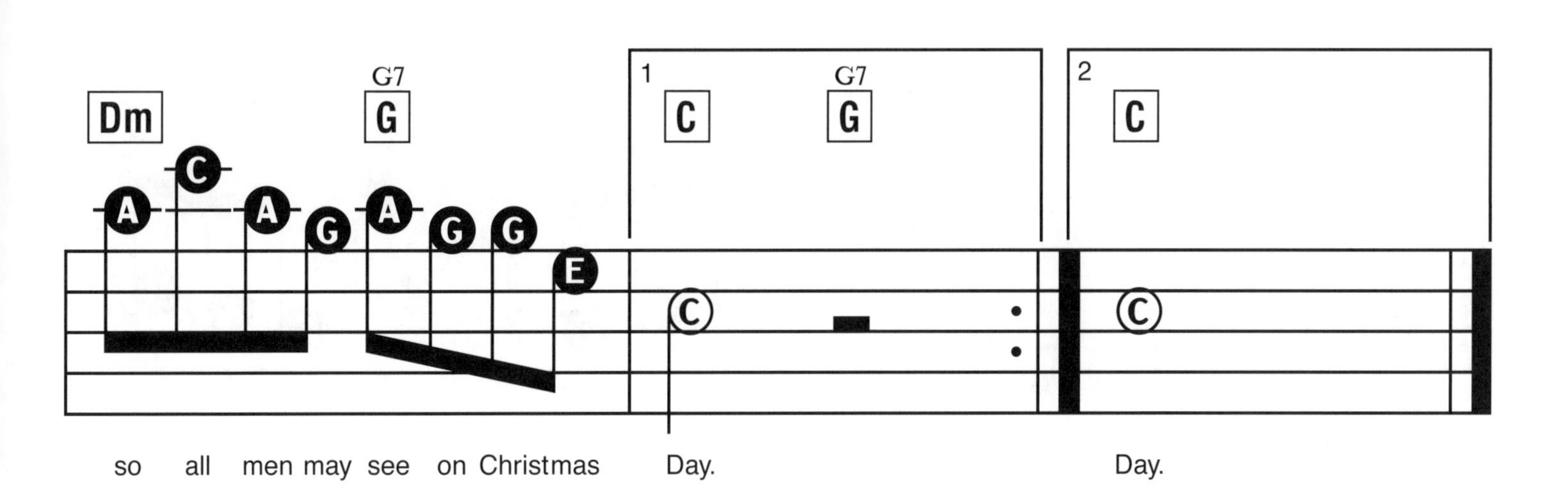
Dm
G7
G
1
C
G7
G
2
C
so all men may see on Christmas Day. Day.

Please Come Home for Christmas

Registration 2
Rhythm: Slow Rock or Fifties Ballad

Words and Music by Charles Brown
and Gene Redd

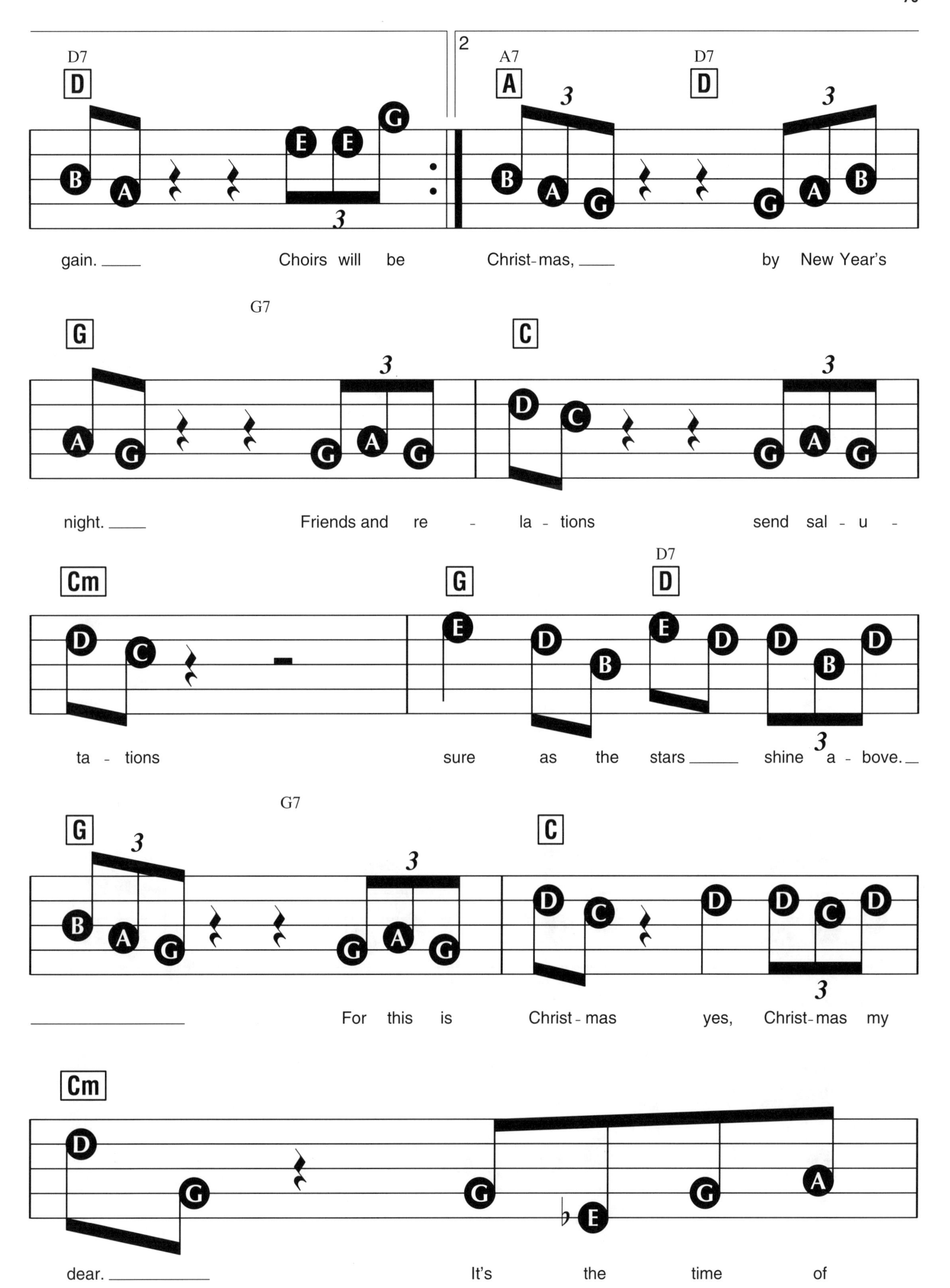
2
D7
D
A7
A
D7
D
3
3
3
gain. Choirs will be
Christ-mas, by New Year's
G
G7
C
3
3
night. Friends and re - la - tions send sal - u -
Cm
G
D7
D
3
ta - tions sure as the stars shine a - bove.
G
G7
C
3
3
3
For this is Christ - mas yes, Christ-mas my
Cm
dear. It's the time of

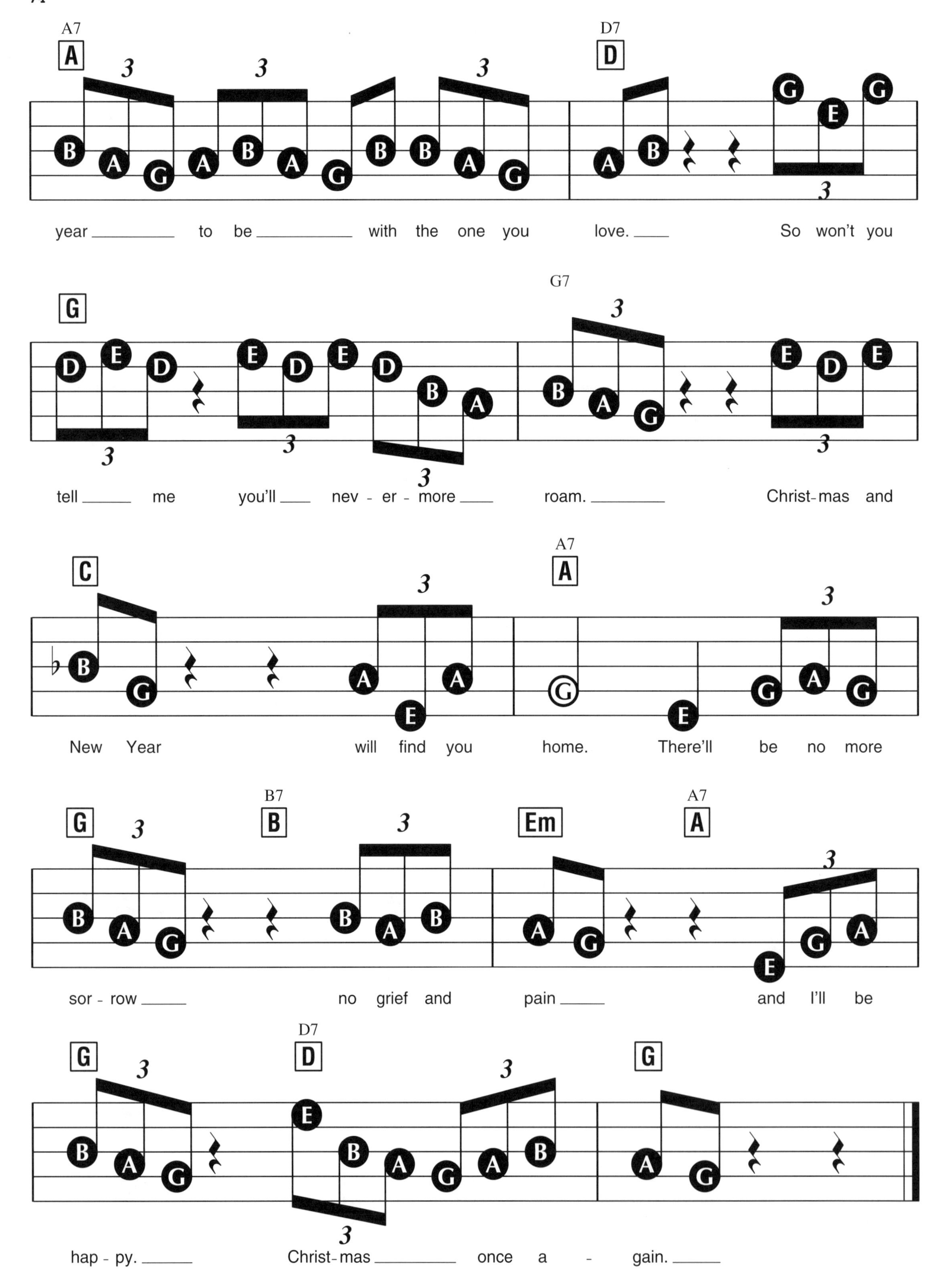
A7
D7
year to be with the one you love. So won't you
G
G7
tell me you'll nev - er - more roam. Christ-mas and
C
A7
New Year will find you home. There'll be no more
G
B7
Em
A7
sor - row no grief and pain and I'll be
G
D7
G
hap - py. Christ-mas once a - gain.

Same Old Lang Syne

Registration 7
Rhythm: Fox Trot or Ballad

Words and Music by
Dan Fogelberg

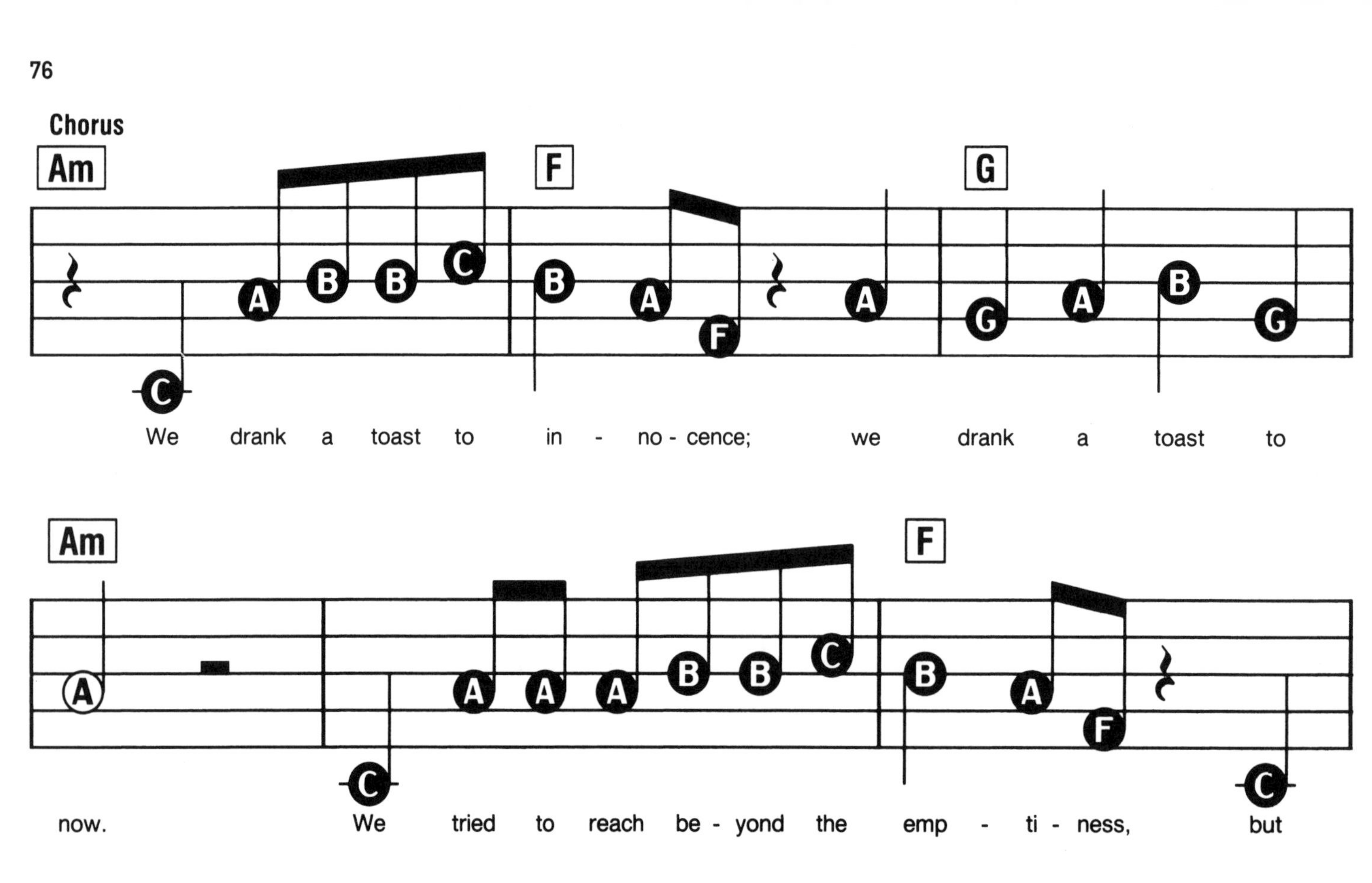
Chorus
Am
F
G
We drank a toast to in - no - cence; we drank a toast to
Am
F
now. We tried to reach be - yond the emp - ti - ness, but

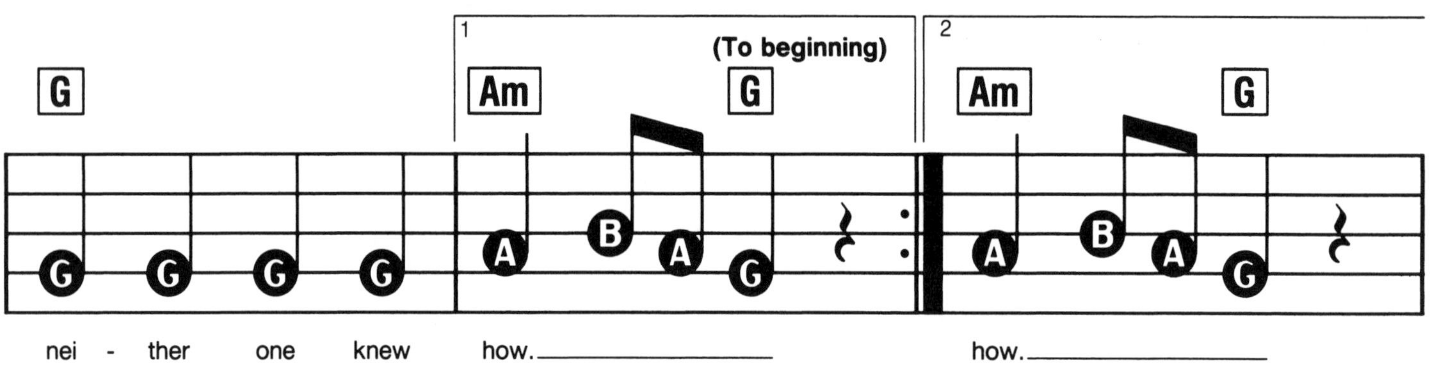
1
2
G
Am
(To beginning)
G
Am
G
nei - ther one knew how.
how.

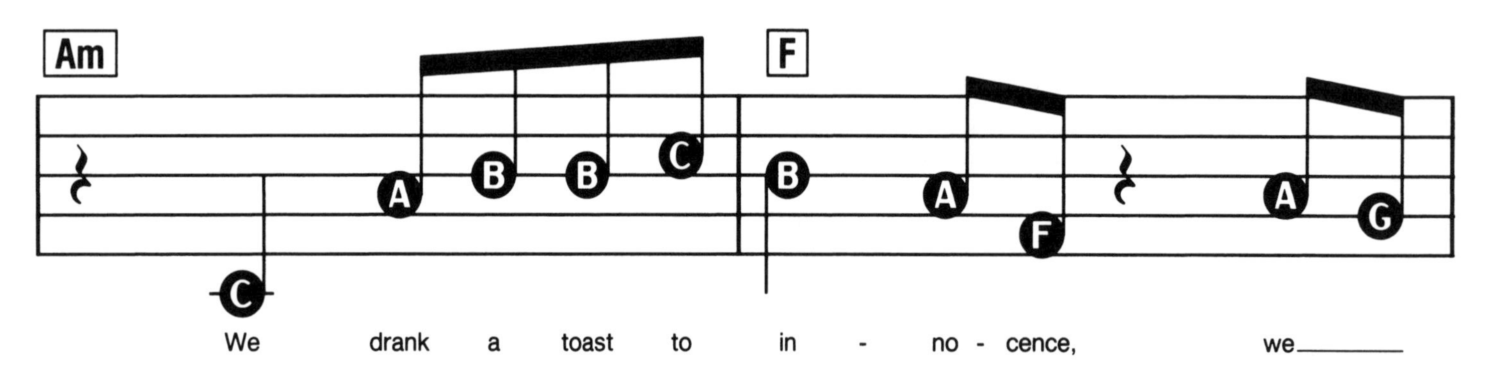
Am
F
We drank a toast to in - no - cence, we

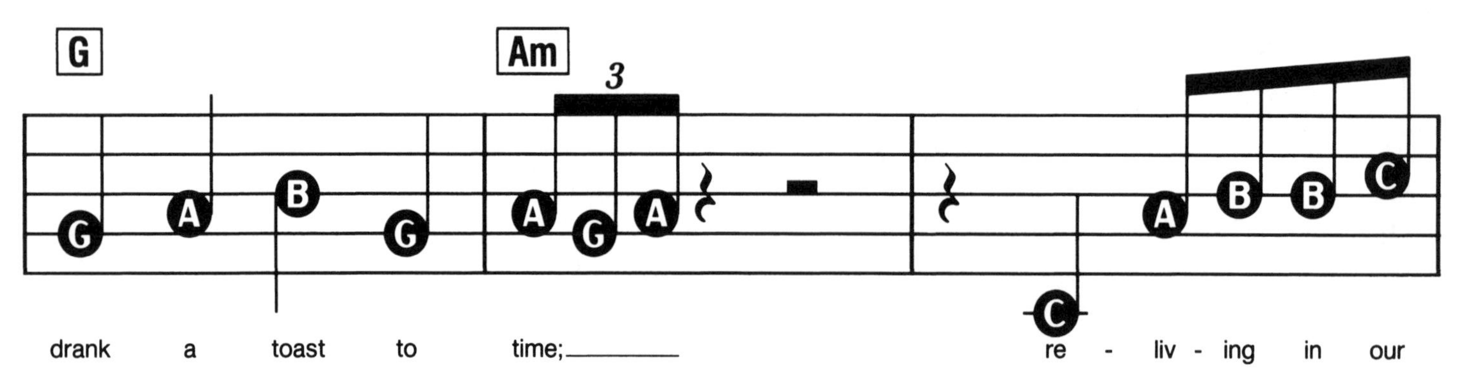
G
Am
3
drank a toast to time;
re - liv - ing in our

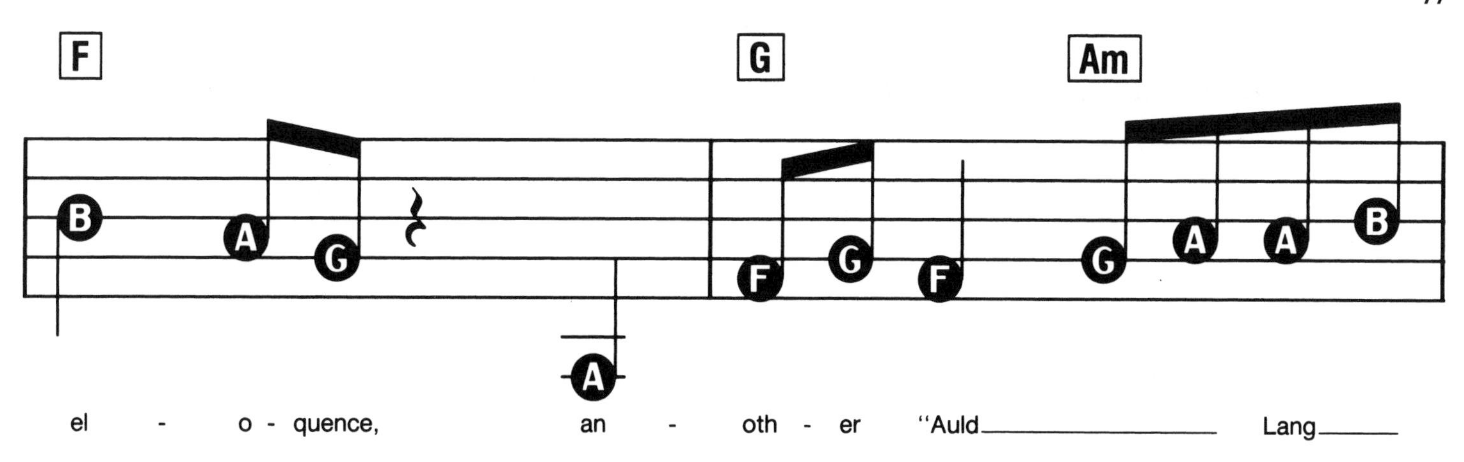

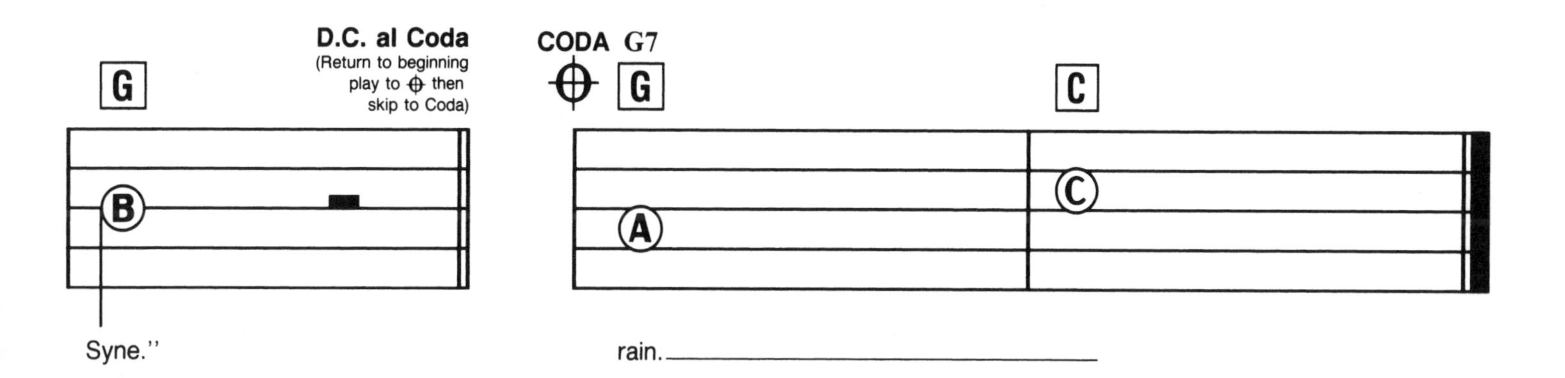

Additional Lyrics

3. We took her groc'ries to the check out stand;
   The food was totalled up and bagged.
   We stood there, lost in our embarrassment,
   As the conversation lagged.

4. We went to have ourselves a drink or two,
   But couldn't find an open bar.
   We bought a six-pack at the liquor store
   And we drank it in her car.

5. She said she's married her an architect,
   Who kept her warm and safe and dry.
   She would have liked to say she loved the man,
   But she didn't like to lie.

6. I said the years had been a friend to her
   And that her eyes were still as blue.
   But in those eyes I wasn't sure if I
   Saw doubt or gratitude.

7. She said she saw me in the record stores,
   And that I must be doing well.
   I said the audience was heavenly,
   But the traveling was hell.

8. The beer was empty and our tongues were tired,
   And running out of things to say.
   She gave a kiss to me as I got out,
   And I watched her drive away.

9. Just for a moment I was back at school
   And felt that old familiar pain.
   And as I turned to make my way back home,
   The snow turned into rain.

Silver Bells

from the Paramount Picture THE LEMON DROP KID

Registration 5
Rhythm: Waltz

Words and Music by Jay Livingston
and Ray Evans

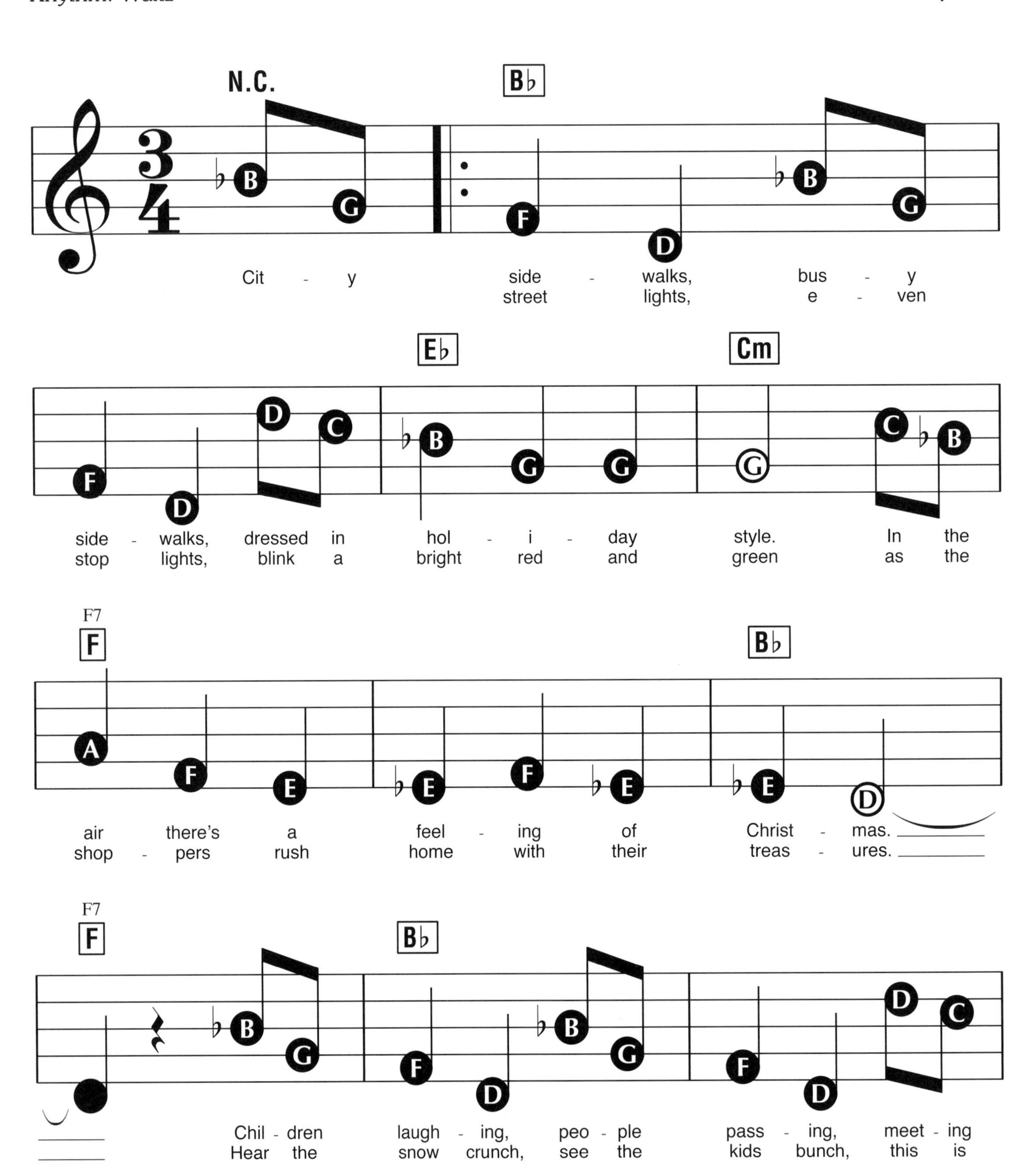

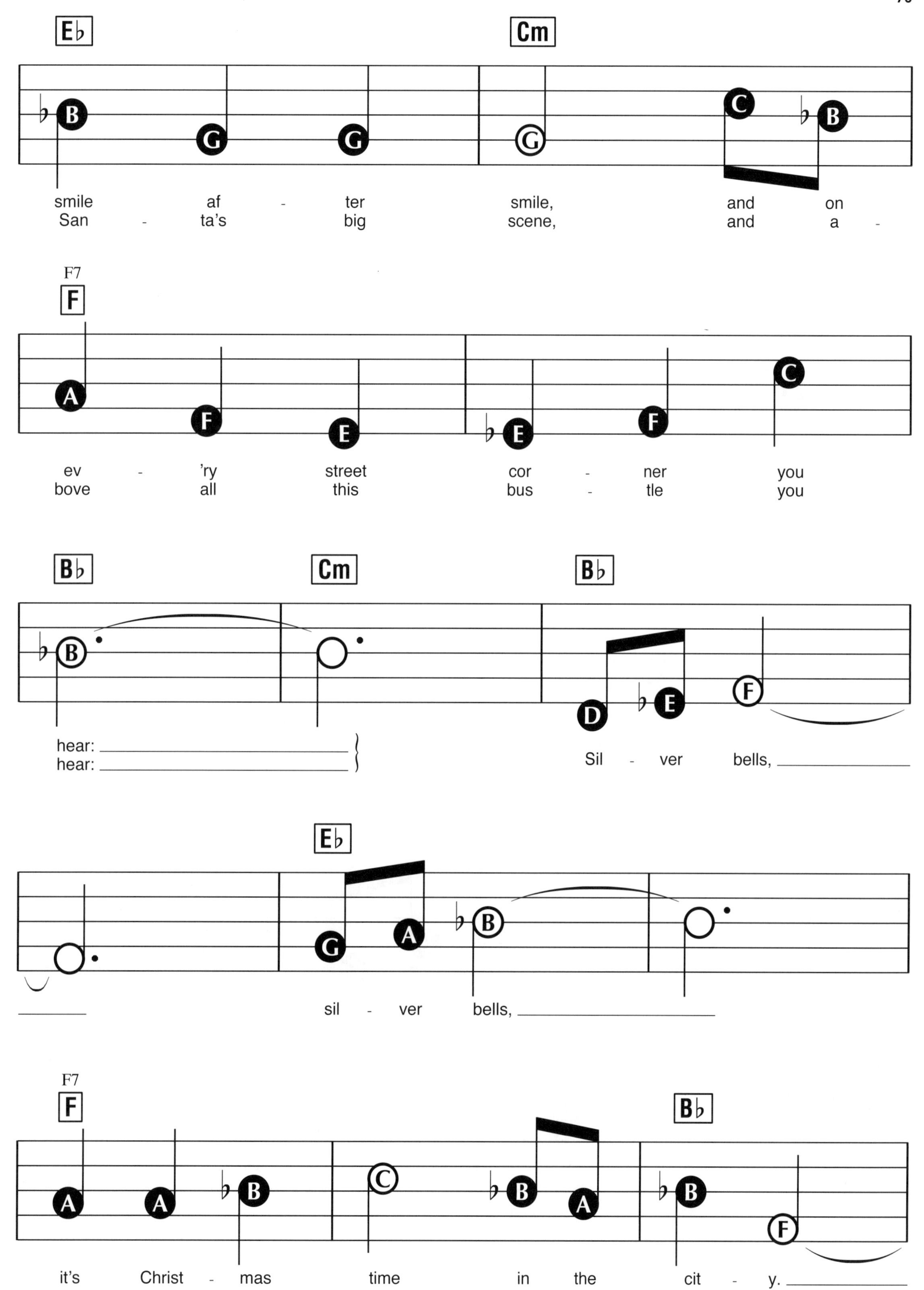
E♭
Cm
smile af - ter smile, and on
San - ta's big scene, and a -
F7
F
ev - 'ry street cor - ner you
bove all this bus - tle you
B♭
Cm
B♭
hear:
hear:
Sil - ver bells,
E♭
sil - ver bells,
F7
F
B♭
it's Christ - mas time in the cit - y.

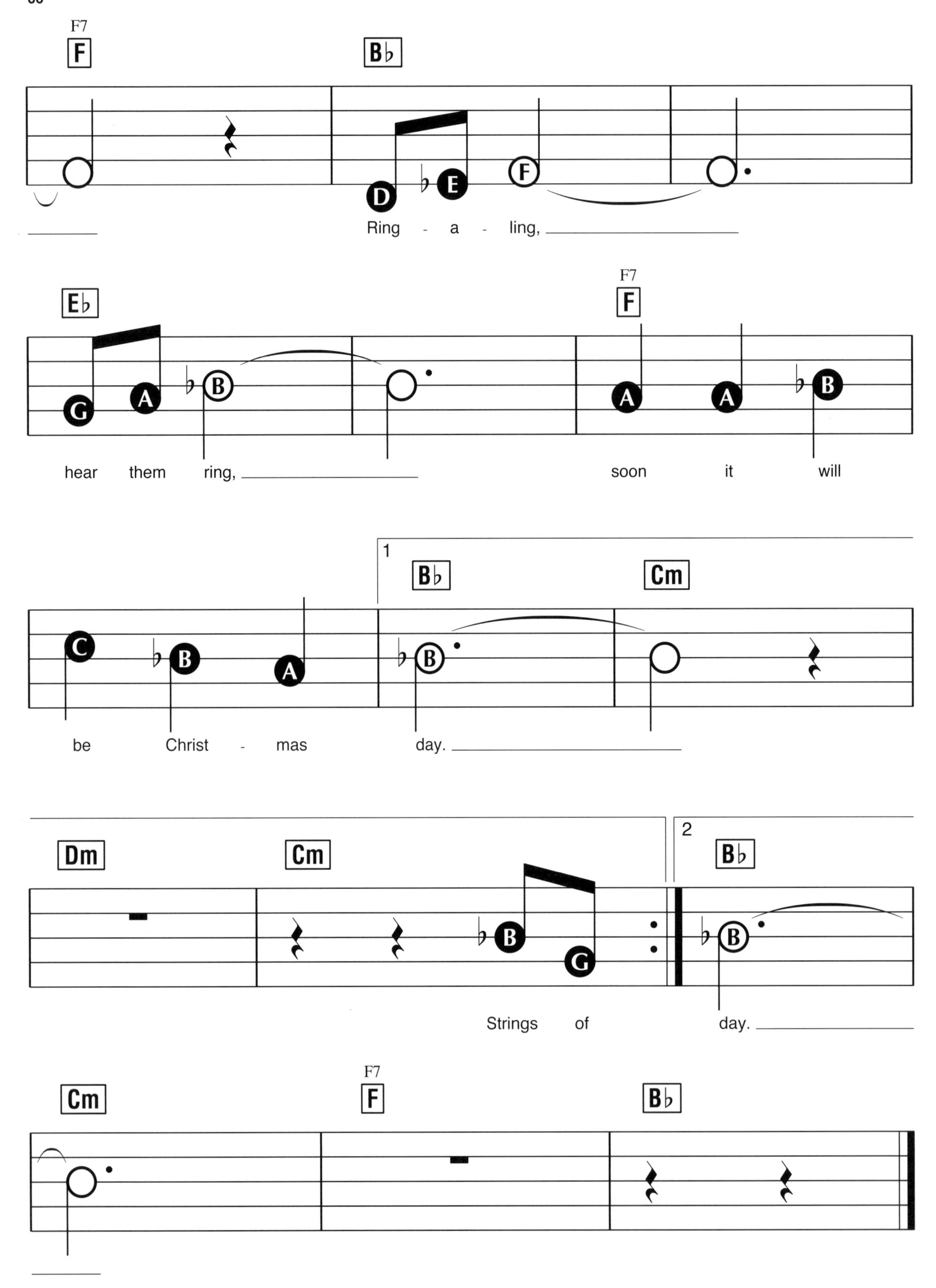
F7
F
B♭
D
E
F
Ring - a - ling,
E♭
G
A
B
hear them ring,
F7
F
A
A
B
soon it will
C
B
A
be Christ - mas
1
B♭
Cm
B
day.
Dm
Cm
B
G
Strings of
2
B♭
B
day.
Cm
F7
F
B♭

Tennessee Christmas

Registration 5
Rhythm: Rock

Words and Music by
Amy Grant and Gary Chapman

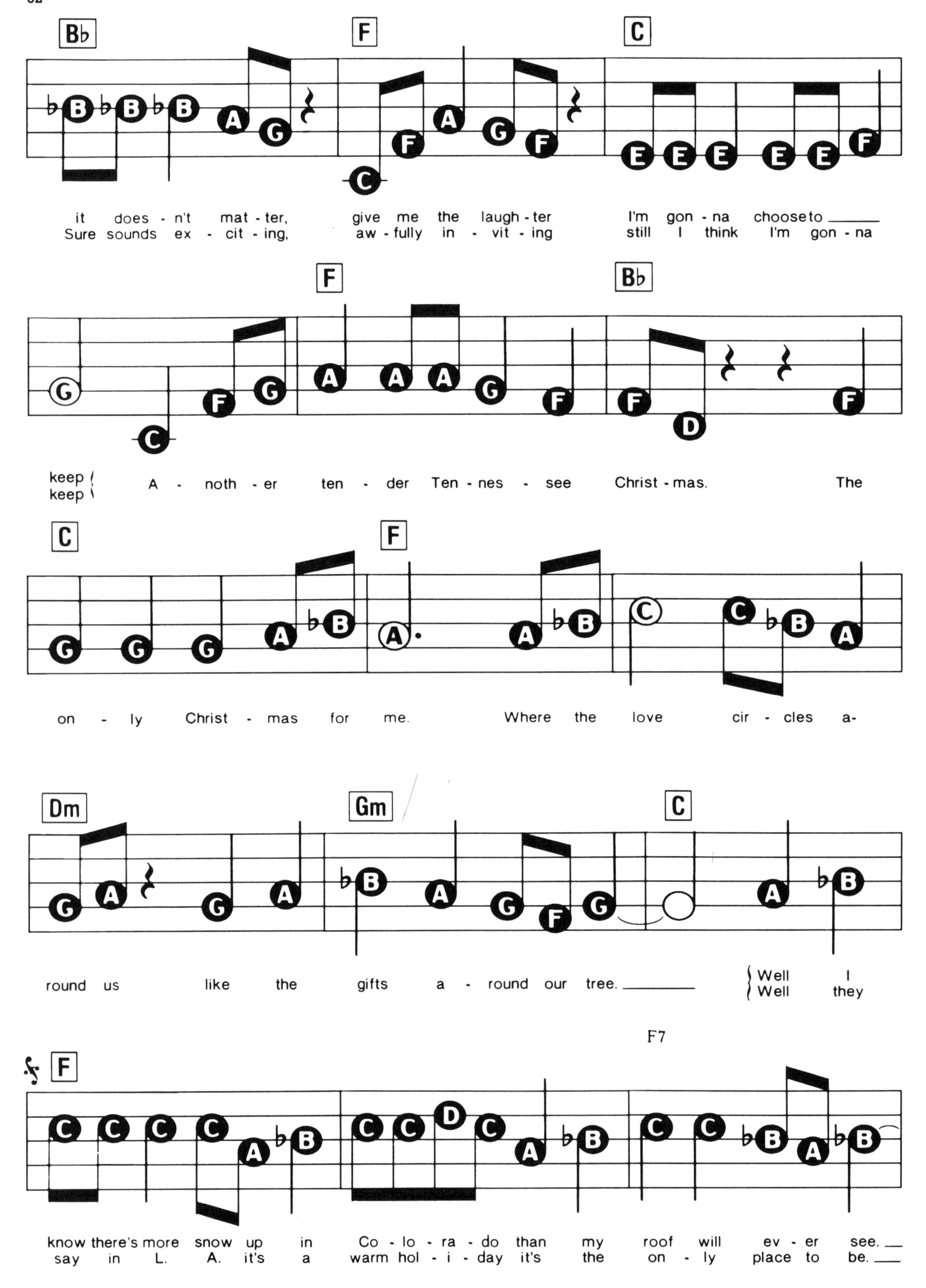
Bb
F
C
it does - n't mat - ter,
Sure sounds ex - cit - ing,
give me the laugh - ter
aw - fully in - vit - ing
I'm gon - na choose to
still I think I'm gon - na
F
Bb
keep
keep
A - noth - er ten - der Ten - nes - see Christ - mas.
The
C
F
on - ly Christ - mas for me.
Where the love cir - cles a-
Dm
Gm
C
round us like the gifts a - round our tree.
Well I
Well they
F7
F
know there's more snow up in Co - lo - ra - do than my roof will ev - er see.
say in L. A. it's a warm hol - i - day it's the on - ly place to be.

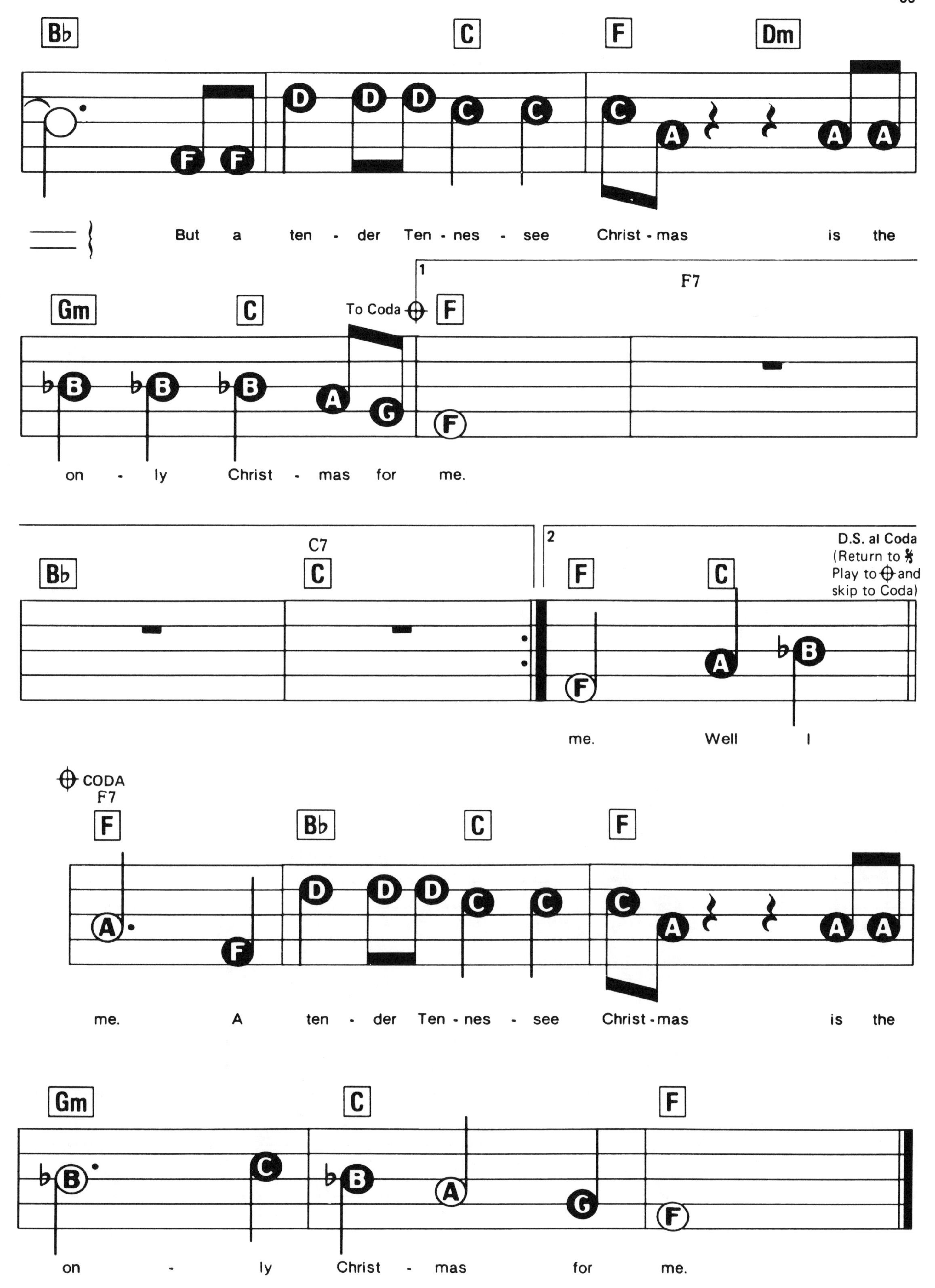

B♭
C
F
Dm
But a ten - der Ten - nes - see Christ - mas is the
Gm
C
To Coda
1
F
F7
on - ly Christ - mas for me.
B♭
C7
C
2
F
C
D.S. al Coda
(Return to 𝄋
Play to ⊕ and
skip to Coda)
me. Well I
⊕ CODA
F7
F
B♭
C
F
me. A ten - der Ten - nes - see Christ - mas is the
Gm
C
F
on - ly Christ - mas for me.

Somewhere in My Memory

from the Twentieth Century Fox Motion Picture HOME ALONE

Registration 3
Rhythm: Ballad

Words by Leslie Bricusse
Music by John Williams

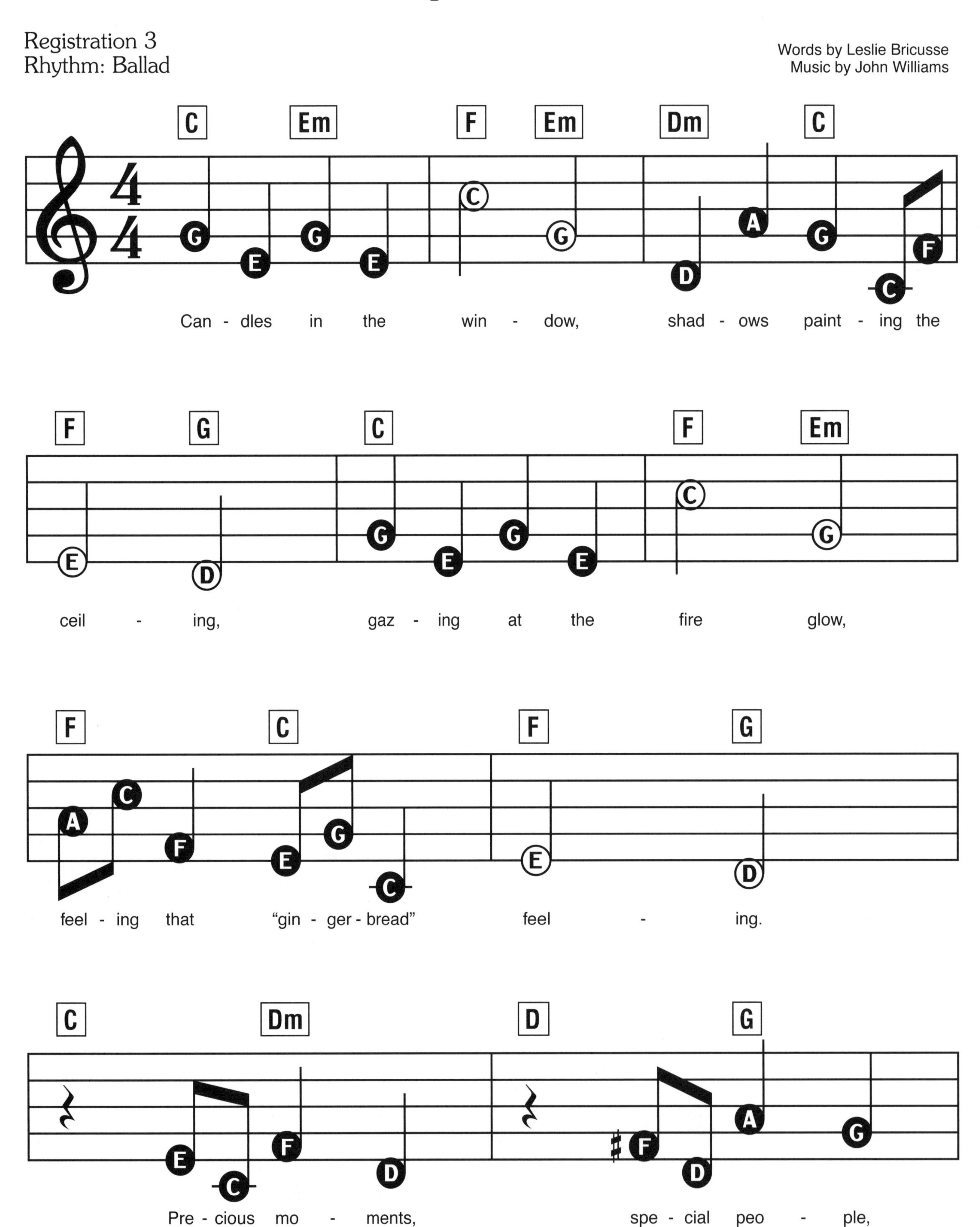

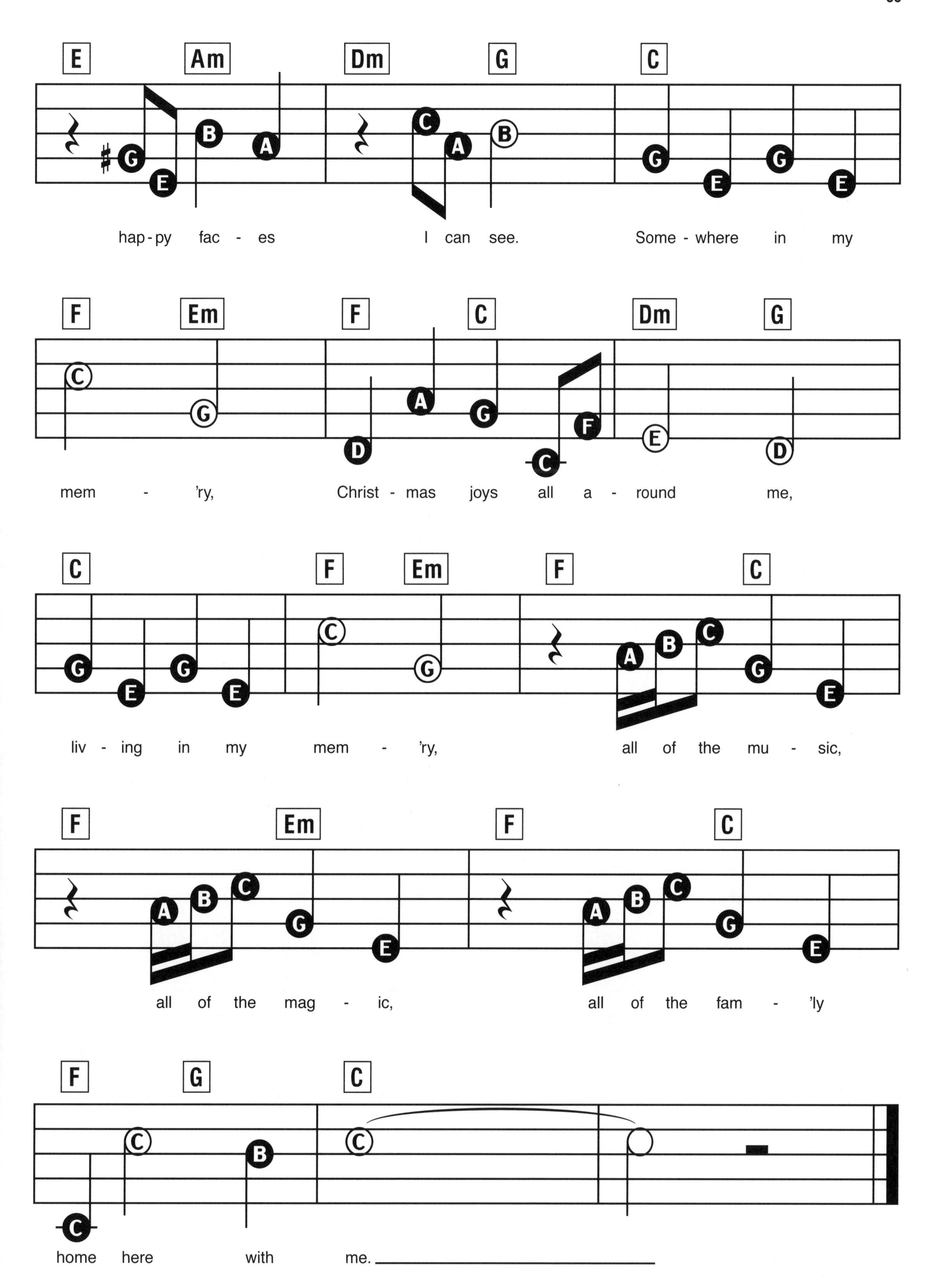
E Am Dm G C
hap - py fac - es I can see. Some - where in my
F Em F C Dm G
mem - 'ry, Christ - mas joys all a - round me,
C F Em F C
liv - ing in my mem - 'ry, all of the mu - sic,
F Em F C
all of the mag - ic, all of the fam - 'ly
F G C
home here with me.

Where Are You Christmas?

from DR. SEUSS' HOW THE GRINCH STOLE CHRISTMAS

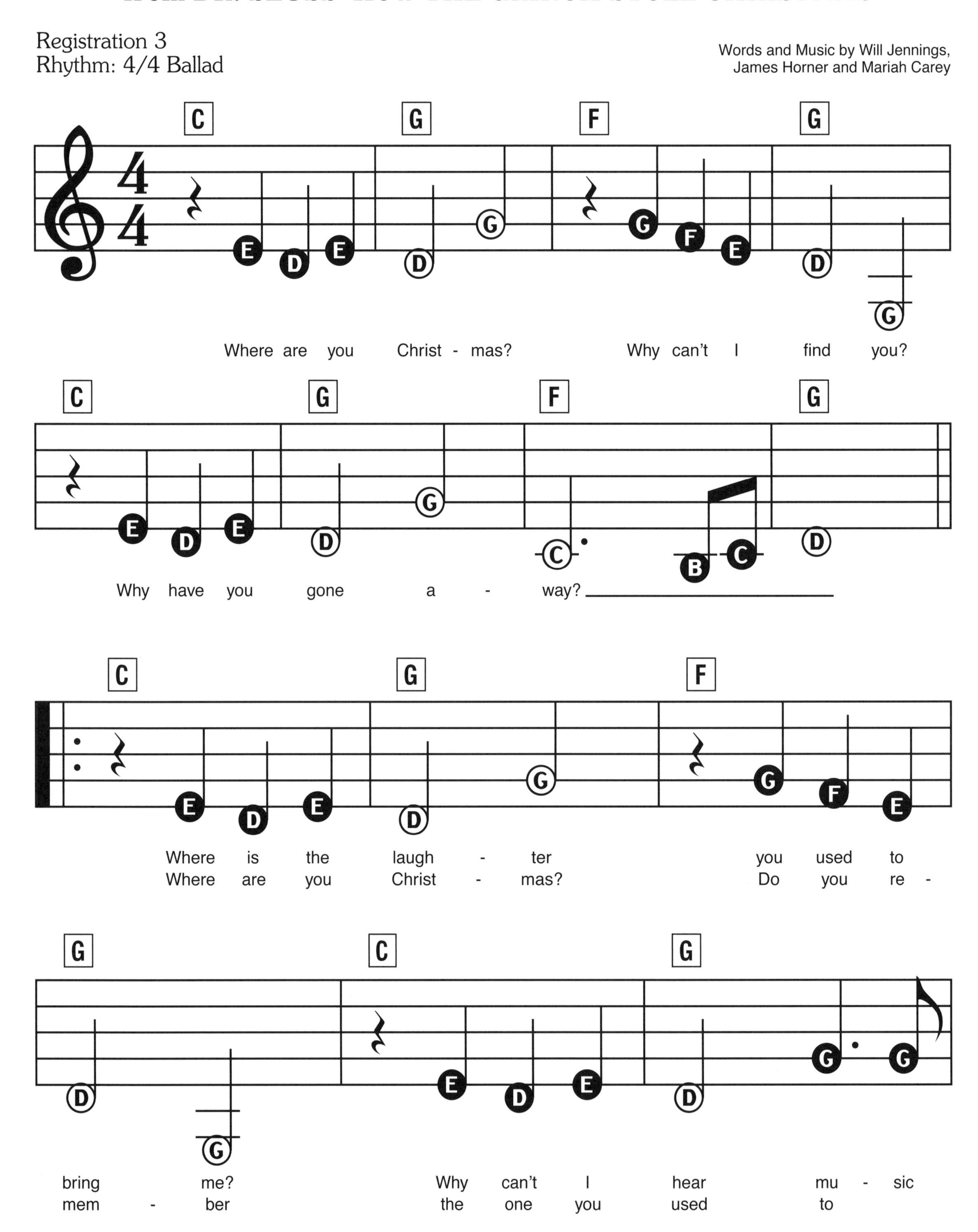

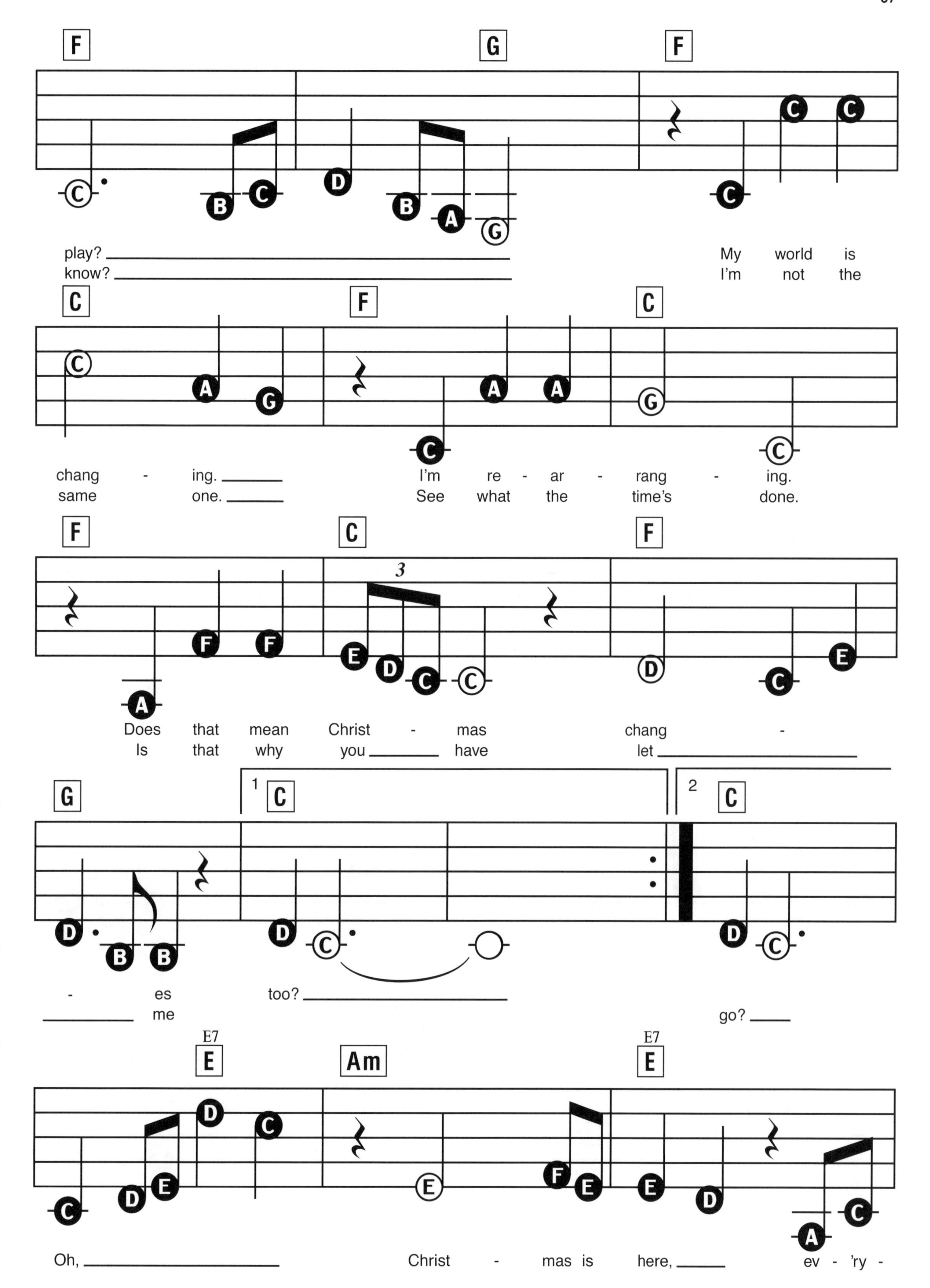
F G F
play? My world is
know? I'm not the
C F C
chang - ing. I'm re - ar - rang - ing.
same one. See what the time's done.
F C F
3
Does that mean Christ - mas chang -
Is that why you have let
G 1 C 2 C
- es too?
me go?
E7 E Am E7 E
Oh, Christ - mas is here, ev - 'ry -

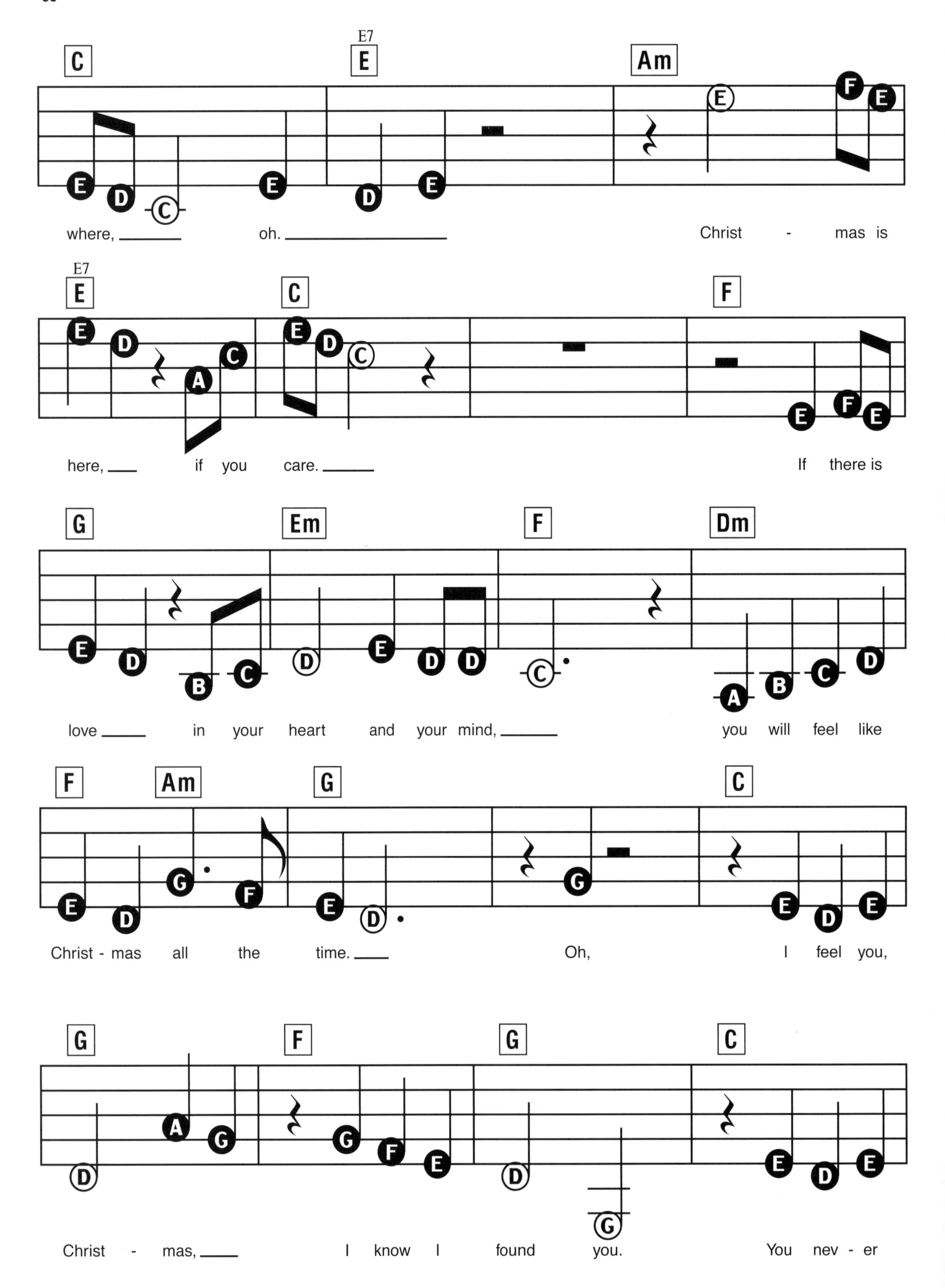
C
E7
E
Am
where,
oh.
Christ - mas is
E7
E
C
F
here,
if you
care.
If there is
G
Em
F
Dm
love
in your
heart and your mind,
you will feel like
F
Am
G
C
Christ - mas all the time.
Oh,
I feel you,
G
F
G
C
Christ - mas,
I know I found you.
You nev - er

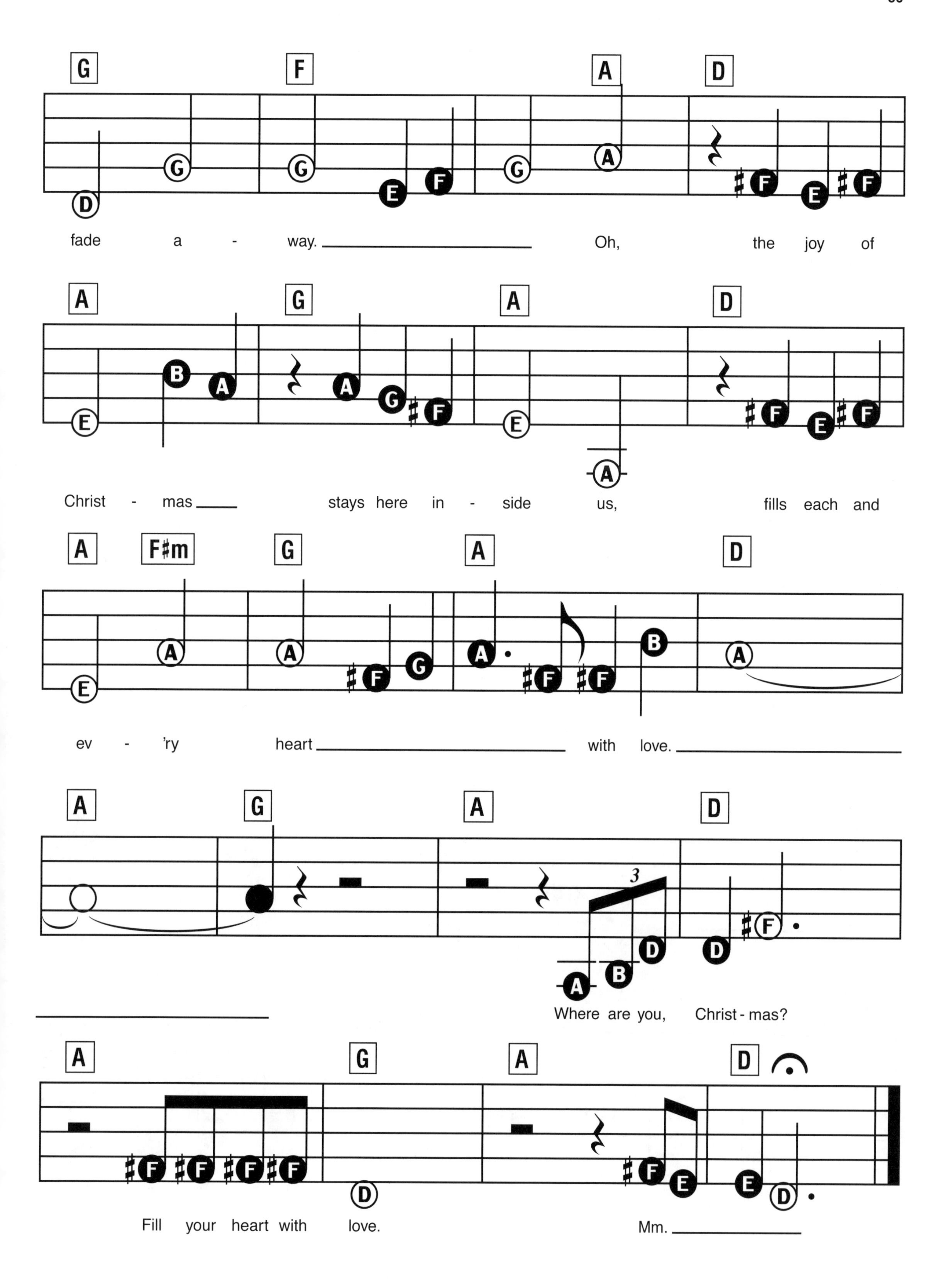
G F A D
fade a - way. Oh, the joy of
A G A D
Christ - mas stays here in - side us, fills each and
A F♯m G A D
ev - 'ry heart with love.
A G A D
Where are you, Christ - mas?
A G A D
Fill your heart with love.
Mm.

White Christmas

from the Motion Picture Irving Berlin's HOLIDAY INN

Registration 10
Rhythm: Rock or Pops

Words and Music by
Irving Berlin

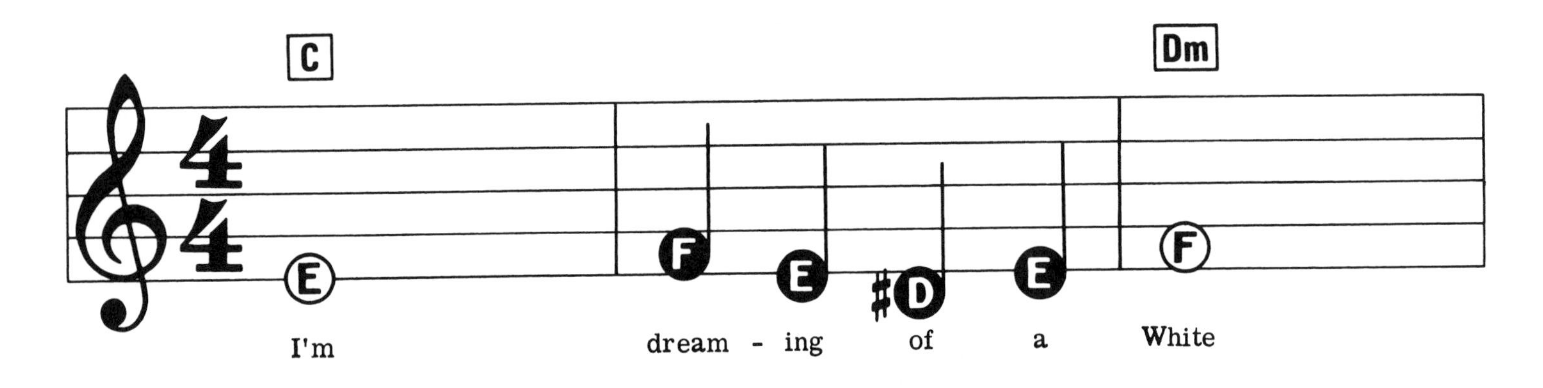

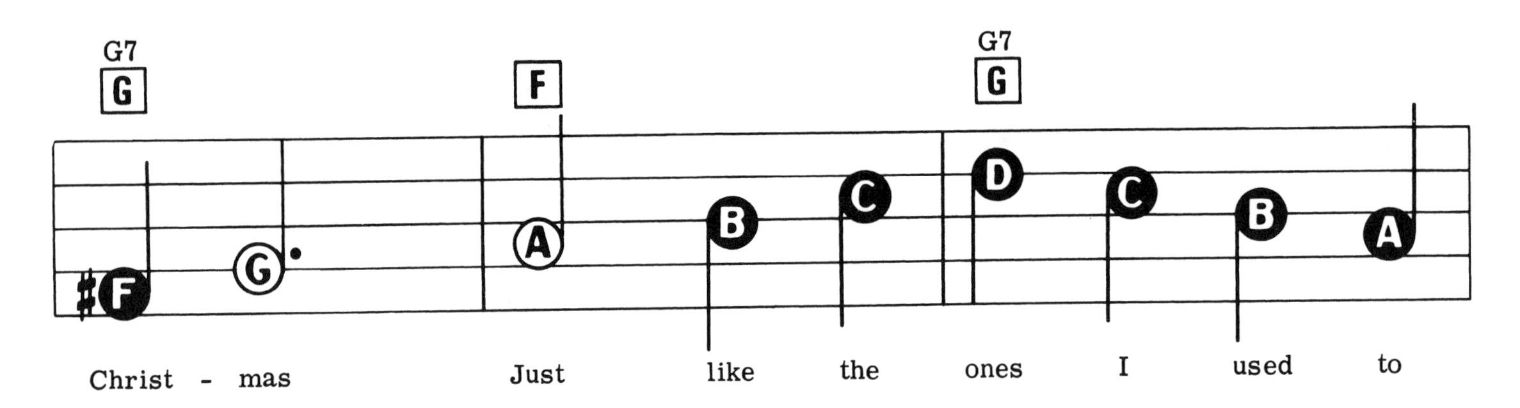

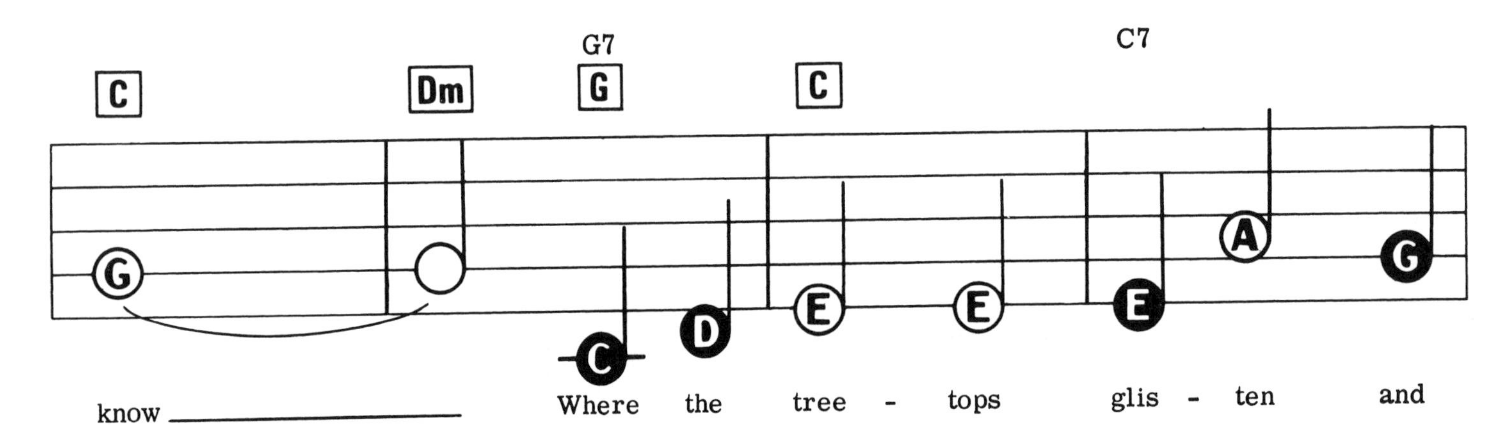

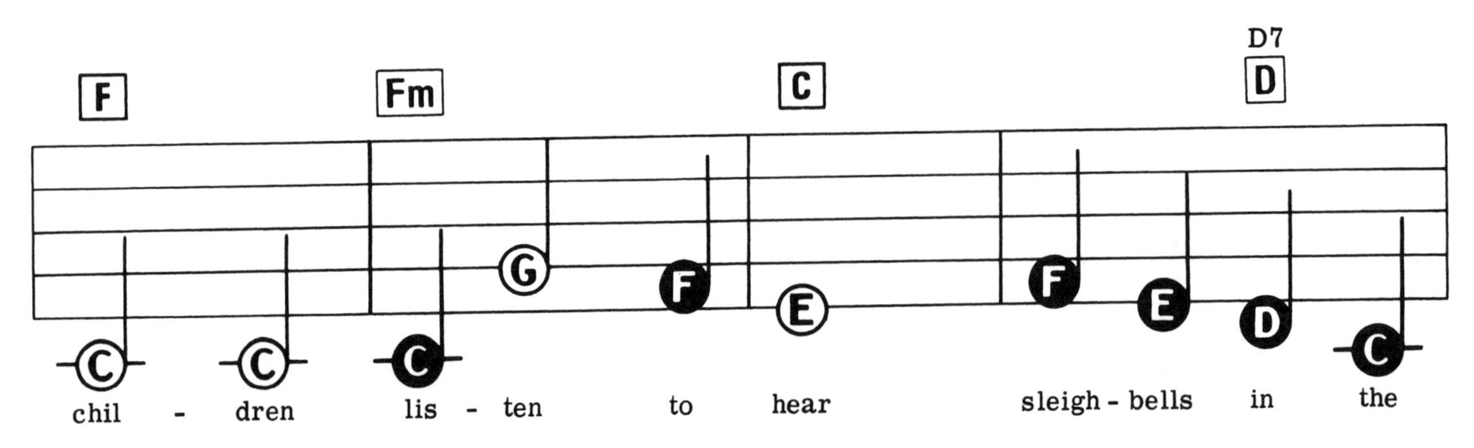

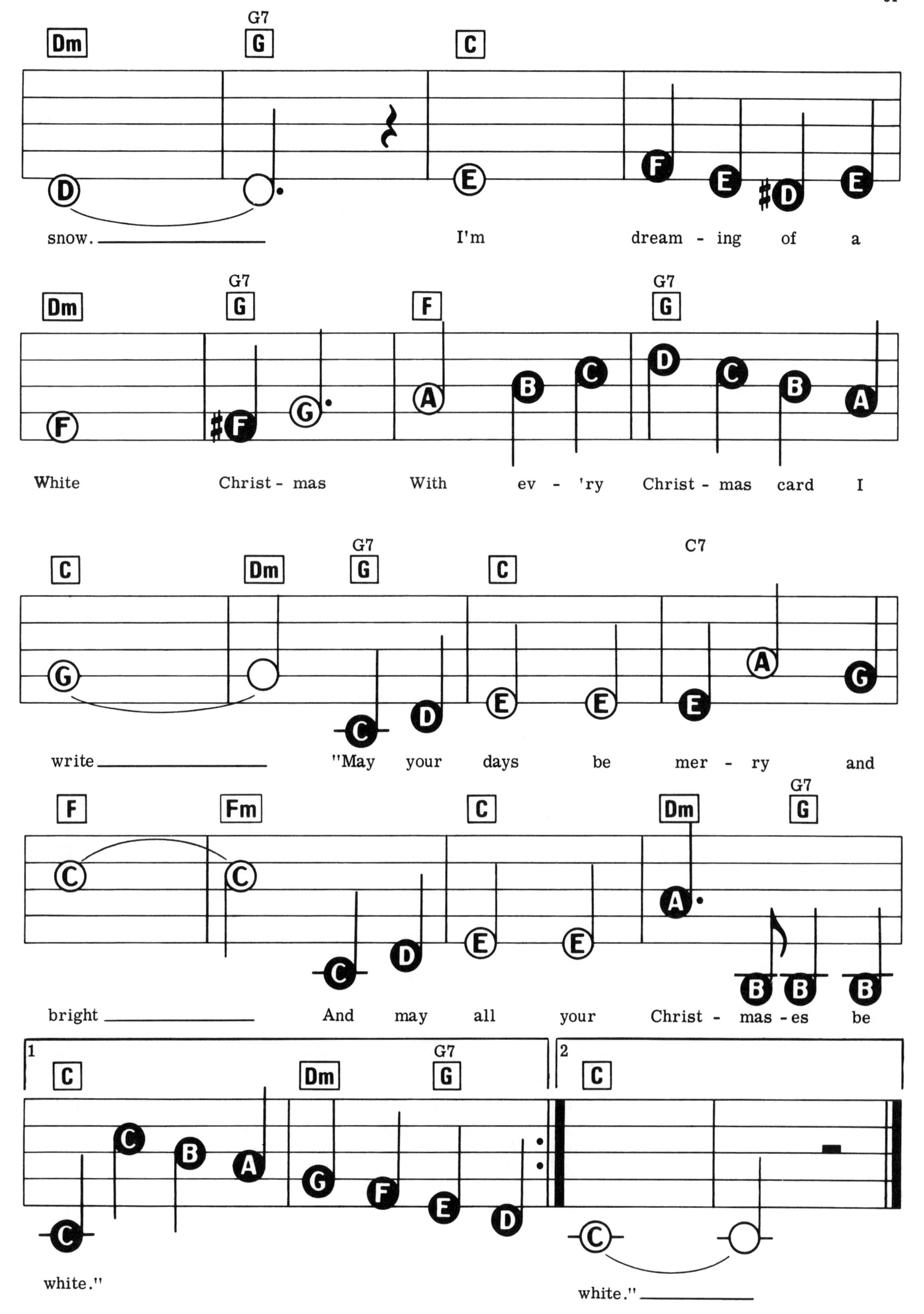
Dm G7 G C
D E F E ♯D E
snow. I'm dream - ing of a
Dm G7 G F G7 G
F ♯F G A B C D C B A
White Christ - mas With ev - 'ry Christ - mas card I
C Dm G7 G C C7
G C D E E E A G
write "May your days be mer - ry and
F Fm C Dm G7 G
C C C D E E A B B B
bright And may all your Christ - mas - es be
1 C Dm G7 G
C C B A G F E D
white."
2 C
C
white."

You're All I Want for Christmas

Registration 3
Rhythm: Pops or Ballad

Words and Music by Glen Moore
and Seger Ellis

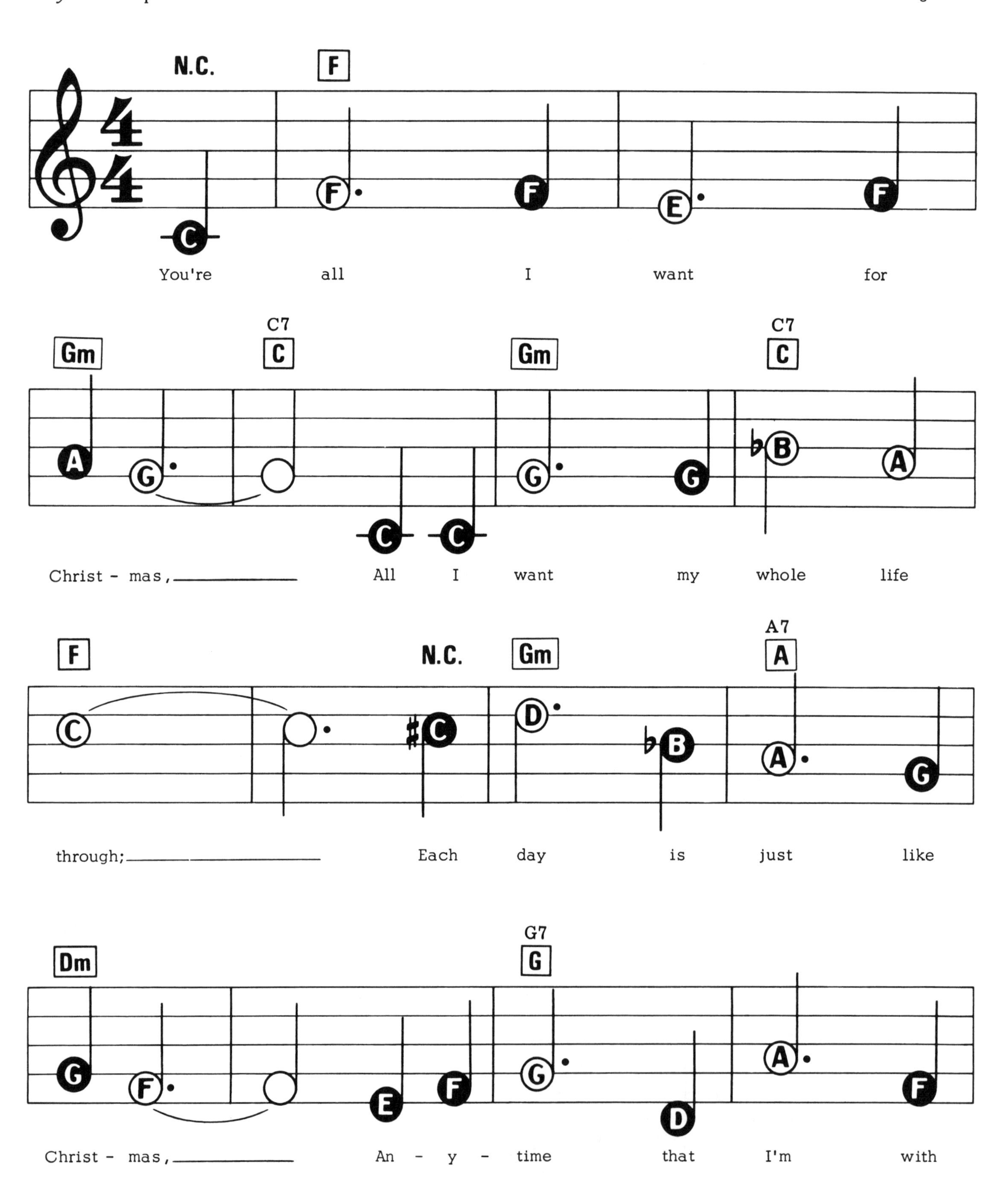

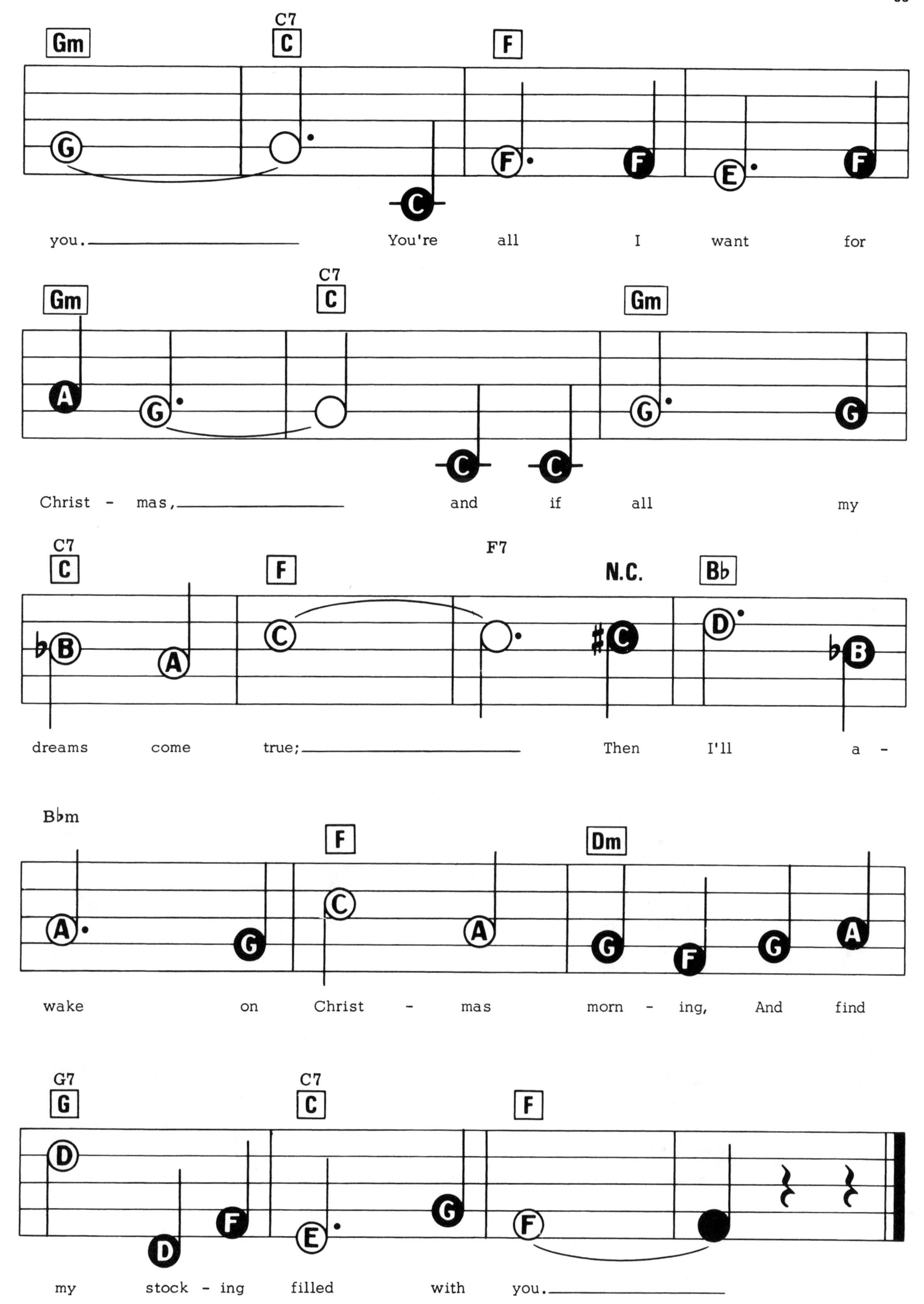
Gm
C7
C
F
you.
You're
all
I
want
for
Gm
C7
C
Gm
Christ - mas,
and
if
all
my
C7
C
F
F7
N.C.
B♭
dreams
come
true;
Then
I'll
a -
B♭m
F
Dm
wake
on
Christ - mas
morn - ing,
And
find
G7
G
C7
C
F
my
stock - ing
filled
with
you.

There's Still My Joy

Registration 8
Rhythm: Waltz

Words and Music by Melissa Manchester, Matt Rollings and Beth Chapman

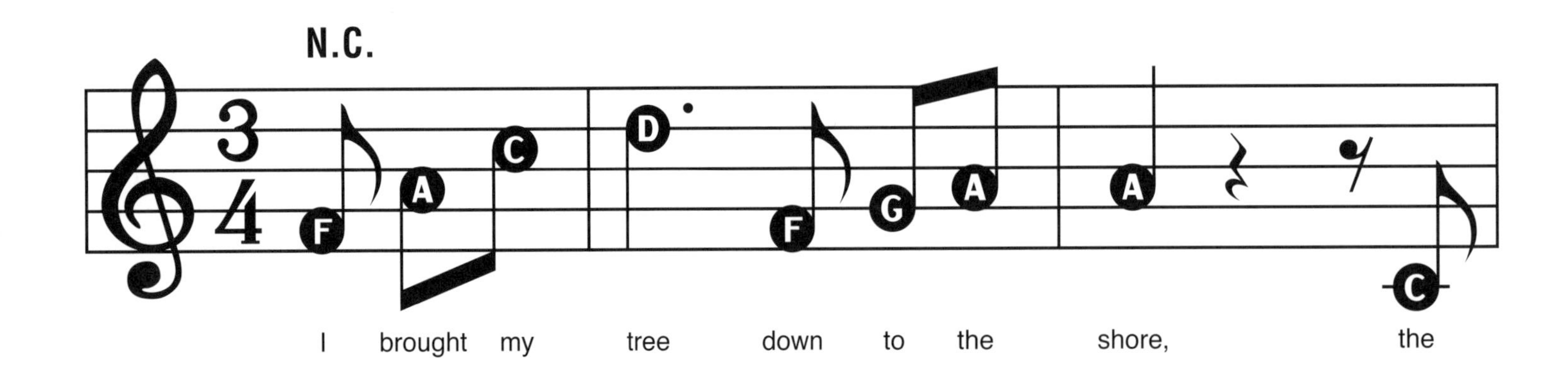

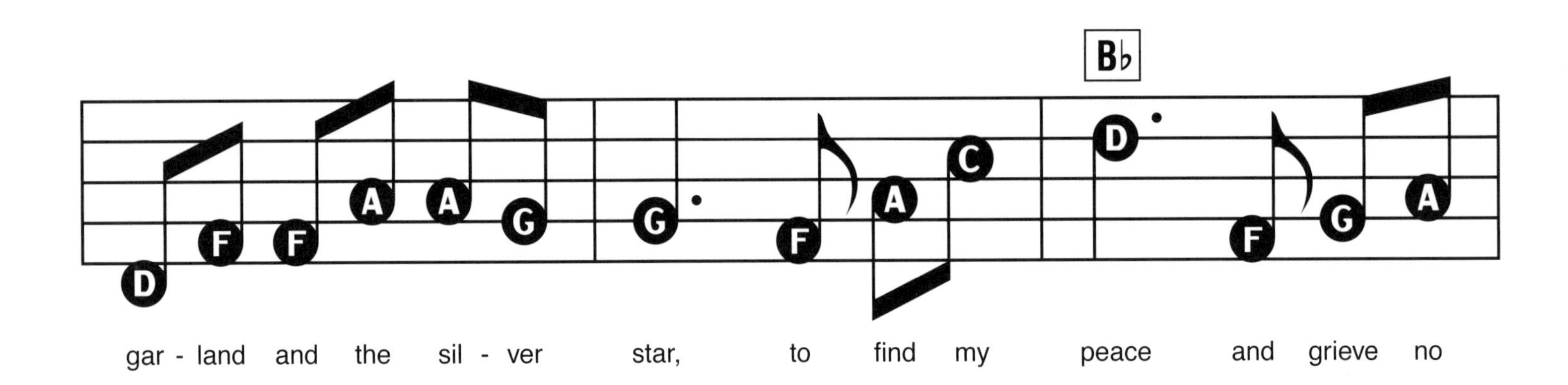

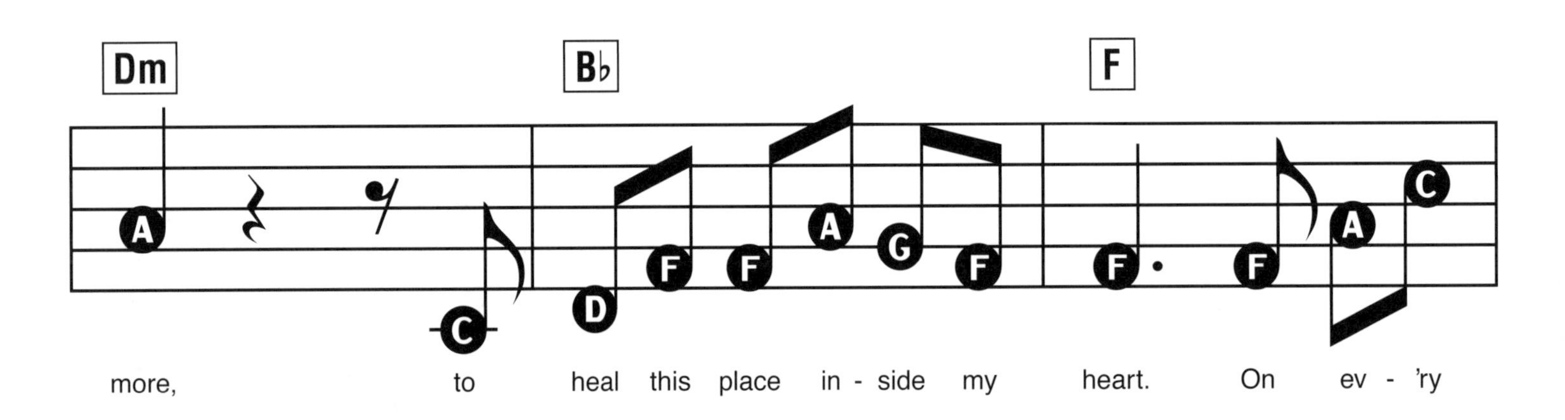

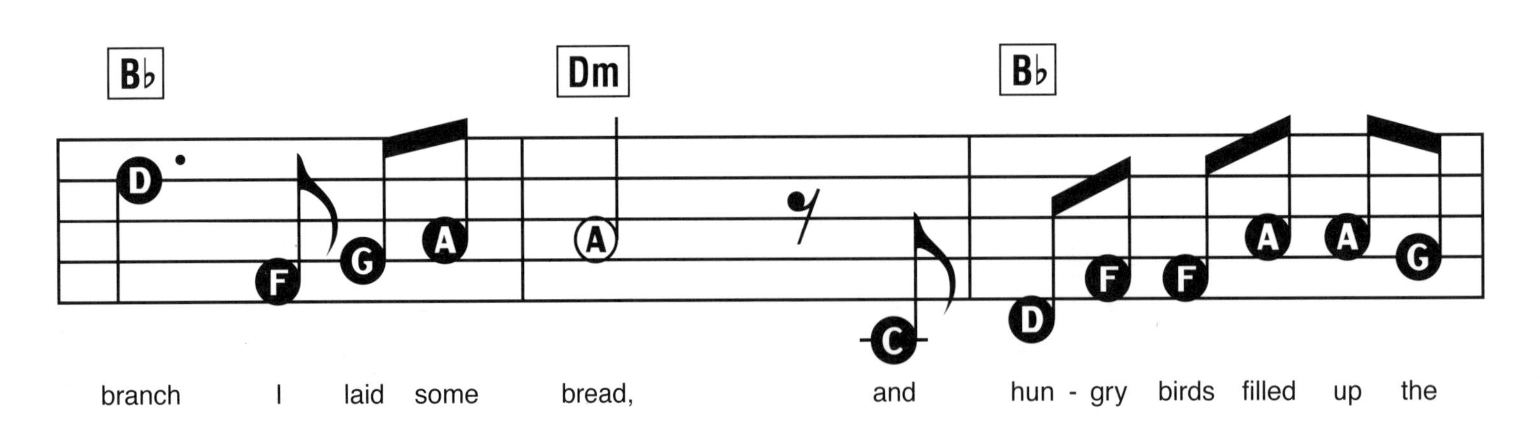

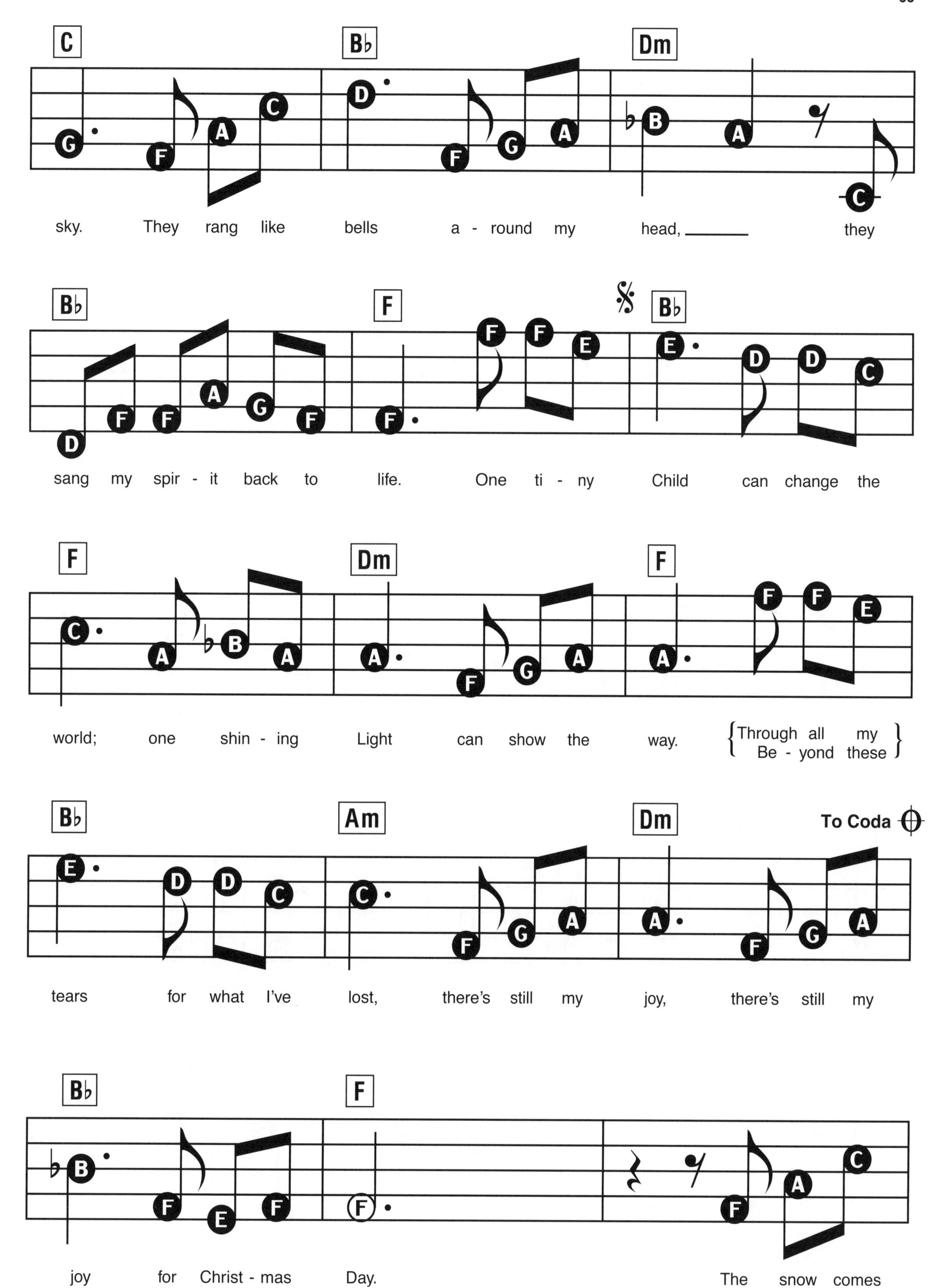
C
B♭
Dm
sky. They rang like bells a - round my head, they
B♭
F
B♭
sang my spir - it back to life. One ti - ny Child can change the
F
Dm
F
world; one shin - ing Light can show the way.
Through all my
Be - yond these
B♭
Am
Dm
To Coda
tears for what I've lost, there's still my joy, there's still my
B♭
F
joy for Christ - mas Day. The snow comes

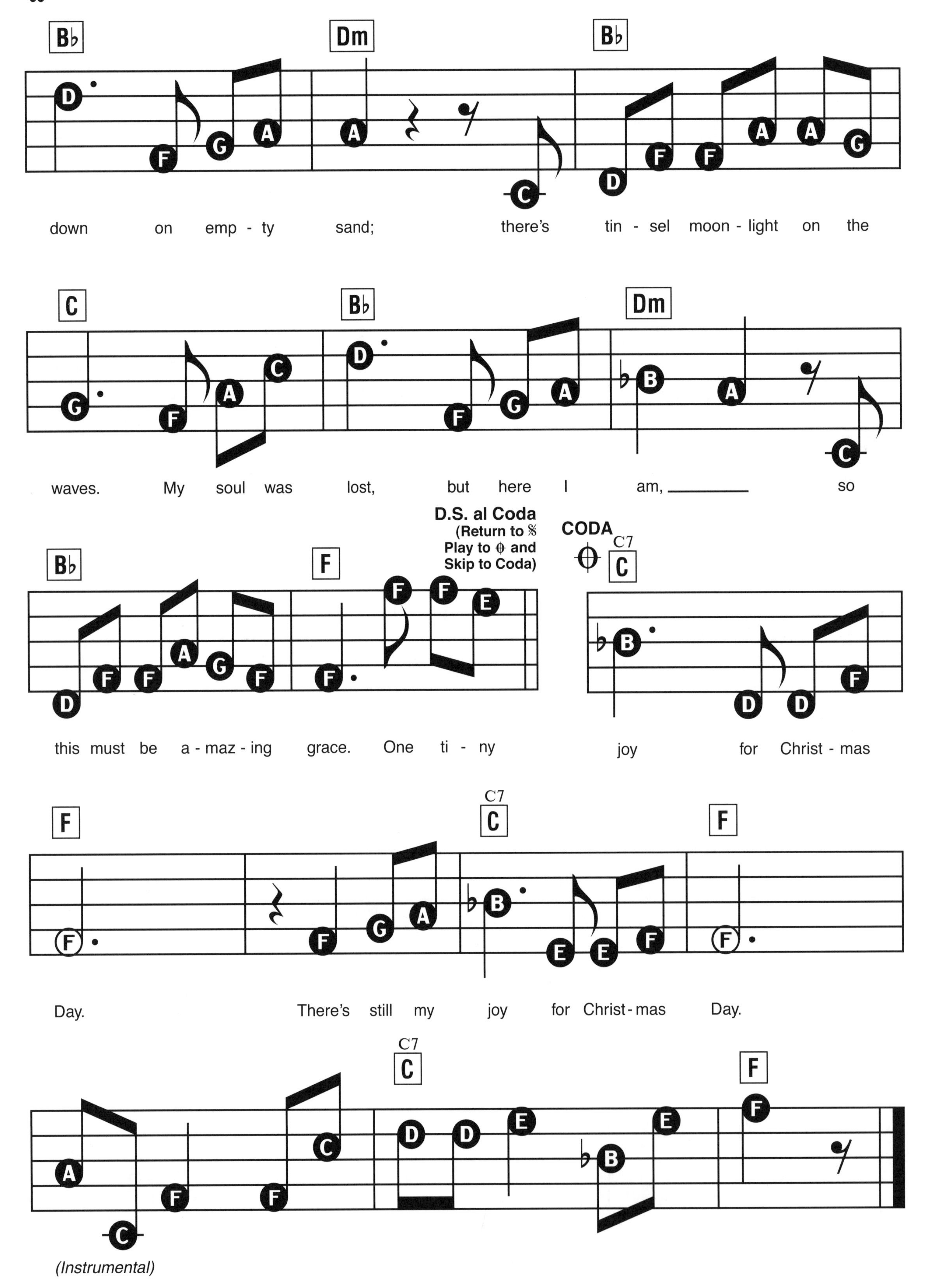

B♭ Dm B♭
down on emp - ty sand; there's tin - sel moon - light on the
C B♭ Dm
waves. My soul was lost, but here I am, so
B♭ F
this must be a - maz - ing grace. One ti - ny
D.S. al Coda
(Return to 𝄋
Play to ⊕ and
Skip to Coda)
CODA
C7
C
joy for Christ - mas
F C7 C F
Day. There's still my joy for Christ - mas Day.
C7 C F
(Instrumental)